LIFE IN THE WHITE HOUSE

BETTY C. MONKMAN

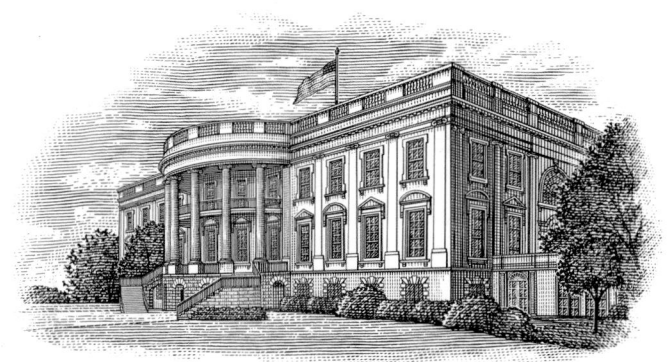

THE **WHITE HOUSE**
HISTORICAL ASSOCIATION

WHITE HOUSE HISTORICAL ASSOCIATION

Board of Directors
John F. W. Rogers, Chairman
Teresa Carlson, Vice Chairperson
Gregory W. Wendt, Treasurer
Anita B. McBride, Secretary
Stewart D. McLaurin, President

Eula Adams, Michael Beschloss, Gahl Hodges Burt, Merlynn Carson, Jean M. Case, Ashley Dabbiere, Wayne A. I. Frederick, Deneen C. Howell, Tham Kannalikham, Metta Krach, Barbara A. Perry, Ben C. Sutton, Jr., Tina Tchen

National Park Service Liaison: Charles F. Sams III

Ex Officio: Lonnie G. Bunch III, Kaywin Feldman, Carla Hayden, Colleen Shogan

Directors Emeriti: John T. Behrendt, John H. Dalton, Nancy M. Folger, Knight Kiplinger, Elise K. Kirk, Martha Joynt Kumar, James I. McDaniel, Robert M. McGee, Harry G. Robinson III, Ann Stock, Gail Berry West

Chief Publishing Officer: Marcia Mallet Anderson
Associate Vice President of Publishing: Lauren McGwin
Editorial Coordinator: Rebecca Durgin Kerr
Editorial and Production Manager: Noella James
Editorial and Production Manager: Margaret Strolle
Editorial Consultant: Ann Hofstra Grogg

Office of the Curator, The White House
Donna Hayashi Smith, Melissa C. Naulin, Nikki Pisha, Corey Purtell

Copyright © 1966, 1967, 1970, 1973, 1975, 1978, 1982, 1987, 1991, 1996, 2003, 2007, 2013, 2017, 2023 by the White House Historical Association. All Rights Reserved

15th Edition

ISBN 978-1-950273-44-7

Library of Congress Control Number 2023940433

All illustrations in this book are copyrighted by the White House Historical Association unless otherwise noted in the Illustration Credits (p. 248) and may not be reproduced without permission. Requests for reprint permissions should be addressed to: Rights and Reproductions Manager, White House Historical Association, P.O. Box 27624, Washington, D.C. 20038.

Printed in Italy

Opposite: Routine maintenance work is under way on the White House, the house built for the ages, 2022.

Page ii: The East Room is filled with flowers as tables are set for the State Dinner in honor of President Yoon Suk Yeol of the Republic of Korea, April 26, 2023.

Page viii: White House Carpenter Ed Watson hangs the Presidential Seal on the South Portico ahead of a planned Congressional Picnic, 2011.

THE WHITE HOUSE

Life in the White House is magical every day. I will never forget the moment President Biden and I walked up the front steps of the White House, passed through the enormous classical columns, and stepped over that marble threshold on Inauguration Day. As the mahogany doors closed behind us, the grandeur of the Entrance Hall caught my breath. Light from the crystal chandelier reflected off the floor to shine on the Presidential Seal above the Blue Room door, a subtle, but powerful, reminder of the journey we were about to take—and the weight of those who had come before.

In the three years since, we have welcomed visitors and guests from around the world to walk these halls alongside us and experience the White House in new ways. Together, we have celebrated historic accomplishments, honored inspiring artists, and bestowed the highest of medals on our most courageous Americans. We have decked the halls for holidays, hunted for Easter eggs, and hosted State Dinners.

The echoes of those moments swirl through the halls, joining addresses and agreements that changed the course of our nation's history. They are all a part of the White House's legacy, a collective memory that shapes our past and promises a future filled with hope.

At the same time, this house is home to those more intimate, quieter moments—family birthdays, graduations, and even a wedding; our cat, Willow, and dog, Commander, play-fighting on the lawn and in the Residence.

We are grateful for the unfaltering work of the chefs, florists, ushers, and staff who come here each day to serve our country—who take pride in caring for our house—"the people's house."

Being first lady is the honor of my lifetime, but it is only a piece of who I am. Education is my life's work. So, I am thrilled that this new edition of *Life in the White House* is sharing ever more stories of these hallowed halls—opening these historic doors wider and wider for more to see inside.

This house belongs to the American people—and it is a privilege to share it with you.

Jill Biden

President Joe Biden, joined by First Lady Jill Biden, signs the Month of the Military Child Proclamation in the White House Library, March 31, 2021.

CONTENTS

XI FOREWORD

1 INTRODUCTION: THE PRESIDENT'S HOUSE, THE NATION'S HOUSE

2 PRESIDENTS AT WORK IN THEIR HOME

36 WHERE HOSPITALITY MAKES HISTORY

96 THE FIRST FAMILY AT HOME

170 IN THE PRESIDENT'S PARK

208 A HOUSE FOR THE AGES

244 CONCLUSION: THE BEST OF BLESSINGS ON THIS HOUSE

248 ILLUSTRATION CREDITS

250 INDEX

FOREWORD

Life, at its fullest, has been lived in the White House for more than two hundred years. Like countless millions of American homes, it is a place where marriages have been celebrated, children have been born and raised, family dinners have been shared, and loved ones have been mourned. Through the years, daily routines have been enlivened by favorite pastimes and brightened by a succession of every kind of pet imaginable. But unlike other American homes, the life lived here unfolds in the shadow of the serious business of the presidency, as the world looks on. The hospitality extended here makes history—whether it be a State Visit by a king or a queen or ten thousand children rolling their Easter eggs. Past residents are never forgotten at the White House: their portraits line the walls, their memories inspire their successors, and the furnishings they leave behind will always belong to the American people.

The story of life as lived in the White House is an ambitious subject for a single book, but with the following pages, we are sharing the big picture—from the laying of the cornerstone to the most recent State Dinner. With this edition, the fifteenth since the book was first released as *The Living White House* in 1966, we have changed the title to *Life in the White House* to best reflect that the focus of the book is wholly on the extraordinary subject of life in the house built for the ages.

Stewart D. McLaurin
President
White House Historical Association

Above: Stewart D. McLaurin pauses at the entrance to the White House Historical Association on Lafayette Square, 2014.

Opposite: President Ronald Reagan makes a State Dinner toast to Australian Prime Minister Malcolm Fraser, June 30, 1981.

INTRODUCTION
THE PRESIDENT'S HOUSE,
THE NATION'S HOUSE

The White House is part of every American's national heritage. As the office and home of the president, it is the place toward which citizens look for leadership from the person they have chosen to act for all. No other elected official is so directly accountable to them. Their problems are his problems; his home is theirs.

John Adams, the first chief executive to live in the White House, once wrote, "People of the United States! You know not half the solicitude of your presidents for your happiness and welfare." "I never forget," said President Franklin Delano Roosevelt in one of his famous fireside chats, "that I live in a house owned by all the American people and that I have been given their trust."

The Executive Mansion has been a focal point of government and a barometer of the political, economic, and social state of the nation ever since it was first occupied in 1800, a decade after Congress had established the country's permanent capital in the fields and forests beside the Potomac River. It has known the tramp and flames of enemy invaders, the pomp of victory celebrations, the pain of economic depressions, the private joy of family weddings, and the somber pageantry of State Funerals.

Unlike the ornate and monumental palaces of Europe's royal past, the porticoed White House stands today with simple dignity amid green and rolling lawns in the heart of Washington, D.C. Since John and Abigail Adams became its first residents, more than forty presidents and their families have lived in this very public building, where hundreds of official events are held each year and thousands of guests and visitors walk through its public rooms and grounds. As author Lonnelle Aikman wrote in the first edition of this book, "Indeed, it is this personal and domestic life, carried on in the fierce glare of national affairs, that gives the White House its fascinating dual character."

A scene from the State Arrival Ceremony for President Emmanuel Macron of the French Republic, December 1, 2022.

Above: President Joe Biden works in the Oval Office with his dog Commander by his side, September 27, 2022.

Opposite: Because it is the home and office of the president, the American people have always been drawn to the White House, as seen in this engraving c. 1861 titled *The Presidential Mansion and Grounds, During the Performance of the Military Bands.*

CHAPTER ONE

PRESIDENTS AT WORK IN THEIR HOME

The White House, whose long-popular name was not officially inscribed on the presidential letterhead until Theodore Roosevelt's time, stands as a living symbol of the nation's power and prestige. As the home and office of the chief executive, it is the keystone of the government. With Congress and the Supreme Court, it is the central theater of action in which national goals are achieved and defended. But the fascination the White House holds for most Americans is in its association with the presidents who have led the United States for more than two centuries.

In this 1930 illustration titled *Building the First White House*, by N. C. Wyeth, George Washington is depicted with architect James Hoban at the White House construction site. Although he oversaw the design of the building, Washington was the only president who did not live in the White House.

4 LIFE IN THE WHITE HOUSE

PRESIDENTS AT WORK
THE PRESIDENT'S
HOUSE IS BUILT

Above: James Hoban is remembered in the White House today by his portrait, a wax silhouette made from life by John Christian Rauschner, c. 1800, which is displayed in the White House Library. On the lowest shelf is a very early illustration of the President's House published as a frontispiece to *A Stranger in America*, c. 1807.

George Washington, though "Father of His Country" and "first in the hearts of his countrymen," was the only president who never lived in the White House. He ended his service as chief executive and died before the federal government moved from Philadelphia to the village capital named in his honor. Even so, Washington left the indelible mark of his own dignity and good taste on this eighteenth-century building with its magnificent setting. He selected its site and gave his prestigious approval to the classical, harmonious design for the mansion submitted by Irish-born architect James Hoban in a democratically open competition. In envisioning the home in which the presidents would live, Washington expressed his vision for the future of the new country: "For the President's House, I would design a building which should also look forward, but execute no more of it at present than might suit the circumstances of this Country when it shall be first wanted. A plan comprehending more may be executed at a future period when the wealth, population, and importance of it shall stand upon much higher ground than they do at present."

From the beginning the "President's House"—the name Washington preferred —was destined to be a stage for events that marked the progress of the nation from thirteen states stretched along the Atlantic seaboard to a preeminent world power reaching into the Pacific Ocean. Here President Thomas Jefferson, in his first term, accepted Napoleon's offer to sell the French-owned port of New Orleans and the vast lands to the west known as the Louisiana Purchase. James Madison faced a far more painful decision in the War of 1812—called "Mr. Madison's War" by his foes. At the darkest hour of the conflict, when Dolley Madison and the cabinet were in flight from the burning capital, the president must have wondered if he had endangered all that the Revolution had won. But the peace that followed unified the nation, and Madison called Hoban back to rebuild the White House exactly as it had been. James Monroe, the fourth president from Virginia, filled it with elegant French furniture and added a South Portico. A few years later Hoban also built the North Portico. This was the White House that would be both home and office for the president for nearly a century, until the 1902 West Wing added office space. The White House itself has never ceased to be the president's home.

PRESIDENTS AT WORK 5

PRESIDENTS AT WORK
MANY ROADS TO THE WHITE HOUSE

The *Commanders in Chief* paintings (above and opposite) by Ross Rossin, 2019 and 2004, imagine the nineteenth- and twentieth-century presidents as if gathered together in the White House. The forty-five men who have served as president of the United States came to the White House from across America. Their roads to the presidency included many different careers: eleven were former generals, several were teachers, many were lawyers, and many served as governors and in Congress.

To the President's House in 1829 came tough Andrew Jackson, hero of the Battle of New Orleans. "Old Hickory" from Tennessee was the first man to reach the top executive office from beyond the Appalachians. His overwhelming presidential victory in 1828 clearly demonstrated the new political power of a growing and more democratically based electorate, and it alerted the aristocratic statesmen of the East that henceforth national leadership would be shared with the people of the West. The campaign of William Henry Harrison rolled to success in 1840 on a bandwagon bearing twin symbols of a log cabin and a barrel of hard cider, despite the fact that Harrison, a descendant of Virginia aristocracy, was not born in a log cabin and had no special taste for cider.

Two decades later, Abraham Lincoln bore the burdens and heartbreak of the "irrepressible conflict" of the Civil War in the vortex of the struggle. Through bitter military reverses and petty partisan politics, in the face of cruel criticism and cartoons picturing him as a clown and a devil, he held together the frayed bonds of union until the nation could again be united.

"I think of Lincoln, shambling, homely, with his strong, sad, deeply furrowed face, all the time," Theodore Roosevelt wrote a friend after he, too, came to live and work in this house of historic memory. "I see him in the different rooms and in the halls . . . he is to me infinitely the most real of the dead Presidents."

Harry Truman recalled his predecessors, too. "I sit here in this old house and work on foreign affairs, read reports, and work on speeches. . . . The floors pop and drapes move back and forth—I can just imagine old Andy and Teddy having an argument about Franklin."

The men who have taken on their country's toughest assignment reflect many different backgrounds. Together their varied lives support the democratic proposition that every American, however humble in origin, has a chance to reach the highest position in the land. Abraham Lincoln was born in a log cabin, as were several other chief executives. The exact number is uncertain because the claim of humble origins—authentic or not—had potent political appeal in the nation's early days.

Eleven presidents were former generals—including George Washington and Dwight Eisenhower. Warren G. Harding was a newspaper publisher; Herbert Hoover was an engineer. Several presidents were teachers or college professors. At least twenty practiced law early in their careers; many served as state governors, members of Congress, and cabinet officers. Eight vice presidents rose to the presidency on the death of incumbents; four of them—Theodore Roosevelt, Calvin Coolidge, Harry S. Truman, and Lyndon B. Johnson—went on to win another term on their own. Gerald Ford was the only vice president to attain the office by the resignation of a chief executive. He replaced Richard M. Nixon, who resigned under threat of impeachment by Congress.

William Howard Taft, defeated for a second term in 1912, was later appointed by Harding to be chief justice of the United States—the only man ever to serve in both high posts. Of the two, Taft preferred the Supreme Court. "I don't remember that I was ever President," he once remarked happily.

PRESIDENTS AT WORK
THE OATH OF OFFICE

Each presidency begins with the Oath of Office. The nation's first president, George Washington, was sworn in on April 30, 1789, in New York City, then the nation's capital. He set a tradition that his successors would follow when he placed his hand on the Bible and took the Oath. Thomas Jefferson was the first to take the Oath at the U.S. Capitol in Washington, D.C., as have most of his successors. When presidents died in office, however, vice presidents have been sworn in where they happened to be. And some circumstances dictated that the Oath be taken in the White House. Rutherford B. Hayes took this precaution, privately sworn in on March 3 because March 4 was a Sunday and the official ceremony would not take place until Monday. And after 1933, when Inauguration Day was moved to January 20, inclement weather occasionally forced the swearing-in indoors.

LIFE IN THE WHITE HOUSE

Among those presidents who took the Oath of Office in the White House (clockwise from opposite top) were Rutherford B. Hayes who was sworn in in the Red Room, March 3, 1877; Gerald R. Ford who took the Oath of Office in the East Room after the resignation of President Richard Nixon, August 9, 1974; Ronald Reagan who was sworn in for his second term in a private ceremony in the Entrance Hall on the landing of the Grand Staircase, January 20, 1985; and Harry S. Truman who took the Oath of Office in the Cabinet Room following the death of President Franklin D. Roosevelt, April 12, 1945.

PRESIDENTS AT WORK
UNENDING DUTIES

Wherever the president goes, the responsibilities of the office go, too. Whether editing a speech aboard *Air Force One* or reading the latest of daily reports at midnight in the study or bedroom, the president works at all hours. The day-to-day duties that never end have steadily increased since John Adams complained that a "peck of troubles in a large bundle of papers . . . comes every day."

As the nation grew from some 5 million people in 1800 to more than 331 million in 2020, each new president has inherited heavier and more complex duties and responsibilities. Behind the stately pillars of the Executive Residence, as in the inconspicuous East and West Wings and in the nearby executive office buildings, where most official business goes on, staff members help their chief meet obligations, great and small. Their tasks include assisting the president with political and legislative agendas, planning domestic and national security policies, gathering and analyzing information, receiving visitors, handling correspondence and documents, and preparing for a constant round of official and social activities.

When John Quincy Adams took on the presidency, the growing paperwork was made almost unbearable by his failure to delegate it. To cope with the minutiae, he used shorthand no one else could decipher, and he impaired his eyesight and health by writing thousands of words a week in official and personal correspondence.

James K. Polk was similarly inclined. "No President who performs his duty faithfully . . . can have any leisure," he declared. "If he entrusts the details . . . to subordinates constant errors will occur. I prefer to supervise the whole operation of the Government myself." Already, however, this had become impossible. Polk's attempt to do the task put such a strain on his frail constitution that he became ill and died at age 53, a few months after leaving office.

Congress was slow to provide funds for executive help. Most early presidents called on a relative to act as private secretary, paying salaries from their own pockets. Congress finally voted money to hire one private secretary for President James Buchanan; then the Civil War suddenly increased the need.

President Abraham Lincoln with his secretaries John Nicolay (left) and John Hay (right), November 8, 1863.

Lincoln acquired two bright and talented young secretaries, John Hay and John Nicolay, and clerks detailed from other government departments. But no one could shield the president from the burdens of a country at war, nor would he permit himself to be sheltered from the avalanche of problems unloaded by officials, generals, war contractors, cranks, wounded soldiers, and tearful wives and mothers.

PRESIDENTS AT WORK
THE NEED FOR DEDICATED SPACE

The West Wing is seen here as it would have appeared during the 1903 New Year's Reception shortly after it was completed. It created a much-needed separation of dedicated work space for the president and private living space for the first family.

Until 1902, when President Theodore Roosevelt built the West Wing to separate his office from his living quarters, all families shared the Executive Mansion with the public, which was freely admitted to ask favors, to seek interviews with the president, or just to shake his hand. Most annoying was the clamor of petitioners for public office, often raised by those without qualifications. Lincoln told of a man who asked for a post as a foreign minister and gradually reduced his demands until he was willing to settle for an old pair of pants. Office seekers, however, had become pests long before Lincoln's presidency. They and their eager sponsors haunted the White House even in the time of John Adams. With each change of administration came fresh hordes, and president after president complained of persecution and senseless waste of time. Jackson openly used the spoils system to reward his supporters. For a time fear stalked the ranks of his opponents in government service; in all, it is estimated, about one-fifth of the entire workforce was replaced. During William Henry Harrison's tenure, a group of men once barred him from a cabinet meeting until he accepted their applications. Yet it was not until after James A. Garfield's murder by a thwarted job hunter that firm action was taken. In 1883 Congress passed the Pendleton Act, the first major reform law to open the way to competitive examinations as the basis for most federal service. The nation was coming of age. Such changes in public attitude toward the obligations and rights of the person in the White House reflected the increasing energy, wealth, and population of the country.

Before the West Wing was built, the Residence was crowded with those seeking an audience with the president. Most troublesome was a seemingly endless flow of office seekers demanding the chief executive's attention. The cartoon (below) pictures the outgoing President Grover Cleveland in 1889 as he leaves his successor Benjamin Harrison struggling to hold back a crowd of office seekers pressing on his door.

PRESIDENTS AT WORK
COMMUNICATION EVOLVES

While President Grover Cleveland (above) and his nineteenth-century counterparts were accustomed to writing their correspondence by hand, the twentieth century brought many changes. Personal computers became widespread during the Carter presidency as seen (right) in 1978. In the twenty-first century, computers are used for most written communications. President Barack Obama himself often sat at the computer to polish text. He is seen in the Outer Oval Office (opposite) as he works on a statement on the compromise to reduce the deficit and avert a default, August 2, 2011.

Gone are the days when Grover Cleveland could write many of his letters and speeches by hand, or when William McKinley and his staff of a dozen people could cope with all of the business. Woodrow Wilson sometimes picked up a letter from a secretary's desk and answered it on his own typewriter. Harding was the first president to hire a professional speechwriter. Computers were introduced into the White House during Richard Nixon's tenure and came into widespread use under Jimmy Carter.

As national issues have increased and grown more complex, the presidential staff has come to include domestic, legal, and national security advisers at the White House, plus economic, technical, and other advisory groups in the neighboring executive office buildings. Late twentieth-century presidents and the first presidents of the twenty-first century, supervising the nerve center of action in the West Wing, have found that new technology only increases the pace of their work.

PRESIDENTS AT WORK
ON THE MOVE

Below, clockwise from top left: A White House courier during the presidency of Theodore Roosevelt, c. 1906, and a messenger on horseback, c. 1890. The first fleet of cars arrived with President William Howard Taft in 1909.

Theodore Roosevelt carried out his dynamic foreign and domestic programs in a period when messengers on horseback or bicycle rushed urgent letters and documents to and from the White House, Congress, and executive departments. Automobiles came in with Taft. The first airplane assigned to the chief executive was specially built, used once by Franklin Roosevelt and later by Truman. Jets and helicopters have been supplied since Eisenhower's time.

Seen (left) in 1947, the Douglas VC-54C Skymaster was the first aircraft purpose-built to fly the president of the United States. Nicknamed the "Sacred Cow," the plane was used by Presidents Franklin D. Roosevelt and Harry S. Truman and flown by the U.S. Army Air Force.

On July 12, 1957, Dwight D. Eisenhower departed from the South Lawn for Camp David (below) on a Bell H-13J, becoming the first sitting president to travel by helicopter.

PRESIDENTS AT WORK
ON THE PHONE

In 1877 Hayes installed a telephone at the mansion after seeing one demonstrated by inventor Alexander Graham Bell. Yet as late as Taft's term only one operator was needed to handle calls. When the operator went to lunch, Taft's young son, Charlie, considered it great sport to take over the switchboard. Today telephone calls and e-mails from those expressing their opinions on current issues and those seeking assistance from the president, regularly flood into the White House.

First installed more than a century ago, the telephone remains essential at the President's House. President William Howard Taft (opposite) is seen using a White House telephone in c. 1908, but it was not until Herbert Hoover's presidency that the telephone was installed on the president's own desk. Hoover (left) is seen with a simple dial telephone in the Oval Office in 1929. Although the telephone has become more sophisticated, the arrangement is very much the same for President Joe Biden, seen here conversing at his Oval Office desk in 2021.

PRESIDENTS AT WORK
MESSAGES BROADCAST

Communicating with the American people has always been a presidential priority, and the White House has been quick to adopt new technology. Calvin Coolidge was the first president to address the nation by radio from the White House, and Franklin D. Roosevelt's fireside chats reassured an anxious nation in the depth of the Great Depression. Harry S. Truman's televised speeches set a precedent for later presidents, who used TV to communicate with the public, notably in times of crisis. The first White House website went live in the Clinton administration, and recent presidents have used social and digital media to get their messages out to the nation.

Below: President Harry S. Truman gave the first televised address to the nation from the White House on October 5, 1947.

Above: President John F. Kennedy addresses the nation by television and radio from the Oval Office, announcing a U.S. naval blockade of Cuba, October 22, 1962.

Left: At 8:30 p.m. on September 11, 2001, President George W. Bush addressed the nation from the Oval Office following the terrorist attacks of the day.

PRESIDENTS AT WORK 21

PRESIDENTS AT WORK
TRAVEL ABROAD

To their regular schedules, presidents in the twentieth century began adding travels abroad. Theodore Roosevelt was the first president to leave the United States, traveling to Panama in 1906. Wilson was the first to go to Europe, attending the peace conference at Versailles following World War I. Franklin D. Roosevelt was first to visit South America and Hawaii, and he attended the historic World War II conferences at Casablanca, Tehran, and Yalta. Truman went to Germany for a conference at Potsdam, held just before the war's end. Since the age of jet travel, presidents have traveled extensively throughout the world for international conferences and State Visits.

Right: President Theodore Roosevelt became the first president to journey outside the United States when he visited work in progress on the Panama Canal in 1906. He is seen here on a Panama Railroad train with Mrs. Roosevelt, who is protected from mosquitoes with netting.

Opposite: Today presidential travel abroad generally begins with a short trip on *Marine One* from the White House to Andrews Air Force Base to board *Air Force One* for a flight overseas. Seen boarding *Marine One* on the South Lawn as the press looks on are (clockwise from top left) Ronald and Nancy Reagan en route to West Germany, 1982; George W. Bush on his way to Latin America, 2005; Barack Obama headed to Saudi Arabia, 2009; and Joe Biden leaving for Europe, 2022.

22   LIFE IN THE WHITE HOUSE

PRESIDENTS AT WORK

PRESIDENTS AT WORK
CABINET MATTERS

President Theodore Roosevelt meets with his cabinet, March 2, 1909.

When formulating and promoting policies, most presidents have shown a high regard for the people's support and understanding. "I shall go just so fast and only so fast as I think I'm right and the people are ready for the step," said Abraham Lincoln. Benjamin Harrison declared that public opinion was "the most potent monarch this world knows." Indeed, public opinion often may weigh more heavily in a president's decision than advice from his cabinet. Chief executives have varied sharply in consulting department heads on important matters—a choice left open by the U.S. Constitution. James Monroe conferred at length with his cabinet, and especially with Secretary of State John Quincy Adams, before pronouncing the

Surrounded by press, President Joe Biden is joined by his cabinet, July 20, 2021.

Monroe Doctrine that warned European powers against further expansion in the Western Hemisphere. Andrew Jackson, on the other hand, largely bypassed his cabinet, preferring to discuss issues with friends, who were disparaged as his "kitchen cabinet" but who served him capably and loyally.

Even during the First and Second World Wars, Presidents Woodrow Wilson and Franklin D. Roosevelt seldom called a cabinet session. Roosevelt, like Jackson, chose to confer with outsiders of differing views and with some of his administrative assistants whose qualifications, he said, were "high competence, great physical vigor, and a passion for anonymity."

PRESIDENTS AT WORK
IN THE OVAL OFFICE

Above: President Calvin Coolidge works at his desk in the Oval Office, August 15, 1923.

Left: Richard M. Nixon calls the moon to speak with Apollo 11 crew members Neil Armstrong and Edwin ("Buzz") Aldrin via telephone-radio transmission, July 20, 1969.

Above: President Donald J. Trump meets by video conference with members of the U.S. military stationed at remote sites worldwide to thank them for their service, Christmas Day, 2018.

Right: President Joe Biden holds a bilateral meeting with President of Finland Sauli Niinistö in the Oval Office, March 4, 2022.

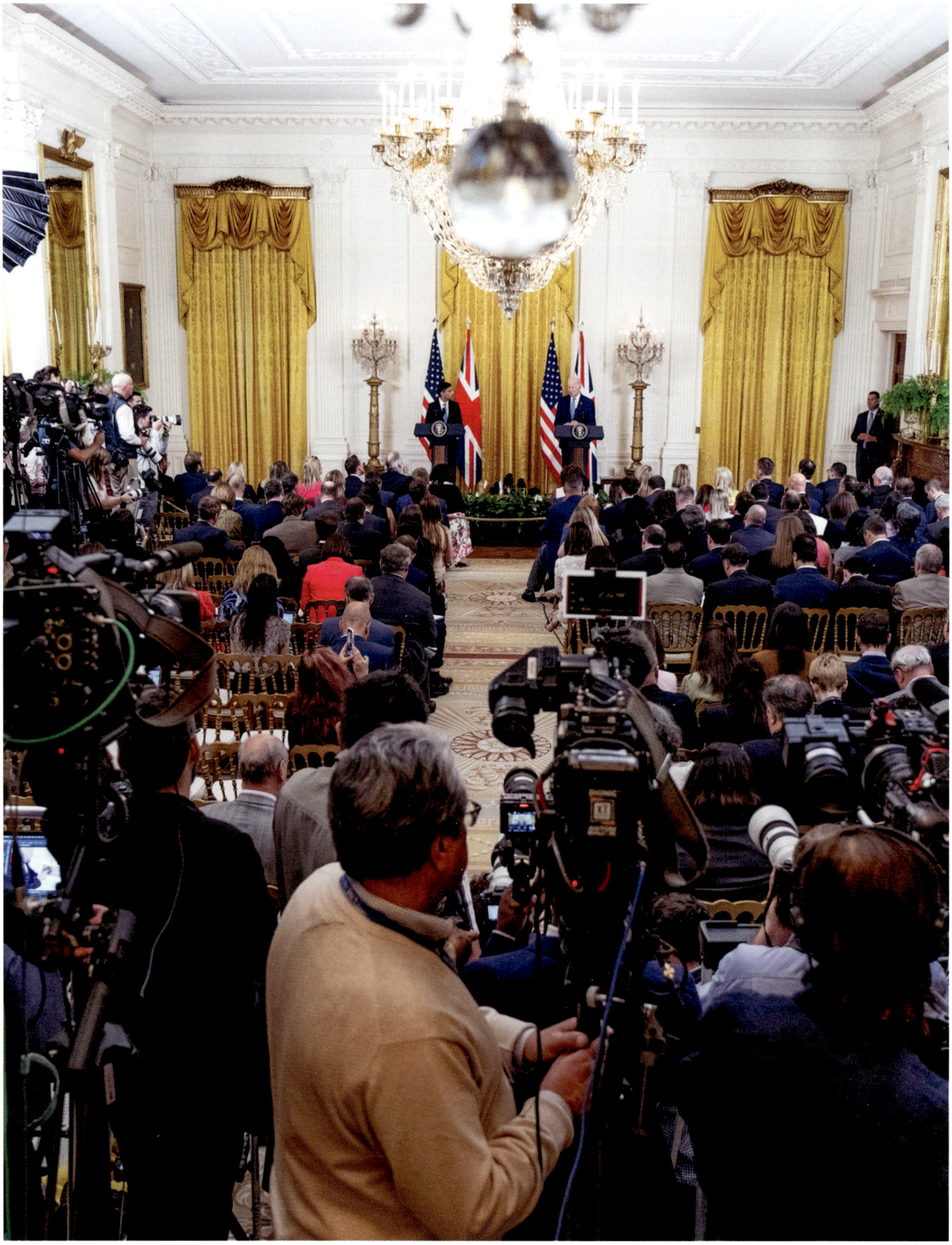

PRESIDENTS AT WORK
THE PRESS KEEPS WATCH

Over the years, the public image projected by every president and first family has been part fiction and part reality, part personal and part official. Cartoons of Teddy Roosevelt, for one, with his toothy grin and round glasses, evoke the earnest conservationist who helped preserve the nation's natural resources and the indomitable David who fought the Goliaths of industrial monopoly. But in the twenty-first century, with 24/7 news coverage on cable and the internet, presidents are not always able to control their own image. Teams of reporters follow them constantly, checking the daily schedule and covering local events and travel abroad.

As an institution, the press conference began when Wilson initiated formal question-and-answer meetings with reporters to explain his programs. It has continued in varied forms, from requiring reporters to submit written queries to the present rapid-fire questioning under television lights. Originally held in the Oval Office, the conferences were moved to the Executive Office Building during the Eisenhower presidency. Now they usually occur in the East Room or West Wing and sometimes in the Rose Garden.

Press accommodations have come a long way since reporters had to pick up what news crumbs they could from outside the mansion's entrance. Theodore Roosevelt provided the first White House newsroom in his new West Wing, reputedly after taking pity on reporters shivering in a winter storm. Further improvements were made in 1970, when a press center was built over Franklin Roosevelt's swimming pool. It includes a briefing room and two floors of booths for writers and broadcasters.

In a world of dire emergencies and instant communications, the White House has become a focal point of the fierce, incessant searchlight of global attention. To meet the demand to know what goes on here, some one hundred reporters and photographers—from newspapers, magazines, television, radio, and digital news outlets—regularly cover activities of the president and first lady. Many others have credentials and attend special events, such as visits of foreign officials.

As the press looks on, President Joe Biden participates in an East Room press conference with United Kingdom Prime Minister Rishi Sunak, June 8, 2023.

In the early twentieth century, press conferences were often held in the Oval Office as seen (right) in 1939 as reporters crowd around Franklin D. Roosevelt at his desk. Today press conferences are often held in the James S. Brady Press Briefing Room, which was created for that purpose. It is seen below as Barack Obama prepares to take questions from student reporters, 2016.

During the COVID-19 pandemic, President Donald J. Trump held outdoor press conferences in the White House Rose Garden (above) with participants seated 6 feet apart, 2020. Presidents also choose to hold press conferences on the State Floor, as in November 2022 (left), when Joe Biden met with reporters in the State Dining Room.

PRESIDENTS AT WORK
THE LONELIEST PLACE

In the morning Franklin Pierce had been escorted to the Capitol by the outgoing chief executive, Millard Fillmore. At noon Pierce delivered his Inaugural Address before a cheering crowd and rode to the White House, where for hours he accepted the congratulations of well-wishers. It was growing late when the last handshaker departed. The house was in disarray, with stacks of soiled dishes and chairs pushed in all the wrong places. The servants had disappeared. Jane Pierce, mourning the recent death of the couple's only child to survive infancy, was still in New Hampshire. Wearily, President Pierce, climbed the stairs by candlelight with his private secretary, Sidney Webster. He was president of the United States, and he stood at the pinnacle of a political man's career. But he was alone.

Taft called the White House "the loneliest place in the world." John Quincy Adams remembered his years at the White House as "the four most miserable" of his life. "What is there in this place," cried James A. Garfield, who was hounded by office seekers and would soon be murdered by one, "that a man should ever want to get in it?" "I enjoy being President," Theodore Roosevelt wrote to his son Kermit, "and I like to do the work and have my hand on the lever." But, after one year in office he confessed, "Everyday, almost every hour, I have to decide very big as well as very little questions, and ... what it is possible ... to achieve." For Jefferson, the presidency was "a splendid misery." For Truman, the President's House was "a great white prison." On his desk stood a sign that read, "*The* BUCK STOPS *here!*"

No matter the support from family and advisers, nothing can relieve the president of the sole responsibility for decision-making. A president's place in history is marked by word and act, with bill signings or vetoes, with economic or military strategy. "No easy matter will ever come to you," Eisenhower told President-Elect John F. Kennedy on the eve of the 1961 Inauguration. "If they're easy they will be settled at a lower level."

The weight of the president's obligations is never so starkly displayed as when it sets the country on a path of life or death, peace or war. Facing such a challenge,

McKinley wept, said a confidant, in pouring out his troubles in the Red Room during the frantic days before the Spanish-American War. Wilson's call for a declaration of war against Germany in 1917 followed sleepless nights of assessing the consequences. After Truman took the awesome responsibility of using the atomic bomb against Japan in World War II, he wrote in his autobiography that he "regarded the bomb as a military weapon and never had any doubt that it should be used." But then came the perilous week in 1962 when the United States and the Soviet Union stood "eyeball to eyeball," H-bombs ready. Kennedy had made his irrevocable decision to block Soviet ships from bringing more ballistic missiles to Cuba. Until the Soviet Union backed off, the world's future wavered in the balance

President Harry S. Truman sits at his White House desk with the sign "*The* BUCK STOPS *here!*," referring to the president's sole responsibility for decision-making.

PRESIDENTS AT WORK

President Lyndon B. Johnson listens to a tape-recorded message sent from Vietnam by his son-in-law Captain Charles Robb, a Marine Corps company commander, July 31, 1968.

During the late 1960s, the riots in American cities and the escalation of the Vietnam War with the deaths of American soldiers weighed heavily on Lyndon B. Johnson, who chose not to run for reelection in 1968.

Five years later, an unprecedented domestic crisis cast its first dark shadow across the Nixon White House with news of a break-in at the offices of the Democratic National Committee in the capital. The seemingly minor incident grew into a series of investigations and criminal indictments that resulted in intense pressure on Nixon to resign in the face of almost certain impeachment. Gerald Ford endured much criticism for his pardon of Nixon and faced challenges related to the economy. Jimmy Carter had to deal with a national energy shortage and the seizure of U.S. embassy staff in Iran. Ronald Reagan was confronted with the bombing of a Marine barracks in Beirut; his dramatic meetings with Soviet President Mikhail Gorbachev produced a treaty signed in the East Room to limit certain nuclear missiles. The Cold War ended following the fall of the Berlin Wall during George H. W. Bush's tenure, but other areas demanded his attention. He sent American troops into Panama when the security of the Panama Canal was threatened, and into Kuwait when Iraq invaded. Bill Clinton sent American forces to Somalia and Bosnia. Then, less than a year after his Inauguration, George W. Bush responded to terrorist attacks by sending American troops into Afghanistan and, in 2003, to war in Iraq.

Barack Obama wound down American involvement in Iraq and Afghanistan but faced uprisings in North Africa and Syria and tensions over nuclear weapons in Iran and North Korea. The COVID-19 pandemic raised unique foreign and domestic policy challenges for the administration of Donald J. Trump. Joe Biden withdrew troops from Afghanistan but sent arms to Ukraine and worked to strengthen the NATO alliance following Russia's unprovoked invasion of its neighbor.

As the representative of all the people, the president must balance the often-conflicting interests of many groups and sections in seeking the common good. At once the ceremonial head of government, leader of a political party, administrator of the nation's laws and domestic affairs, director of foreign policy, and commander in chief of the armed forces, the chief executive can seldom, if ever, escape the pressures of the job. How this many-faceted power has been used has depended on the era, and the character and conscience of each president.

President Ronald Reagan and Soviet President Mikhail Gorbachev sign the Intermediate Range Nuclear Forces (INF) Treaty in the East Room, 1987.

Dancers perform in the East Room (above) during a Diwali reception hosted by President and Dr. Biden, October 24, 2022. And Diana, Princess of Wales, dances with actor John Travolta (opposite) at a White House dinner during the Reagan presidency, 1985.

CHAPTER TWO

WHERE HOSPITALITY MAKES HISTORY

Whatever their personal style, no first family can ever forget that they act as the nation's official hosts. The distinctive architecture of the Executive Residence, with its spacious rooms and elegant parlors, lends itself to both casual and formal gatherings. Though each administration leaves its own distinctive social imprint on White House entertaining, the hospitality always retains its symbolic meaning in the house that belongs to all Americans.

WHERE HOSPITALITY MAKES HISTORY
EARLY TRADITIONS

Recognizing their responsibility for setting national standards of hospitality, John and Abigail Adams required guests to show the kind of deference to the new republic that subjects accorded rulers of monarchies abroad. During their short stay in the village capital, the Adamses practiced the formal court etiquette that had been adopted for a similar reason by George and Martha Washington in New York and Philadelphia. Mrs. Adams remained regally seated to greet the town's leading citizens and foreign diplomats who attended the president's levees, or receptions. By her side, dressed in a black velvet coat, John Adams bowed solemnly to arrivals, who then took designated seats around the wall.

Such formality went out the window when Thomas Jefferson became president. He emphasized, instead, his cherished ideals of equality and democracy. In his words, he "buried...levees, birthdays, royal parades" and replaced them with two main White House receptions that were open to all, on New Year's Day and the Fourth of July.

Jefferson entertained Jérôme Bonaparte, Napoleon's youngest brother and the future king of Westphalia, after that impetuous young man married the Baltimore belle Betsy Patterson. Jefferson once invited his butcher to dinner. The man brought his son, explaining that the boy could use the place vacated by a guest who was ill. And the president made both feel welcome among the distinguished company. Jefferson's dislike for ceremony, however, only highlighted his refined taste. He served fine wines and hired a French chef to prepare foods unfamiliar to Americans. Around his small, informal table, he assembled the wittiest, most knowledgeable men and women to be found in the city or coming from abroad to visit the strange young capital.

President Andrew Johnson receives callers at a New Year's Reception in 1866.

In learning and accomplishments, Jefferson himself was unique. His interests ranged from music and history to farming, astronomy, anthropology, and architecture. And it was this erudition that President John F. Kennedy referred to in his famous toast at a 1962 dinner honoring Nobel Prize winners. His guests, said Kennedy, made up "the most extraordinary collection of talent, of human knowledge, that has ever been gathered together at the White House, with the possible exception of when Thomas Jefferson dined alone."

Jefferson replaced the custom of bowing with the more democratic practice of shaking hands. The greeting proved so popular that no successor could abandon it, despite the painful pressure from thousands of hands embracing the privilege. Slight James K. Polk, once described as the "merest tangible fraction of a president," found a way to avoid a painful grip. "When I observed a strong man approaching," he said, "I generally took advantage of him by being a little quicker . . . seizing him by the top of his fingers, giving him a hearty shake."

Abraham Lincoln performed the task, in the words of an observer, "as though . . . splitting rails as of yore." On January 1, 1863, before signing the Emancipation

This modern watercolor depicts a reception during the presidency of John Adams. Visitors entered the Oval Room (known today as the Blue Room) from a temporary wooden balcony on the south side of the house. The South Portico was not added until 1824.

Proclamation, he shook hands for three hours at the usual New Year's Reception. Upstairs in his cabinet room, he spread the official document on the table, dipped his pen in ink, and paused. "I never . . . felt more certain that I was doing right," he said, looking at Secretary of State William H. Seward. "But . . . my arm is stiff and numb. . . . If they find my hand trembled, they will say, 'he had some compunctions.' But, anyway, it is going to be done!" Then, slowly and carefully, Lincoln wrote the bold signature that appears at the end of the document.

Besides shaking hands with the public at special events, most presidents regularly made themselves available to the public. Calvin Coolidge opened the White House doors for this purpose weekly. Rather surprisingly, the taciturn New Englander thoroughly enjoyed the contact. "On one occasion I shook hands with nineteen hundred in thirty-four minutes," Coolidge recalled in his autobiography. "Instead of a burden, it was a pleasure and a relief to meet people in that way and listen to their greeting, which was often a benediction."

President and Mrs. Abraham Lincoln (above) shake hands with guests during the 1862 New Year's Reception. Sixty-five years later, in 1927, hundreds of visitors form a line (below) along the North Drive to shake hands with President Calvin Coolidge at the New Year's Reception, continuing the annual tradition.

When Herbert Hoover and his wife, Lou, opened the White House for a traditional New Year's Day Reception in 1930, six thousand people appeared. By 1932, the annual open house and handshaking had become such an ordeal that the Hoovers decided to be out of town the following year. The custom was never revived.

No one ever took more delight in receiving people and making them welcome than did vivacious Dolley Madison. Even before she became first lady, she sometimes served as official hostess for the widowed Jefferson while her husband, James Madison, was secretary of state. After she moved into the mansion in 1809, Dolley Madison made the President's House the rallying point of Washington's fast-burgeoning social life. In the "blazing splendor" of her drawing room, as the writer Washington Irving described it, were gathered, said another guest, "all these whom fashion, fame, beauty, wealth or talents, have render'd celebrated."

While "the great little Madison" met with his cabinet, Mrs. Madison often entertained the wives at "dove parties." Taking no sides in political disputes of the day, she was cordial to Federalist and Republican leaders alike. To callers in general, she served refreshments of seedcake and hot bouillon in winter, punch in summer. Perhaps compensating for the subdued dress of her Quaker girlhood, Dolley Madison arrayed herself in rich silks and satins and accentuated her height with magnificent turbans, sometimes decked with ostrich plumes. Yet so obvious was her honest friendliness that everyone found her appealing, notwithstanding her exaggerated dress and mannerisms. "'Tis here the woman who adorns the dress," said a contemporary commentator; "in her hands the snuff-box seems only a gracious implement."

First Lady Dolley Madison, as depicted in 2011 by artist Peter Waddell, hosts one of her weekly parties in the "Elliptical Saloon," now known as the Blue Room.

WHERE HOSPITALITY MAKES HISTORY

The White House is seen engulfed in flames on the night of August 24, 1814, during the War of 1812, in this watercolor painted in 2004. The blaze, set by British troops who hurled flaming torches through the windows, gutted the interior and was finally extinguished by a raging thunderstorm.

Then suddenly, brutally, the mansion's "Golden Age," as some called the Madison era of entertaining, came to an end. The War of 1812 had broken out five months before Madison's reelection. It dragged on, mostly in sea engagements far from Washington, until the electrifying news struck the capital on a hot August 23, 1814, that the British had landed troops in Maryland. Gathering members of his cabinet, President Madison went off early the next day to join the American forces near Bladensburg, Maryland. Meantime, Mrs. Madison remained at the White House, overseeing preparations for a dinner for the president and watching through a spyglass for her husband to return, "ready at a moment's warning to enter my carriage and leave the city," as she wrote her sister in an hour-by-hour letter.

"I am still here within sound of the cannon!" she added at 3:00 in the afternoon. "Two messengers covered with dust, come to bid me fly; but I wait for him." Friends finally persuaded Mrs. Madison to leave and escorted her across the Potomac into Virginia, where she eventually would join the president. Her flight came none too soon. Having scattered the Bladensburg defenders, the British troops marched into Washington that evening and put the torch to the White House, the Capitol, and other public buildings. A torrential thunderstorm saved the city from more devastating destruction, but the Executive Mansion was reduced to a blackened, burned-out shell.

Rebuilding took three years. During the remainder of Madison's administration, the couple lived in rented houses, where the incomparable Dolley held court and the president conducted executive affairs in an atmosphere of renewed confidence following the country's second confrontation with the British.

When James Monroe and his family moved into the rebuilt White House in the fall of 1817, its partially rebuilt exterior had again been painted a gleaming white. Handsomely restored inside, it contained elegantly carved and gilded furniture and decorative objects in the State

The exterior walls were all that remained of the White House after the fire of 1814. The burned, soot-covered shell is seen in this watercolor by George Munger, c. 1814–15.

Rooms, many of them ordered by Monroe from France. Nor were the appearances deceptive. The new facade and furnishings marked a return to the pomp of earlier days.

Guests at the first New Year's Reception had a preview of the changed rules when foreign diplomats were greeted with elaborate protocol before the public was admitted. From then on, Monroe insisted, as had Washington and Adams, that respect be shown the United States by placing foreign ministers "upon much the same footing . . . of form and ceremony" as that required of American ministers at European courts. This meant that diplomats would come to the White House only by invitation or after requesting a formal audience with the president.

First Lady Elizabeth Monroe adopted a chillier social tone. She refused to continue the exhausting custom of making first calls to cabinet wives or women in the city, or even returning them. Eliza Hay, the Monroes' married daughter who lived in the White House with her husband, carried on her own feud with Diplomatic Corps wives over the etiquette of paying calls. The drastic change from the Madisons' warmth and accessibility alienated Washington's social leaders. They retaliated by boycotting the Monroes' "at homes." "The drawing room of the President was opened last night to a 'beggarly row of empty chairs,'" wrote Sarah Gales Seaton, wife of a prominent Washington newspaper editor. "Only five females attended, three of whom were foreigners."

In long-range social prestige, however, the White House always wins. Washington society eventually accepted the Monroes' rules of etiquette, along with their hospitality. Moreover, future first ladies would be forever indebted to Elizabeth Monroe for freeing them from the demands of local sociabilities.

The Monroes' successors, John Quincy Adams and his wife, continued the high style of

Social entertaining was limited during the Monroe presidency as First Lady Elizabeth Monroe refused the custom of making first calls to the cabinet wives and women in the city. The announcement of the wedding of their daughter Maria to Samuel Laurence Gouverneur is found in only a brief newspaper notice.

MARRIED,
On Saturday evening last, by the Rev. Mr. Chase, Mr. Matthias Mount, to Miss Fanny E burn, both of this city.
At Washington, on Thursday evening last, Samuel Lawrence Gouveneur, Esq. of New-York, to Miss Maria Hester Monroe, youngest daughter of James Monroe, President of the United States.

entertaining, bringing to it a background of the longest and most varied diplomatic and social experience abroad that any president has ever had. John Quincy, son of the first president to live in the White House, had served in United States missions at many courts, including Prussia, the Netherlands, and England. His wife, Louisa Catherine Adams, born in London to an American father and an English mother, was a brilliant scholar and an accomplished hostess. Well read in Greek, French, and English literature, she wrote verse in French, played the harp and spinet, and maintained her equanimity under the heavy pressure of official entertaining.

"This evening was the sixth Drawing-Room," President Adams wrote in his diary after one of the public levees that were held every other week. "Very much crowded—Sixteen Senators, perhaps sixty Members of the House of Representatives, and multitudes of Strangers.... These parties are becoming more and more insupportable."

As a conscientious New Englander, however, Adams never shirked his duty. He met punctiliously with his guests and served even more elaborate refreshments than had his predecessor. The loaded trays carried by waiters threading their way through crowded State Rooms held ice cream, coffee, tea, cakes, jellies, wines, and liqueurs—plus various imported Caribbean fruits in season.

Perhaps the most notable dinner presided over by John Quincy Adams was one in 1825 honoring the Marquis de Lafayette on his sixty-eighth birthday. The French hero of the Revolutionary War, who was paying a return visit to America, responded thus to the president's toasts to his and George Washington's birthdays: "To the Fourth of July," he said, "the birthday of liberty in both continents."

John Quincy Adams ended his one-term presidency in deep chagrin over his defeat by the West's magnetic general, Andrew Jackson. He did not linger to attend

First Lady Louisa Catherine Adams was an accomplished White House hostess. Here she is shown with her gilded mahogany harp and bound collection of music in this c. 1824 painting by Charles Bird King.

the inaugural ceremonies, which culminated in the most boisterous celebration ever seen at the White House.

The enthusiastic followers of the hero of the Battle of New Orleans poured into Washington from far and near to see the "People's President" installed in the highest post of the land. Frontiersmen, clerks, and bankers, some with wives and children, jammed the boardinghouses and hotels. "It was like the inundation of the northern barbarians into Rome," said one eyewitness.

After applauding Jackson's Inaugural Address at the Capitol, the crowd moved on to enjoy the White House reception—to the accompaniment of crashing china and glassware. Attendants lured many of the unruly guests out to the lawn for punch served from buckets. Inside, merrymakers stood in muddy boots on satin upholstered chairs to catch a glimpse of their new leader, while would-be handshakers backed him against the wall. The president escaped the mob's further embrace only by slipping out and spending the night at the "Wigwam," as capital residents had nicknamed the nearby Gadsby's Hotel. Yet the rude opening of the Jackson administration was far from an accurate foretaste of "Old Hickory's" tenure in the White House.

At his official receptions and suppers, Jackson also offered guests sumptuous repasts, including the best wines and liqueurs, and every kind of meat and fowl the lush new land afforded. The last open house held by Jackson was almost as crowded as his first. On the eve of leaving office in 1837, he was presented with a 1,400-pound cheese. Placing the huge gift in the Entrance Hall, he invited the public to come and eat as much as they liked in celebration of George Washington's birthday. The people came in droves. What they did not eat dropped on the floor and was trod into the carpets; the smell lingered for weeks.

President Andrew Jackson invited the public to feast on a 1,400-pound cheese, which was placed in the Entrance Hall in February 1837. Jackson had been given the cheese in celebration of George Washington's birthday.

The whole affair, some said, effectively discouraged public entertaining by incoming President Martin Van Buren, who was Jackson's vice president and his handpicked choice for the nation's top office. Whatever his reason, Van Buren—a widower for years—discontinued all public receptions except those on New Year's Day and the Fourth of July. Instead of the openhanded hospitality of the Jackson era, he arranged small, exclusive dinner parties, where both friendly and opposing political leaders traded lively repartee.

The president's four bachelor sons, who lived with him and shared his social and political interests, presented an irresistible challenge to Washington matchmakers. Dolley Madison—by now an aging but still romantic widow—won the prize by introducing Van Buren's eldest son, Abraham, to Angelica Singleton, a lovely young relative of hers then visiting the capital from South Carolina. As Mrs. Abraham Van Buren, charming Angelica made a perfect hostess for her father-in-law. But the president's enemies found a rich lode of political capital in what they pictured as selfish high living in the Executive Mansion while the country suffered from a severe depression. Congressman Charles Ogle of Pennsylvania led the attack in blocking an appropriation of $3,665 for the mansion's maintenance. In what would become famous as the "Gold Spoon Oration," Ogle described Van Buren as one who used "knives, forks, and spoons of gold that he may dine in the style of the monarchs of Europe." He spent "the People's cash in . . . green finger cups, in which to wash his pretty tapering, soft, white lily fingers," and ate fancy French foods instead of good American "'hog and hominy,' 'fried meat and gravy' . . . with a mug of 'hard cider.'" Van Buren's defenders assembled figures to prove that their man actually was costing the taxpayers less for house expenses than had any other president. But the gold-spoon image had

Pictured holding a glass of champagne and living in high style, President Martin Van Buren was caricatured by his opponent during the presidential campaign of 1840.

WHERE HOSPITALITY MAKES HISTORY

The White House Collection contains this campaign textile from the presidential election of 1840, which pictures a log cabin and a barrel of hard cider, symbols for successful candidate William Henry Harrison, pictured at the bottom.

been created, and in 1840 the voters elected the president's opponent, William Henry Harrison, candidate of the Whig "Log Cabin and Hard Cider" Party.

Harrison's wife, Anna, was the only first lady who never acted in her official role. She did not even see the White House. At the time of the Inauguration she was unable to stand the rough coach-and-steamer trip from her home in western Ohio. She was about to leave when a messenger rode up with news of the president's death one month after his Inauguration. It was too late to attend the State Funeral for her husband. She remained in Ohio, where Harrison had made his career—and where their grandson, Benjamin Harrison, would start on his path to the presidency nearly half a century later.

Thus the White House received an unexpected resident in John Tyler, who as the vice presidential candidate had been the last half of Harrison's catchy campaign slogan, "Tippecanoe and Tyler Too." President Tyler, labeled "His Accidency" by unkind critics, was destined to remain in the mansion only a single term. But he brought to it in turn two wives as different as they could be. Gentle Letitia, his first wife and mother of eight children, led a retiring life until her death in 1842. Acting in her stead, her daughter-in-law Priscilla (married to son Robert) performed as a highly successful official hostess on such glittering occasions as the State Dinner and ball given for the Prince de Joinville, son of King Louis Philippe of France.

Tyler's second wife, lighthearted 24-year-old Julia Gardiner—a belle at home and abroad before her marriage—frankly enjoyed the attention she received as the nation's first lady. Seated in a large armchair on a platform in the Blue Room, the erstwhile "Rose of Long Island" greeted guests with the air of a queen. In a white satin ball gown and gleaming headdress adorned with diamonds and ostrich feathers, she led the dancing in the East Room as gentlemen whirled their partners in the then-daring waltz. At one reception she introduced a bouncy Bohemian dance called the polka and started it toward wide popularity. After an especially triumphant evening, Julia Tyler wrote her mother with girlish delight, "The British Minister, Pakenham, was there . . . and devoted to me. At least fifty members of Congress paid their respects to me, and all at one time."

To pleasure-loving members of the capital's higher echelons, the dancing steps of the second Mrs. Tyler gave way far too quickly to the dogged tread of all-work-and-no-play President James K. Polk and his attractive but strait-laced wife Sarah, a devout Presbyterian. New rules banned dancing, card playing, and similar diversions. The proper Polks did their duty, offering the required number of formal dinners and grand receptions, but no food or beverages refreshed the great dry public gatherings, which were famous for sedateness and sobriety. A guest who ventured to compliment the first lady on the "genteel assemblage" at one of these receptions received Sarah Polk's dignified reply: "Sir, I have never seen it otherwise."

This early daguerreotype captures President and Mrs. James K. Polk with their guests at the White House in 1849. From left to right: future president James Buchanan; Harriet Lane (Buchanan's niece); Joanna Rucker (Mrs. Polk's niece); postmaster general Cave Johnson; First Lady Sarah Polk; Secretary of the Treasury Robert Walker; President Polk; former First Lady Dolley Madison; and Matilda Childress Polk (Mrs. Polk's cousin).

WHERE HOSPITALITY MAKES HISTORY

The next three presidents—Zachary Taylor, Millard Fillmore, and Franklin Pierce—had little chance to enliven the Washington social scene. The popular former general, "Old Rough and Ready" Taylor, died after only sixteen months in office. During that time his delicate wife, Margaret, had relied on their married daughter, Betty Bliss, to do the honors at official functions.

Ailing Abigail Fillmore also was forced to delegate many of her hostess chores to her daughter, Mary Abigail. Yet, as the president's wife, she managed to put in an appearance and to greet guests at a surprising number of dinners and receptions in spite of delicate health and the pain that came from standing on a permanently injured ankle.

One of the gloomiest periods in White House entertaining prevailed during the Pierce administration, which began two months after the Pierces had witnessed the death of their last surviving child, Benjamin, killed in a railroad accident. Naturally limited at first, White House social functions continued thereafter in a stiff and somber atmosphere, which extended even to Jane Pierce's large table bouquets of rigidly wired japonicas.

The return of what a reporter called "joy and gladness in the Executive Mansion" came, ironically enough, in the ominous pre–Civil War term of James Buchanan. One cause for joy was Buchanan's beautiful young niece and ward, Harriet Lane. As his official hostess, she presided over so many brilliant balls and sumptuous banquets that the White House was compared to a European court.

The Buchanan White House frequently drew titled travelers. Journalists wrote about the first diplomatic mission to Washington from Imperial Japan in the spring of 1860. Delivering a commercial treaty, the sixty-member entourage created a sensation in the mansion's East Room, where curious Americans viewed the envoys' exotic clothing and hairstyles. As a final social coup in his politically weak administration, President Buchanan welcomed the Prince of Wales, later Britain's Edward VII, as a houseguest. Harriet Lane arranged a State Dinner with royal protocol, followed by fireworks on

Opposite: The first envoys from Imperial Japan pay their respects to President James Buchanan and his cabinet during an East Room reception in 1860.

WHERE HOSPITALITY MAKES HISTORY

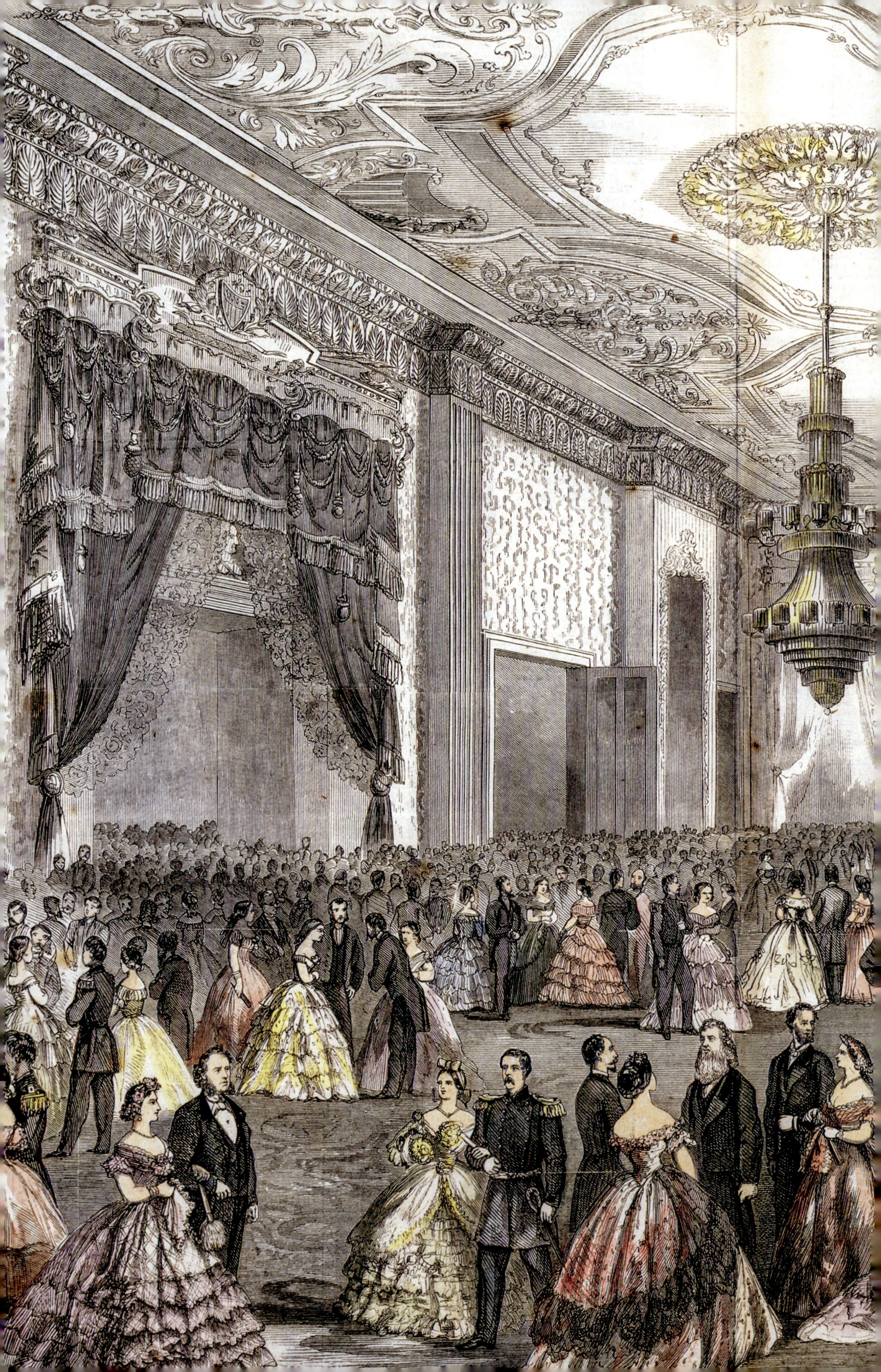

the lawn. But the public reception for the prince turned into a roughhouse. "The Royal party have certainly seen Democracy unshackled for once," wrote a New York correspondent. "The rush . . . was terrible. People clambered in and jumped out of the windows."

During the Civil War, White House entertaining took a new direction. The Union capital was crowded with Union army and navy officers, war contractors, and assorted visitors who came to see President Lincoln and to share the first family's hospitality. Special dinners and receptions were given for high government officials, staff officers, and diplomats. To the weekly public levees came crowds of soldiers and day laborers along with the most fashionable ladies and gentlemen. Attired "with gloves and without gloves; clean and dirty," they all pressed toward "the tall, rapidly bobbing head of the good 'Abe,' as he shook hands with his guests," recalled one bystander; and "when anyone he knew came along, he bent himself down to the necessary level, and seemed to whisper a few words in the ear, in pleasant, homely fashion."

First Lady Mary Todd Lincoln held afternoon receptions, too, and carefully planned major social events. But nothing she did could please her relentless critics. If she served fine food, the first lady was wasting money while brave boys died at the front. If she held only a reception instead of a formal dinner, her critics said she must have been saving money for the personal finery that everyone knew to be her weakness. Yet the same public committed shocking acts of vandalism in the president's home. Guests at Lincoln's second inaugural reception cut souvenirs of floral designs from brocaded window draperies and lace curtains; damage was extensive. After Lincoln's assassination, ruthless collectors ravaged the house. "Silver and dining ware were carried off," wrote an eyewitness. "It was plundered not only of ornaments but of heavy articles of furniture. Costly sofas and chairs were cut and injured."

Mary Todd Lincoln strived to transform the aging White House into an elegantly appointed mansion suitable for such fine entertaining as the "Grand Presidential Party at the White House" held by the Lincolns on February 5, 1862.

WHERE HOSPITALITY MAKES HISTORY
THE VICTORIAN ERA

Following the Civil War, White House hospitality continued to reflect the attitudes of each new set of residents as they adapted themselves and their house to changing times. When Andrew Johnson and his family moved into the shabby building in the summer of 1865, they brought to its renovation a sturdy common sense that might well have served as an example to politicians during the turbulent days of Reconstruction.

"We are plain people from the mountains of Tennessee," said the Johnsons' older daughter, Martha Patterson, who directed most of the work and took over as official hostess for her ailing mother. "I trust too much will not be expected of us," she added, and then proceeded to extend the family's hospitality with natural good taste and a charm that surprised and won over many Washington sophisticates. The Johnsons also showed how "plain people" could stand with dignity during the terrible weeks before the president's impeachment trial ended in his vindication. But it was a miserable time for all.

The Inauguration of popular Union general Ulysses S. Grant on March 4, 1869, finally opened the floodgates for long-deferred capital celebrations. Julia Grant relished her role as mistress of the White House. She found it, she wrote, "a garden spot of orchids . . . a constant feast of cleverness and wit, with men who were the brainiest . . . and women unrivalled for beauty, talent and tact."

The Grants entertained often and lavishly. In 1874 King David Kalakaua of the Sandwich Islands—now Hawaii—became the first ruling monarch to visit the White House. At a State Dinner in his honor, three of the king's retinue stood behind him, and one examined each dish before the king accepted it.

If the Grant administration typified mid-Victorian style in multiple table courses and intricate decor, President and Mrs. Rutherford B. Hayes followed as perfect examples of the era's ideal of moral rectitude. Few White House scenes were ever more sedate than the Sunday evening hymn sings and prayers that congressional and cabinet friends shared with the presidential family. After an April 1877 dinner for Grand Duke Alexis, son of the

Russian czar, no alcoholic beverage, including wine, was served at White House functions—a prohibition that later earned Mrs. Hayes the nickname of "Lemonade Lucy" and brought a quip from one guest that "water flowed like wine."

The more relaxed yet intellectual social atmosphere that marked the beginning of James A. Garfield's term as the next president is often obscured by the tragedy of his assassination. Both he and his wife, Lucretia, were warm, cultured people. A classical scholar, Garfield sometimes performed the trick of simultaneously writing Greek with one hand and Latin with the other. Mrs. Garfield was perhaps the first first lady to initiate serious research on White House history. Then, without warning, the bright four-month tenure of the Garfields ended on July 2, 1881, with shots fired by a demented office seeker. Garfield died two months later.

The new chief executive, former Vice President Chester Arthur, was a debonair widower who became the most eligible catch in town. His huge wardrobe and handsome carriage with his coat-of-arms on the door were topics of conversation, his elegant dinners the most sought after. Mary Arthur McElroy, his youngest sister, came from her home in Albany, New York, to assist him as hostess.

King David Kalakaua of the Hawaiian Islands, the first head of state to visit the White House, greets President Ulysses S. Grant at a reception in December 1874.

First Lady Lucy Webb Hayes greets her guests in the Blue Room in 1877.

The people's next choice was America's second bachelor president, Grover Cleveland, who soon chose as his bride his young ward Frances Folsom. As a hostess, she proved as capable as she was beautiful. She organized functions well in advance and showed her stamina by shaking hands with an estimated nine thousand guests at one public reception. She arranged at-home days so that all women who wished to meet her could. She held two receptions a week, one on Saturdays so that working women could attend. Indeed, energetic Mrs. Cleveland so enjoyed life in the White House that she left tearfully in 1889, remarking to a member of the house staff that she and her husband would be back. Four years later she kept her promise. Cleveland was reelected and became the only president to serve nonconsecutive terms.

The Victorian Age gave us two more first ladies, each representative of the period in her own way. Caroline Scott Harrison, wife of Benjamin Harrison, brought to her new role the same energy she had shown in church and club work back in Indiana. A model of domesticity, she presided over the White House with genteel efficiency. She assembled pieces of White House china used by previous families, thus beginning the preservation of the historic White House China Collection.

President William McKinley's wife, Ida, embodied a no less typically Victorian image of the delicate female. Though in poor health, she made valiant efforts to cope with official schedules. She attended exhausting State Dinners, at which the usual seating arrangement was changed to place her beside her devoted husband, who could thus see to her needs. From a chair near the receiving line at receptions, Mrs. McKinley greeted guests but held a bouquet to foil handshakers.

President and Mrs. Grover Cleveland welcome guests at an Army and Navy Reception held in 1888.

WHERE HOSPITALITY MAKES HISTORY

WHERE HOSPITALITY MAKES HISTORY
ENTERTAINING IN THE TWENTIETH CENTURY

Social history at the White House in the twentieth century clearly revealed how life in the Executive Residence is colored by each family's personality and background.

As the twentieth century arrived, it was no coincidence that the dynamic character and deeds of Theodore Roosevelt reflected America's exuberance, growing power, and influence. By moving his offices to the new West Wing and remodeling the mansion's State Rooms after the simple elegance of the early nineteenth century, the president at once gained quarters for increasing executive business and created a more appropriate setting for the nation's official entertaining.

From December 1902, when the renovation was completed, social functions began to take on the more regulated character of modern times. The Roosevelts employed the first White House social secretary, and the president delegated a government official to untangle sticky problems of precedence involving diplomatic and political rivalries.

Roosevelt imparted his own ebullience to every White House event—from a reunion with the Rough Riders of the Spanish-American War to a Japanese jujitsu exhibition in the East Room, or to formal state functions, such as the reception and spectacular stag dinner for Prince Henry of Prussia. Roosevelt also made history with his 1901 dinner invitation to Booker T. Washington, the first African American to receive a social invitation to the President's House. TR's charming wife, Edith, brought to her official duties a poise that led the president's military aide, Archie Butt, to write that she spent seven years as first lady "without ever having made a mistake."

President and Mrs. William Howard Taft were the first to entertain on the roof of the terrace

President Theodore Roosevelt prepares to toast the guest of honor Prince Henry of Prussia at a dinner in the East Room, 1902.

58   LIFE IN THE WHITE HOUSE

leading to the new west extension, where they sat at wicker tables under Chinese lanterns swaying in the breeze. The social highlight of their White House years was the celebration of their twenty-fifth wedding anniversary on June 19, 1911, when they gave a large evening garden party on the South Lawn for several thousand people.

Woodrow Wilson, who like John Tyler became a widower while in office and who also brought a second wife to the mansion, had firm ideas of his role as host. Regardless of pressures, he refused to invite anyone to the White House to advance even the most precious of his programs. "I will not permit my home to be used for political purposes," Wilson declared. And although he presided with good humor at official parties, he preferred small dinners in the Jeffersonian manner—animated by witty and intellectual conversation. Wilson found with his second wife, Edith, a renewal of happiness he had never expected to know again. Without her "love and

President William Howard Taft with his family were caught laughing in this candid photograph from their twenty-fifth anniversary. Several thousand guests were invited to celebrate the occasion on the South Lawn, 1911.

President Warren G. Harding poses with visiting members of the Crow Tribe, c. 1921–23.

care... I don't believe he could live," Mrs. Wilson's social secretary, Edith Benham, wrote in the dark days after the strain of his stubborn but futile League of Nations campaign had left him a paralyzed, broken man.

After the grim days of World War I and the gloom of Wilson's long illness, the arrival of genial Warren G. Harding seemed to bring back the pleasant days of "normalcy" he had promised. Not only did the new president and his wife, Florence, reopen the doors for large and frequent official gatherings, but they also dined almost daily with Harding's card-playing cronies and other close friends. They also opened the mansion to public tours once again after it had been closed during World War I; on such occasions, Mrs. Harding sometimes appeared unexpectedly and shook hands with astonished, delighted sightseers. Though she suffered from a chronic kidney ailment, she energetically went about her duties as first lady. Then, suddenly, following the president's death during a trip to the West in 1923, the convivial period ended.

To the Executive Mansion came the rock-ribbed New Englander and former vice president, Calvin Coolidge, and his charming wife, Grace. Social life during the Coolidge administration was notable for the many anecdotes it produced concerning the granite reserve and wry humor of the president. The early morning breakfasts to which Coolidge invited members of Congress—often to the dismay of late sleepers—gave capital raconteurs some of their best stories. One told of the time the president poured coffee and cream into his saucer. As a few guests followed suit, Coolidge calmly put the saucer on the floor for his dog.

The most famous guest of the time, loquacious Queen Marie of Romania, was entertained at a State Dinner in 1926. According to Chief Usher Ike Hoover, the queen made strenuous efforts to get "Silent Cal" to talk, but "was not any more successful than others who had tried it before." The whole affair was odd, the chief usher noted, for the visit, including ceremonial greetings, the meal, and farewells, took only an hour and forty-five minutes.

Yet, in the matter of etiquette, President Coolidge inaugurated what has become an indispensable aid in conducting State Visits. Following an awkward incident in which wartime enemies were seated together at an official dinner, he established a Protocol Office in the State Department to handle procedures for such visits. Today its staff arranges programs, determines precedence, and suggests food preferences to fit the specific needs of each delegation.

President and Mrs. Calvin Coolidge pose with military and naval aides who assisted in the New Year's Reception, January 1, 1927.

White House entertaining reached new heights when President Herbert Hoover assumed office amid a seemingly endless boom economy. Even after the stock market crashed in the autumn of 1929, the wealthy president and his wife, Lou, continued to invite a record number of guests for breakfast,

WHERE HOSPITALITY MAKES HISTORY

President Herbert Hoover presents aviator Amelia Earhart with a gold medal for her solo trans-Atlantic flight, 1932.

lunch, and dinner, though they personally met the expenses not only for their private parties but also for many of the official ones.

No one could assume, however, that such hospitality marked indifference to the nation's problems. The Quaker president had long shown his humanity in war and postwar relief work in food distribution, and he labored to solve the country's gargantuan economic troubles. At times he would gulp his meals so fast, a member of the domestic staff recalled, that "the servants made bets on how long it would take . . . 'nine minutes, fifteen seconds,' or whatever."

Franklin Delano Roosevelt and his big, gregarious clan came next, to meet the challenge of the Depression and usher in the longest, most varied social period yet. Eleanor Roosevelt in her book *This I Remember* listed a staggering number of official and personal luncheons, teas, dinners, receptions, and other programs. In one year alone, President and Mrs. Roosevelt put up 323 houseguests, served meals to 4,729 people, and offered refreshments at teas and receptions to 14,056 others. The assorted guests pouring into and out of the mansion between March 1933 and April 1945 included students, poets, playwrights, labor leaders, nuclear scientists, prime ministers, and presidents. During World War II, British Prime Minister Winston Churchill came often and stayed in the White House, and the mysterious visitor of 1942, known only as Mr. Brown, turned out to be Soviet Foreign Minister V. M. Molotov on a mission to speed up the opening of an Allied second front in Europe.

World War II gave a regal dimension to the Roosevelts' hospitality with the appearance of royal refugees fleeing Nazi occupation in Europe. Some, such as the Crown Prince and Princess of Norway and Queen Wilhelmina of the Netherlands, became temporary houseguests. Others,

Above: President Franklin D. Roosevelt and Winston Churchill during a May 1943 meeting at the White House.

Left: First Lady Eleanor Roosevelt with guests at a lawn party honoring U.S. soldiers in 1942.

Below: The arrival of Prime Minister Liaquat Ali Khan of Pakistan at Blair House in 1950. The residence on Pennsylvania Avenue was used by the Trumans during the three and one-half year renovation of the White House.

Opposite: President and Mrs. Dwight D. Eisenhower greet Great Britain's Queen Elizabeth II and Prince Philip at the North Portico on their arrival for a four-day stay in October 1957.

such as the kings of Greece and Yugoslavia, were briefly feted. Older Washingtonians recalled the White House visit of Britain's King George VI and Queen Elizabeth just before war erupted in 1939. Down the hall from the family rooms on the Second Floor, the king occupied the Lincoln Suite, his queen, the Rose Suite, later called the Queens' Bedroom. Screens separated the royal and presidential quarters.

By the time of President Harry S. Truman and his wife, Bess, the "season" had expanded to include half a dozen State Dinners and as many congressional and other large receptions. Some were so well attended that guests stood almost shoulder-to-shoulder. At a reception in 1948, the chandelier in the Blue Room tinkled a warning that the structure was in critically shaky condition. During the following three and one-half years, while the White House underwent reconstruction, the Trumans lived across the street in the government's guest residence, Blair House, and large official dinners and receptions took place in local hotels. In 1951 Britain's Princess Elizabeth and her husband, Philip, Duke of Edinburgh, spent several days at Blair House with the Trumans.

The next year, the presidential family moved back into the restored Executive Mansion just in time to welcome as houseguests Queen Juliana of the Netherlands and her consort, Prince Bernhard. But capital life was changing in the postwar era. State visitors came so frequently from newly independent nations and as a result of foreign policy conferences and fast modern transport that the White House could no longer accommodate them.

Since the latter part of the Eisenhower administration, most official guests have stayed at Blair House, across Pennsylvania Avenue from the White House, during their State Visits. In fact, only once during

64 LIFE IN THE WHITE HOUSE

WHERE HOSPITALITY MAKES HISTORY

Dwight Eisenhower's second term did guests sleep in the mansion—when Elizabeth II, queen of Great Britain, and Prince Philip occupied the same suites as had her mother and father nearly twenty years before. President and Mrs. Eisenhower enjoyed the formal ceremonial role of official entertaining that reflected their years of military life.

Under the lively direction of John F. and Jacqueline Kennedy in the early 1960s, official entertaining changed further. President Kennedy banished receiving lines whenever possible and chatted informally with guests in the connecting State Rooms. At round tables, rather than the more formal U-shaped ones, shorter dinners with fewer courses, prepared by a French chef, allowed the guests more time to dance and to watch performances of internationally known musicians, ballet dancers, opera singers, jazz stars, and Shakespearean actors.

Then came the crack of rifle shots in Dallas—and a dark interlude of international mourning for the bright,

Grand Duchess Charlotte of Luxembourg and First Lady Jacqueline Kennedy compliment actor Basil Rathbone and members of the consort players who had presented an evening of Elizabethan poetry and music in the East Room, April 1963.

66 LIFE IN THE WHITE HOUSE

lost promise of a murdered president. When social life returned to the White House, the new host brought with him a quarter century of capital friendships and service, first as representative and senator from Texas, then as vice president. It was not surprising that an atmosphere of Texas Americana pervaded the private and official parties of Lyndon B. Johnson and his wife, Claudia, better known by her childhood nickname, "Lady Bird."

In January 1969 the spotlight on executive entertaining moved from the Johnsons to the Nixons, another family with two daughters. But the resemblance ended there, for Richard and Pat Nixon, like those who went before, soon produced an entertainment pattern all their own. One innovation was a series of Sunday morning worship services attended by associates and friends of the family. Held in the East Room and presided over by leaders of various faiths, the services were followed by a social hour and refreshments in the State Dining Room. As events unfolded over the next years, the

Above: President and Mrs. Richard Nixon pose with guests the Duke and Duchess of Windsor at a White House dinner, 1970.

Below: President and Mrs. Gerald R. Ford listen to an impromptu performance by legendary bandleader Harry James, June 1975.

WHERE HOSPITALITY MAKES HISTORY

President and Mrs. Jimmy Carter frequently entertained outdoors. In June 1978 they held a jazz festival on the South Lawn featuring Eubie Blake performing ragtime.

Nixon administration ended in political scandals and the president's resignation—and a new family in the old house.

From August 1974 to January 1977 the Gerald Fords made their own brand of White House history. Guests remembered lively dinners capped by dancing in the Entrance Hall, where Betty Ford, who once studied modern dance with the noted Martha Graham Dance Company of New York, whirled gracefully with the president and other partners. During the nation's Bicentennial celebrations in 1976, the Fords hosted numerous heads of state and held many events in the White House to commemorate the country's history.

With the Georgia Carters, still another regional design went into the tapestry of White House hospitality, which never ceases to repeat the infinite variety of American life. "Natural," "spontaneous," and "family oriented" were terms often used by the media to describe Jimmy and Rosalynn's southern style. Their creative entertaining was enhanced by the world-famous American and European performers they introduced in the East Room. On a memorable evening following the ceremonial signing of the Panama Canal Treaties, the Carters' dinner guests included eighteen heads of Latin American states and twenty-five U.S. senators.

Ronald and Nancy Reagan brought Hollywood glamour and Hollywood guests to the White House. They also hosted a vast array of foreign officials, including Prime Minister Margaret Thatcher of Great Britain, King Juan Carlos I and Queen Sophia of Spain, President François Mitterrand of France, and, in a historic visit, the Soviet leader Mikhail Gorbachev. In the early 1980s the Reagans celebrated the birthdays of former Presidents Franklin D. Roosevelt and Harry S. Truman and of former First Lady Eleanor Roosevelt at White House luncheons.

Trees ablaze with tiny lights offer a glittery backdrop for the barbecue given by President and Mrs. Jimmy Carter on the West Terrace during a visit of the Japanese prime minister in May 1979.

Above: President and Mrs. Ronald Reagan with Frank Sinatra at a White House performance, 1982.

Left: President George H. W. Bush hosts a State Dinner for Queen Elizabeth II, 1991.

George H. W. and Barbara Bush had several official dinners and luncheons, but they often entertained at large receptions. Their traditional style of entertaining was reminiscent of their years of diplomatic service and their lives in Texas and on the Maine coast. In 1989, some four hundred foreign ambassadors and their spouses attended an elegant white-tie reception held in honor of the Washington Diplomatic Corps. Mrs. Bush hosted several receptions in the State Rooms to highlight the work of many nonprofit organizations, and President Bush initiated a presidential lecture series with noted presidential biographers that was televised from the East Room. In 1992 they presided over the two hundredth anniversary of the laying of the White House cornerstone and submitted letters and mementos for a White House time capsule.

First Lady Hillary Clinton described the White House entertaining style of the Clinton presidency as both "respectful of tradition" and "fun and informal." In November 2000, she and Bill Clinton hosted a historic dinner in the East Room to celebrate the two hundredth anniversary of life in the President's House. With Lady Bird Johnson, Gerald and Betty Ford, Jimmy and Rosalynn Carter, and George H. W. and Barbara Bush in attendance, President Clinton could announce, "In the entire two hundred years of the White House's history, never before have this many presidents and first ladies gathered in this great room."

A few days earlier, President Clinton had presided over a ceremony marking the arrival of John Adams at the President's House in 1800. "For two centuries now," he stated, "Americans have looked to the White House as a symbol of leadership in times of crisis, of reassurance in times of uncertainty, of continuity in times of change, of celebration in times of joy.... We are still in the business of forming that more perfect union of our Founders' dream. I hope and believe John Adams would be pleased."

In celebration of the two hundredth anniversary of the White House, President and Mrs. Bill Clinton hosted a special Anniversary Dinner on November 9, 2000. Their guests included seven former presidents and first ladies. Posing together in the State Dining Room are (left to right): President and Mrs. George H. W. Bush, Lady Bird Johnson, President and Mrs. Clinton, President and Mrs. Gerald R. Ford, and President and Mrs. Jimmy Carter.

WHERE HOSPITALITY MAKES HISTORY

President Joe Biden welcomes guests to the annual dinner in honor of the nation's governors in the State Dining Room, February 11, 2023.

WHERE HOSPITALITY
MAKES HISTORY
IN THE TWENTY-FIRST
CENTURY

Since the turn of the century, the recent presidents and first ladies have enjoyed sharing the White House with guests and the public. The guest lists of President and Mrs. George W. Bush included writers, historians, and students; religious leaders of many faiths; and aspiring ball players and their families who came to T-ball games on the South Lawn. President and Mrs. Obama opened the White House to a wide variety of Americans, with a special emphasis on military families and young people. President and Mrs. Donald Trump welcomed visiting heads of state and many groups, from the Boy Scouts of America to the winners of the Super Bowl. President and Dr. Biden have hosted world leaders, educators, innovators, sports champions, and representatives of nonprofits and charitable organizations.

The nation's governors and their spouses are welcomed by the president to the White House each winter. The Bidens continued this tradition in February 2023 with a black-tie dinner in the East Room.

The Medal of Honor, the nation's highest recognition of military valor, has been presented in moving East Room ceremonies, most recently by President Biden.

During an East Room ceremony, March 3, 2023, President Joe Biden presents the Medal of Honor to retired U.S. Army Colonel Paris Davis for his heroism during the Vietnam War.

WHERE HOSPITALITY MAKES HISTORY
HOLIDAY TRADITIONS

Below: President Lyndon B. Johnson decorates the White House Christmas tree with the help of schoolchildren, 1964.

Opposite top: First Lady Pat Nixon poses with her White House staff in the Entrance Hall for a holiday photograph, 1973.

Opposite bottom: First Lady Betty Ford and daughter Susan decorate Christmas cookies in the Solarium on the Third Floor of the White House, 1975.

Not until 1889 did the first Christmas tree appear in the President's House. That year Benjamin and Caroline Harrison, with several grandchildren in residence, placed the tree, lighted with candles, in the oval room on the Second Floor, the family sitting room. Theodore Roosevelt, an ardent conservationist, did not approve of cutting trees, but one year his young children snuck a small tree into the White House to be unveiled on Christmas morning. The first tree to appear on the State Floor was placed in the Blue Room by the Taft children. Most nineteenth- and early twentieth-century presidential families celebrated the holiday with private family festivities on Christmas Day, although an open house on New Year's Day welcomed the public from 1801 to 1932. Like most American homes, the White House in these years was decorated with fresh greens and fruit, but on a simple scale.

Most recently, the White House has been a festive place during the holiday season, alive with beautiful music and decorations. Mamie Eisenhower had more than twenty-five trees decorated with tinsel and lights placed in the East Room and other areas of the house, including the laundry room. In 1961, Jacqueline Kennedy had the Blue Room tree decorated with ornaments inspired by *The Nutcracker* ballet of Pyotr Tchaikovsky, and that started a tradition. Now each year the first lady selects a special holiday decorating theme, which is documented in detail for television viewers throughout the world. First ladies have borrowed toys from museum collections, commissioned art school and architectural students, and called on volunteers

WHERE HOSPITALITY MAKES HISTORY

President and Mrs. Jimmy Carter pose with their daughter, Amy, in front of the Blue Room Christmas tree, 1978.

from the states, territories, and the District of Columbia to make ornaments for the nearly 18-foot high Blue Room tree. Talented and creative needlepointers and craftspeople have made thematic ornaments of natural plant materials, paper, fiber, ceramics, metal, and wood.

Laura Bush chose a variety of holiday themes. In 2001, with the theme of "Home for the Holidays," models of presidential birthplaces and homes were made for the East Room mantels and tables throughout the public rooms. Other themes featured first family pets, classic children's stories, American Christmas carols, and the beauty of the natural world with plants, trees, fruit, and flowers reflecting the country's bounty. Michelle Obama selected themes with an emphasis on honoring and paying tribute to the Armed Forces.

First Lady Nancy Reagan climbs a ladder in the Blue Room to hang the Official White House Christmas Ornament, a replica of the dove of peace on the Mount Vernon weather vane, 1982. First issued by the White House Historical Association with the support of Mrs. Reagan in 1981, the annual ornaments are now hung on millions of trees each year, including those at the White House.

76   LIFE IN THE WHITE HOUSE

First Lady Barbara Bush sets the star on top of the National Christmas Tree on the White House Grounds, 1989.

President and Mrs. Bill Clinton and their daughter, Chelsea, decorate a Christmas tree in the Yellow Oval Room, 1994.

First Lady Laura Bush stands in front of the White House gingerbread house display in the State Dining Room, 2003.

First Lady Michelle Obama joins children from military families as they decorate Christmas cookies, November 30, 2011.

During the Donald Trump presidency, First Lady Melania Trump chose to decorate the White House to feature the themes "Time-Honored Traditions," "American Treasures," "The Spirit of America," and "America the Beautiful."

In 2021, First Lady Jill Biden selected "Gifts from the Heart" as the inspiration for her first White House holiday decorations. The theme focused on small acts of kindness that lifted spirits during the COVID-19 pandemic. Each element of the special decor represented what brings people together during the holidays and throughout the year. In 2022, Dr. Biden turned to words from the famous preamble to the Constitution, "We the People," to create holiday displays that represent Americans coming together each year in fellowship and faith, reminding us that we are stronger in community than we are apart.

The traditional gingerbread house, made each year by the White House pastry chef, is displayed in the State Dining Room. In 2022 it featured a design based on the "We the People" holiday decor and included a replica of the Constitution itself. The display weighed more than 300 pounds, with 100 pounds of sugar and 30 pounds of chocolate.

The White House Christmas tree is traditionally delivered by horse-drawn carriage and accepted for the Blue Room by the first lady. First Lady Melania Trump is seen (opposite) accepting the 2020 tree.

First Lady Jill Biden reads to a group of elementary school students (right) in the State Dining Room during the 2021 holidays.

The traditional White House gingerbread display in the State Dining Room was expanded to include a replica of Independence Hall in 2022 (below) in keeping with the "We the People" theme of the holiday decor displayed throughout the house.

WHERE HOSPITALITY MAKES HISTORY

A selection of White House Christmas cards sent through the years is displayed in the White House Bookseller's Area, 2018.

In 1953, the Eisenhowers sent the first official presidential Christmas cards. Each year, presidential cards, including the most recent, are displayed during the holidays. Harpists, choirs, string ensembles, and other musical groups from across the country add to the joyful holiday spirit for visitors and staff alike. "The whole White House smells like Christmas trees, and the wonderful music puts a smile on every face!" observed Laura Bush.

Recent presidents have also commemorated the Jewish holiday of Hanukkah, "The Festival of Lights." Menorahs lent to the White House were lighted and exhibited in the West Wing. Since 2001, they have been on public view in the East Wing, and in recent years on the State Floor. In 2022 the White House acquired its own menorah, made out of wood that had been removed from the building during the Truman renovation. It was created by the White House Carpentry Shop and is the first Jewish artifact to be added to the White House Collection.

President and Mrs. George W. Bush watch as a candle on the menorah is lit (right) during the first Hanukkah celebration in the Executive Residence, 2001.

First Lady Jill Biden (below) speaks during a Hanukkah holiday reception in the Entrance Hall, 2022.

WHERE HOSPITALITY MAKES HISTORY

The Marine Band performs holiday music in the Entrance Hall, 2022.

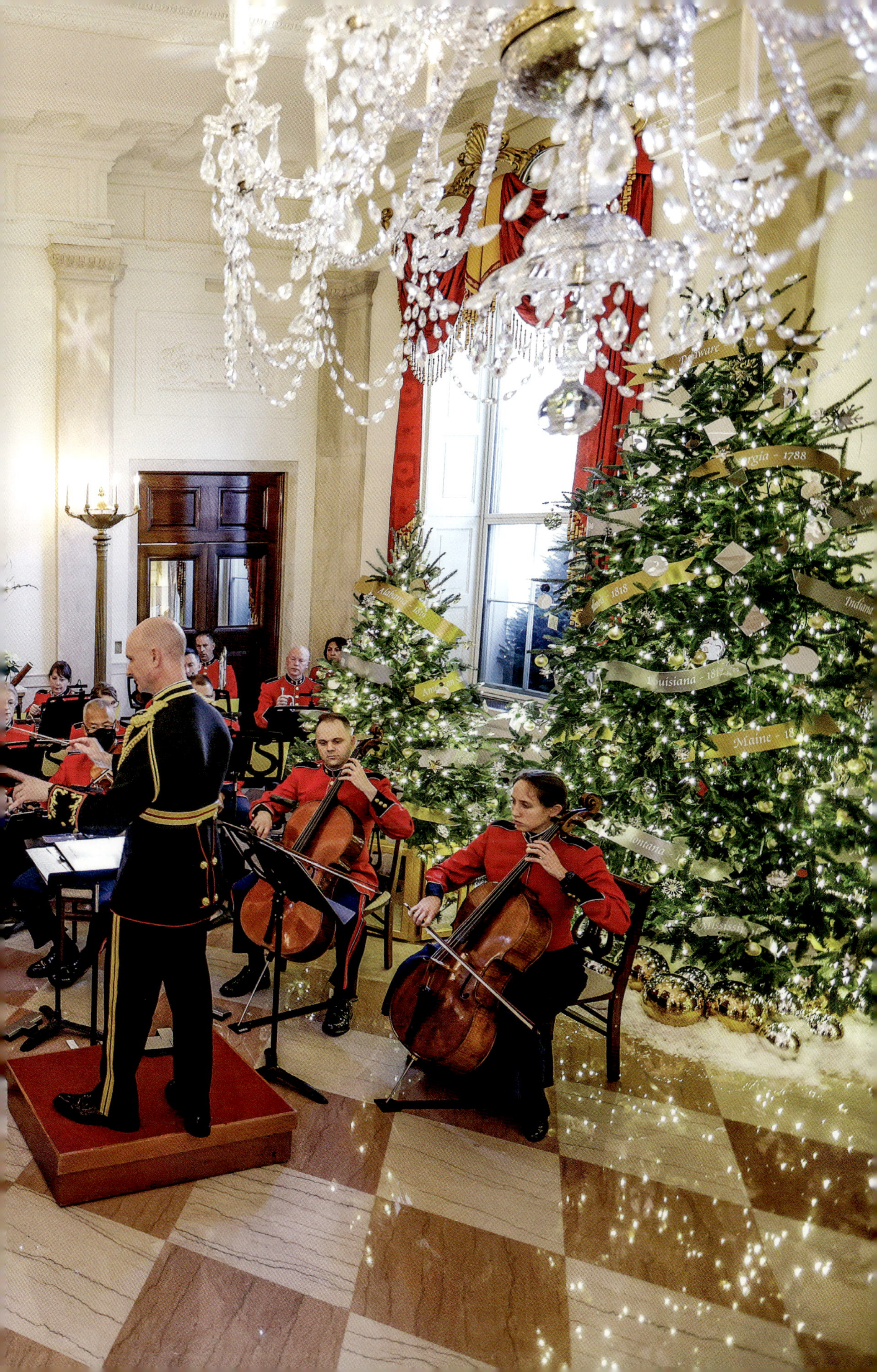

WHERE HOSPITALITY MAKES HISTORY
STATE VISITS

Since World War II, an ever-lengthening procession of foreign leaders has come to 1600 Pennsylvania Avenue to confer on global problems. These dignitaries are often formally entertained at the White House, and an invitation to attend such a function is highly coveted. Certainly a State Dinner to honor a visiting head of government or a reigning monarch is one of the most glamourous of White House affairs, an event that also showcases global power and influence. Today the term "State Dinner" is reserved for events in honor of heads of state, though in the nineteenth century most official dinners, even without a foreign official, were called State Dinners.

Today's State Dinner begins with a morning Arrival Ceremony that was first introduced by John F. Kennedy and remains largely unchanged. In his time, it also included helicopter service to transport guests to the Ellipse. Lyndon B. Johnson, Richard M. Nixon, Gerald R. Ford, and Jimmy Carter maintained the helicopter arrival, though less frequently, and the practice has now largely been abandoned. Most state guests arrive in Washington the day before and are driven through the Southwest Gate toward the white-columned South Entrance of the White House. There the president and his wife greet their guests of honor with a red carpet and often a twenty-one gun salute. The evening of the State Dinner, the president and first lady greet their guests under the North Portico and escort them to the Yellow Oval Room on the Second Floor. There they meet with other top-ranking guests, such as the secretary of state. Meanwhile, about one hundred other guests are arriving at the mansion's east entrance. Passing through the East Wing, these guests ascend the marble stairway to the State Floor. On their way they are presented with cards explaining seating arrangements. Then they

President Joe Biden and First Lady Jill Biden are joined by President of the Republic of Korea Yoon Suk Yeol and his wife, Kim Keon Hee, on the Blue Room Balcony (below), following the State Arrival Ceremony on the South Lawn (opposite), April 26, 2023.

are conducted to the East Room by social aides, officers chosen from the armed forces. The president and first lady with their honored guests descend the Grand Staircase to the sounds of Ruffles and Flourishes and then greet the assembled guests in protocol order. Finally, the president and first lady escort the visitors to the State Dining Room, where the other guests await them.

Decorations and table settings for formal dinners in the White House are classic and elegant. Frequently in use is the red and gold-rimmed set of china acquired during the Reagan administration as well as the Johnson plates with wildflowers. The Clintons selected a set of gold-rimmed ivory china to commemorate the two hundredth anniversary of the White House in 2000. Laura Bush and Michelle Obama selected specially designed services to reflect their interests.

The public does not have to wait long to learn details of the dinner. As an aid to the news media, Lyndon Johnson

The United States Army Old Guard Fife and Drum Corps performs during the State Arrival Ceremony for the Republic of Korea, April 26, 2023.

WHERE HOSPITALITY MAKES HISTORY

In scenes from the December 1, 2022, State Dinner hosted by President and Dr. Biden in honor of French President Emmanuel Macron and his wife, Brigitte Macron, the Bidens await the arrival of the Macrons at the North Portico (opposite); guests are seated for dinner in a tent on the South Lawn (above); and musician Jon Batiste performs (left).

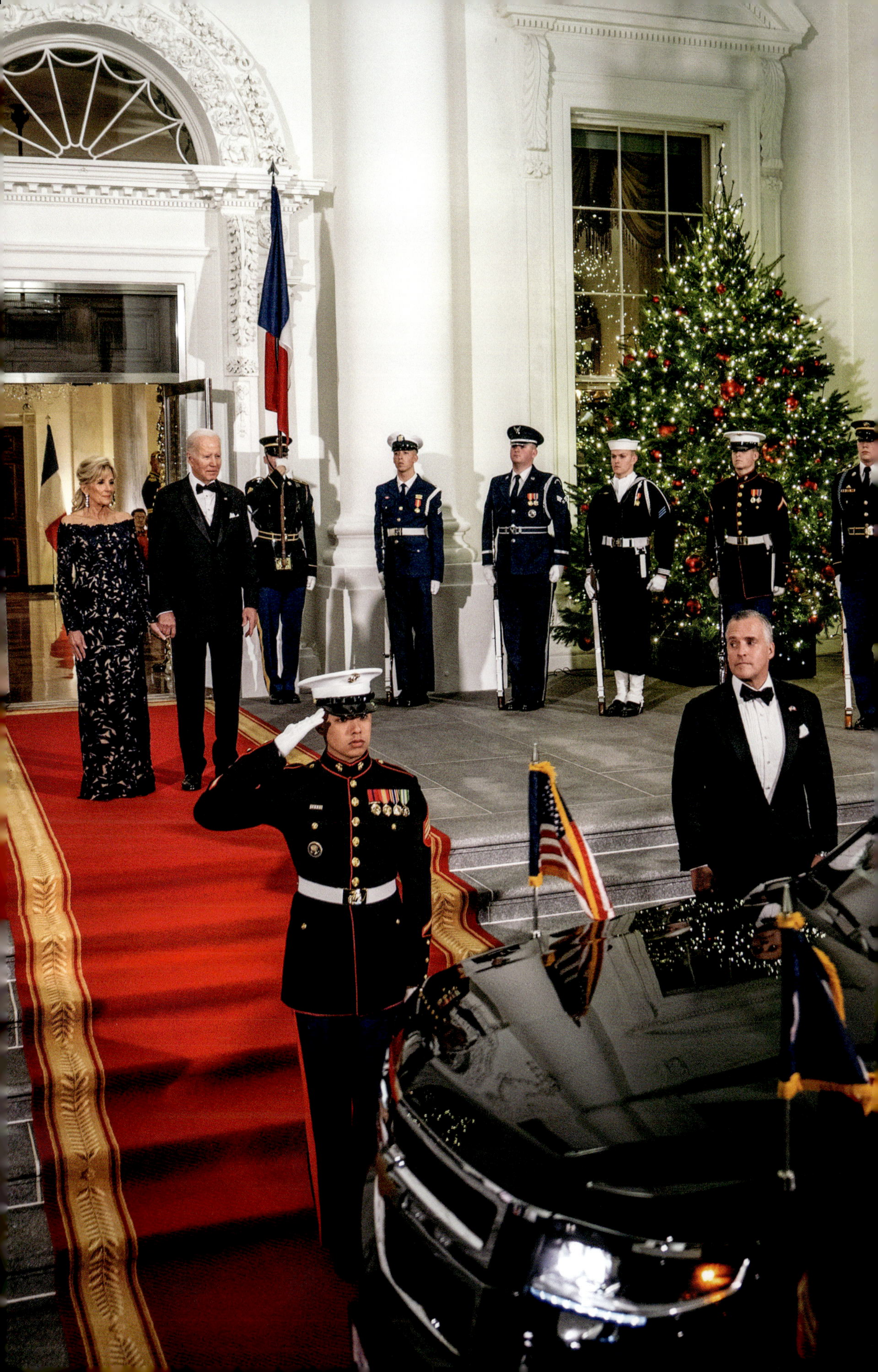

had an electronic system installed so that reporters assembled in another room could hear the traditional exchange of toasts. More recently, some foreign leaders have arranged for coverage of the dinners for later television broadcast in their home countries. Newscasts and next-day newspapers often carry pictures and stories on the guests, menu, and entertainment. To obtain such information and to add firsthand descriptions to their coverage, a few White House reporters have long been permitted to attend the after-dinner entertainment and to chat with the guests.

Behind the glitter and ceremony of such state affairs is elaborate planning that tailors each aspect of the event to the national cultures and individual tastes of the guests of honor. These formal dinners involve the creation of guest lists, menus, flowers, table settings, and entertainment for the evening. To assure the success of the meal, the Reagans even tried out and tasted the complete dinner, down to the last detail, a week or ten days before the event.

First Lady Jill Biden has also worked closely with the White House social secretary and the Executive Residence staff to coordinate every detail for special occasions, while Executive Chef Cristeta Comerford prepares menus.

President Joe Biden and Narendra Modi, the prime minister of India, exchange toasts during a State Dinner in honor of India, June 22, 2023 (opposite). Prior to the dinner, the press was invited to a preview of the food and table settings. Executive Chef Cristeta Comerford and Executive Pastry Chef Susan Morrison (right) explain the menu. Floral arrangements and table settings were also on display during the press preview (below).

Former President Harry S. Truman performs in the East Room of the White House during the Kennedy administration, 1961.

WHERE HOSPITALITY MAKES HISTORY
SHOWCASE PERFORMANCES

American musicians have performed at the White House for more than two hundred years, and the showcase performances have often reflected the musical tastes of first families or their guests. The Marine Band has been a presence at the President's House since it first played for John and Abigail Adams's New Year's Day Reception in 1801, and many other military groups such as the Air Force Strolling Strings and the Army and Navy Choruses have performed.

Jefferson considered music "the favorite passion of my soul" and often played the violin, as did another Virginian, John Tyler. Dolley Madison purchased the first piano for the house, and James Monroe ordered one from Paris in 1817. Louisa Adams played the harp; Caroline Harrison and Florence Harding were practicing musicians. Lincoln loved opera, Franklin D. Roosevelt enjoyed folk music, Truman and Nixon played the piano, and Clinton played the saxophone.

Music ranging from classical, folk, and country to gospel, opera, and jazz has all been heard in the East Room or on the South Lawn. Often, performers visiting Washington are invited to perform for the president, his family and guests. Beginning in the 1840s, the Hutchinson family singers went on to sing for seven presidents. In 1882, the Fisk Jubilee Singers sang for Chester Arthur. Edith Roosevelt initiated a series of classical music recitals; the cellist Pablo Casals performed one evening in 1904 and returned more than fifty years later to play for President and Mrs. Kennedy and their guests. When Franklin D. Roosevelt and Eleanor Roosevelt entertained the king and queen of England in 1939, they included a concert of American music that highlighted folk and concert musicians. Among the performers were Kate Smith, the

The United States Army Old Guard Fife and Drum Corps performs during a reenactment of the arrival of President John Adams at the White House on the two hundredth anniversary of the event in November 2000.

North Carolina Spiritual Singers, and Marian Anderson. Nixon hosted a special dinner for Duke Ellington's seventieth birthday in 1969 and, at the after dinner concert, sat down at the White House Steinway to play "Happy Birthday" to him.

John and Jacqueline Kennedy brought some of the finest artists to the White House to "demonstrate that the White House could be an influence in encouraging public acceptance of the arts," according to a 1962 newspaper report. Their programs often reflected the first lady's cultured tastes. The Kennedys also initiated a series of "Concerts for Young People by Young People." At one of them in 1961 opera singer Grace Brumby, just 25 years old, made her American debut, to rave reviews.

Jimmy and Rosalynn Carter demonstrated their love of classical music by establishing a series of concerts titled "In Performance at the White House" that has been broadcast over public television from the East Room. Rosalynn Carter explained that the idea for this program

President Richard Nixon plays "Happy Birthday" to Duke Ellington during an East Room performance in 1969 when Ellington received the Presidential Medal of Freedom.

LIFE IN THE WHITE HOUSE

President and Mrs. John F.
Kennedy greet Pablo Casals
after his performance in the
East Room in November 1961.

Above: Cellist Yo-Yo Ma and pianist Kathryn Stott provide after-dinner entertainment for the dinner in honor of Charles, Prince of Wales and Camilla, Duchess of Cornwall, 2005.

Left: Harry Connick Jr. and his big band perform during the Governors' Ball in the East Room, 2010.

Opposite: American singer Gladys Knight performs in the East Room following the U.S.–Africa Leaders Summit Dinner, 2022.

LIFE IN THE WHITE HOUSE

"came about because Jimmy and I knew there were so many people who had never been to the White House. . . . We wanted all of America to enjoy the White House as we did." The distinguished pianist Vladimir Horowitz opened the series, followed by Mstislav Rostropovich, Leontyne Price, Mikhail Baryshnikov, and Andrés Segovia.

Barack and Michelle Obama supported the "In Performance at the White House" series with a wide variety of musical genres. Entertainment at State Dinners included Grammy Award vocalists John Legend, Jennifer Hudson, and Beyoncé as well as the National Symphony Orchestra and the U.S. Marine Band. Performers at the Trump White House included the Washington National Opera; and the "President's Own" United States Marine Chamber Orchestra, the United States Army Herald Trumpets, the United States Navy Band Sea Chanters, the United States Air Force Strings, and other military bands. During the Biden presidency, State Dinners have included appearances by musician Jon Batiste, singers Norm Lewis, Jessica Vosk, and Lea Salonga, and violinist Joshua Bell.

President Abraham Lincoln gives his son Tad a reading lesson (above). Francis Bicknell Carpenter was inspired to make this small painting in c. 1873 after Tad's untimely death at age 18. President Biden is joined by his family on the South Portico to watch fireworks celebrating the Fourth of July, 2021 (opposite).

CHAPTER THREE

THE FIRST FAMILY AT HOME

Despite all the comforts and privileges that come to a presidential family, living in a house that is also a national monument has its challenges. When Calvin Coolidge arrived at the White House in 1923, he tried to continue his after-dinner habit of sitting on his front porch, watching people go by. But so many stopped to stare at him that he gave up this pleasant relaxation. To have a personal life in such a place is a struggle. Indeed, the attention commanded by the presidency intensifies the normal joys and sorrows of everyday family experience, the high moments of birth and the despair of death that are part of life here as in any other home. Nearly every president has known the frustration, especially in periods of national stress, of trying to find enough time to be with family. When James Garfield's son Harry was 17 and fell in love with the daughter of one of his father's best friends, a month passed before young Garfield was able to get the president alone to talk about it. Eleanor Roosevelt wrote that at times the Roosevelt boys had to make appointments to see their father. "I doubt if the public realizes," she observed, "the price that the whole family pays in curtailment of opportunity to live a close family life."

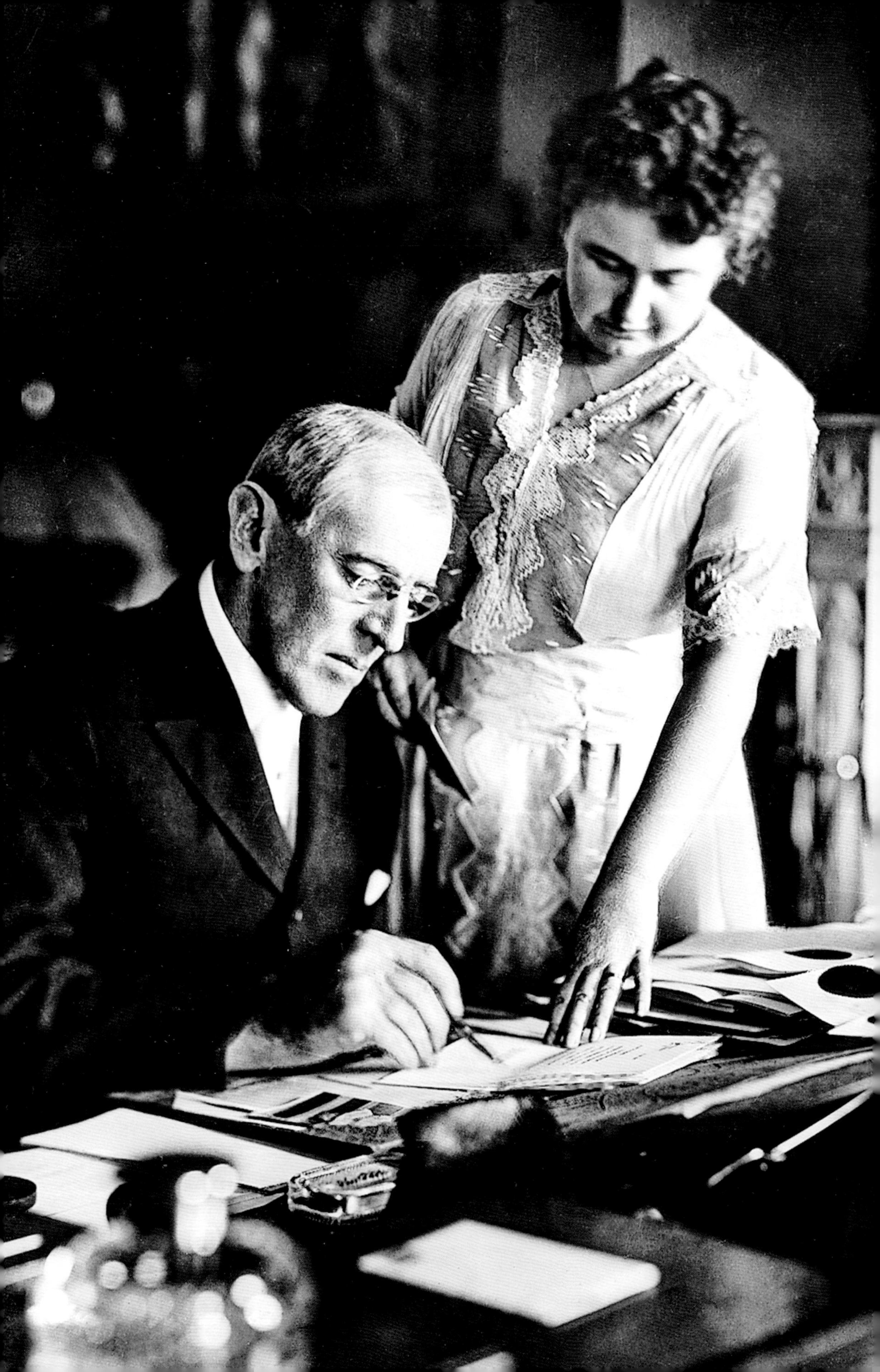

THE FIRST FAMILY AT HOME
FIRST LADIES ON A NATIONAL STAGE

Accentuated challenges face each first lady in her highly visible role. The public is keenly interested in, and often feels free to voice opinions on the projects she chooses to support and the way she runs the house, selects her clothes, or styles her hair. Lou Hoover told of receiving a letter from an indignant tourist who complained about a mended curtain she had seen in one of the rooms. Eleanor Roosevelt remarked that she sometimes felt she was no longer clothing herself "but dressing a public monument."

The clothes and styles of a first lady may sway fashions everywhere. Jacqueline Kennedy's style was copied around the world. When designers drastically lengthened skirts in 1970, reporters asked Pat Nixon just how far from the floor she would wear her hems. Betty Ford, who made her living as a model when she was a young woman studying dance, stayed in step with—and sometimes ahead of—current vogues. Some of Rosalynn Carter's clothes came from top American designers, but she also brought her own sewing machine with her to the White House. Nancy Reagan, who favored classic daytime suits and elegant evening gowns, endured some criticism for her large wardrobe of designer clothes.

In John Adams's time, critics felt that witty, politically sophisticated Abigail Adams had too much influence on the president. To one of them she was "Her Majesty" and "Mrs. President." After that, and throughout the nineteenth century, most wives avoided a political role, limiting themselves to charity and to mild support of such broad issues as temperance and women's suffrage. Dolley Madison helped found and direct a capital orphanage, to which she was said to have contributed "$20 and a cow." Sarah Polk worked as the president's private secretary, clipping and summarizing war news and political reports for him. In the early twentieth century Edith Wilson protected her ill husband by screening his visitors and

Opposite: First Lady Edith Wilson assists her husband President Woodrow Wilson at his desk in June 1920.

Below: First Lady Eleanor Roosevelt with her secretary, Malvina Thompson, and social secretary, Edith Helm (standing), on the Second Floor of the White House, 1941.

official papers so persistently that critics called her "Mrs. President," too. Florence Harding, who had worked with her husband at his Ohio newspaper, advised him during his 1920 election campaign. In the White House, she made herself accessible to the press and was the first first lady to give radio interviews. A former teacher of the deaf, Grace Coolidge had a warm personality and interest in people that complemented her taciturn husband in the political milieu of Washington. Lou Hoover, well educated, well traveled, and with broad interests, was long active in the Girl Scouts and served as its president while her husband was secretary of commerce.

The first wife of a president to participate actively in national affairs was Eleanor Roosevelt. She offered the first press conferences for newswomen, produced prime news during these sessions, and wrote a newspaper column for years. She traveled so much on lecture tours, visits to overseas troops, and as the "eyes and ears" of FDR that her White House code name was "Rover."

First Lady Lady Bird Johnson meets in the Treaty Room with her Committee for a More Beautiful Capital, 1966.

Since then, many of America's first ladies have stepped up to the podium to help shape the presidency and the nation. They have their own staff support to assist with projects, handle press inquiries and correspondence, and plan social events, unlike many nineteenth-century first ladies, who had to call on daughters and friends to address invitations to White House social events.

Jacqueline Kennedy hired the first press secretary on the first lady's staff. With the increasing public interest in her efforts to make the White House a place filled with the echoes of past residents and the finest American works of art and furnishings, she also appointed the first curator to oversee the museum functions of the President's House.

Lady Bird Johnson turned out to be another "Woman Doer," to use the title she created to honor outstanding women, including those active in her own programs to beautify the landscape and to give needy children a preschool boost to education through Head Start. Pat Nixon emphasized volunteer work and became a goodwill ambassador to Latin America in 1970. After an earthquake shook a vast area of Peru, she flew into the devastated region in a cargo plane carrying emergency supplies.

Betty Ford, with her personal warmth and interest in people, made friends for her husband and her country as she traveled with him at home and abroad. She gave strong support to women's issues and the performing arts. Rosalynn Carter embarked on many far-reaching programs, including a national drive to improve the care of the mentally ill. Nancy Reagan worked to fight drug abuse among children. Barbara Bush devoted much time to promoting literacy. Hillary Rodham Clinton advocated human rights, health care, historic preservation, and economic empowerment for women on her

Surrounded by schoolchildren, First Lady Pat Nixon views a presentation of the "Summer in the Parks" program, 1970.

Above: First Lady Betty Ford greets a blind March of Dimes poster child during a White House event, 1974.

Left: First Lady Rosalynn Carter reports to the President's Commission on Mental Health, 1978.

Above: First Lady Nancy Reagan presides over a conference in the East Room on drug abuse, April 1985.

Right: First Lady Hillary Rodham Clinton speaks on health care reform on the South Lawn of the White House, September 1993.

THE FIRST FAMILY AT HOME

First Lady Michelle Obama hosts local children on the South Lawn as they attempt to break the Guinness World Record for the most people doing jumping jacks in a twenty-four hour period, 2011.

goodwill trips abroad. In 2000 she was elected by the people of New York State to the U.S. Senate and served as secretary of state from 2009 to 2013. As a former public school teacher and librarian with a passion for reading and education, Laura Bush visited many schools. She collaborated with the Library of Congress to host the first National Book Festival in Washington, D.C., which continues to draw thousands of book lovers each fall. She promoted opportunities for women around the world and supported women and children in Afghanistan and human rights in Burma.

Michelle Obama led a nationwide effort to unite the country around children's health and to create support for families to lead healthier lives. Her initiatives included the White House Kitchen Garden, the "Let's Move" program, and the first "Kids' State Dinners" at the White House. She, along with Dr. Jill Biden, wife of then Vice President Joe Biden, engaged with military families to address the unique challenges they faced. Mrs. Obama led the "Joining Forces" initiative to hire and train military veterans and military spouses, encouraged national service, and worked to promote the arts and arts education in schools.

First Lady Melania Trump was dedicated to the many issues affecting children across the nation, from online safety to opioid abuse. She established "Be Best," an awareness campaign dedicated to ensuring a better future for children. She also joined the president on many international visits and met with foreign diplomats, heads of state, and their spouses to share solutions to the issues impacting children globally. Her appreciation for the military and their families led her to military bases domestically and overseas, and she worked with Second Lady Karen Pence to expand the American Red Cross Comfort Kit program. In 2020, Mrs. Trump played an integral role in honoring the one hundredth anniversary of the ratification of the Nineteenth Amendment, which gave women the right to vote.

Children join President Donald J. Trump and First Lady Melania Trump in the Oval Office for the announcement of the first lady's "Be Best" initiative, 2018.

Above: First Lady Jill Biden speaks at a "Cancer Moonshot" event in the East Room, February 2, 2022.

Opposite: First Lady Jill Biden encourages runners taking part in a "Joining Forces" military kids workout on the South Lawn, April 29, 2023, during the Month of the Military Child.

Dr. Jill Biden, a classroom teacher for more than thirty years, is the first presidential spouse to maintain her career while living in the White House. As first lady, she has continued teaching English and writing at Northern Virginia Community College, where she has been a professor since 2009, when her husband Joe Biden became vice president.

As first lady, Jill Biden has also continued to champion causes that support military families. Through the "Joining Forces" initiative, she has advocated for increased economic opportunities for military spouses and for additional educational programming for military children. She has also focused on health and wellness in the military community, promoting improved resources for survivors and their caregivers, including military and veteran children in caregiving homes.

Dr. Biden has reinvigorated "Cancer Moonshot," an initiative her husband launched as vice president in 2016 to accelerate progress against cancer. She encourages Americans to prioritize cancer screenings and has worked to reduce health inequities in cancer diagnosis, treatment, research, and outcomes.

THE FIRST FAMILY AT HOME

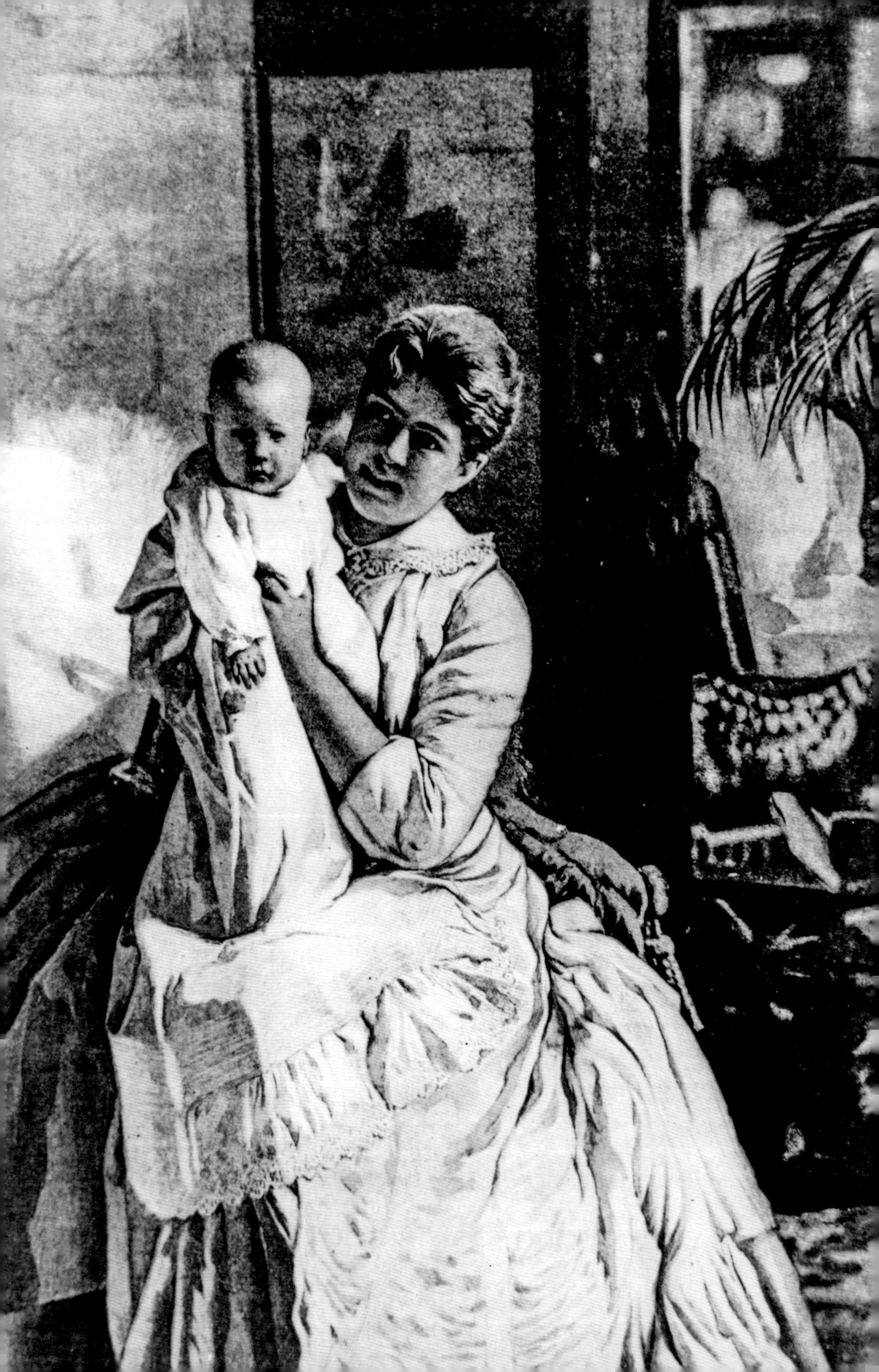

THE FIRST FAMILY AT HOME
CHILDREN IN THE WHITE HOUSE

One of the most endearing aspects of life in the Executive Mansion can be glimpsed from the hundreds of stories that have come down through the years about the many children who have lived, and sometimes grown up, in the White House, where something new and exciting is always happening.

The very young ones were usually grandchildren, since few men have reached the top rung of the political ladder in their early years. And the first of all these children whose shouts and laughter echoed through the mansion's broad corridors was the four-year-old granddaughter of John and Abigail Adams. Little Susanna arrived in November 1800 in the carriage bringing her grandmother, who was belatedly joining President Adams in the unfinished building. The little girl distressed her grandparents soon afterward by developing whooping cough, but she recovered and lived to tell her own small granddaughter Susanna of her adventures in the White House.

Thomas Jefferson's eight years in the presidency were cheered and brightened by the visits of his married daughters, Martha Randolph and Maria Eppes. On one of these visits, in the winter of 1805, Mrs. Randolph gave birth to her eighth child—named James Madison Randolph. In her chronicles of early Washington life, Margaret Bayard Smith recalled Jefferson's remark when she mentioned the amusement that children afforded adults. "Yes," he said, "it is only with them that a grave man can play the fool."

It is probable that the first child born in the White House was to Ursula Hughes, an enslaved woman, in 1802. Five children of enslaved women were born in the President's House during Jefferson's time.

Though Andrew and Rachel Jackson never had children of their own, the widowed president surrounded himself with Rachel's visiting nieces and nephews and their offspring. Three of the six or more youngsters usually

Opposite: First Lady Frances Cleveland poses with baby Marion at the White House, 1896.

Below: President Woodrow Wilson with his first grandchild, Ellen Wilson McAdoo, in his arms, 1915.

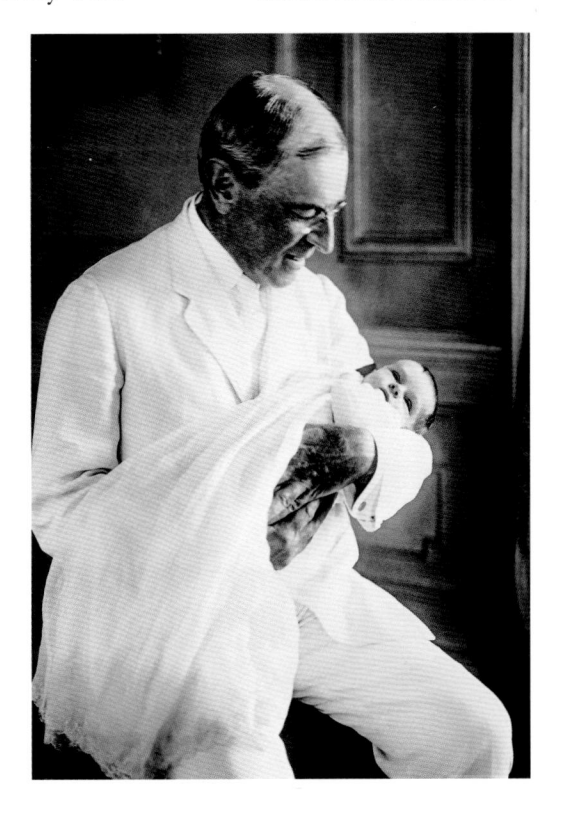

on hand were born in the White House. They were children of Rachel's nephew Andrew Jackson Donelson, who stayed with the president as his private secretary, and his wife, Emily, who served as Jackson's official hostess.

"Uncle Andrew," as the children called the president, often attended personally to the needs and wants of his adopted family; he rolled their baby carriages through the halls, comforted them in teething, and frequently joined in their games. Golden-haired Mary Emily Donelson wrote long afterward about a happy Christmas season she spent with the president and of a party that Jackson gave for the youngsters, their playmates, and other Washington children. Though the world knew him as a man of "iron will and fierce, ungovernable temper," she said, "he was the gentlest, tenderest, most patient of men at his own fireside."

It may surprise many who recall pictures of Abraham Lincoln's lined and aging face that he and his wife, 52 and 43 respectively, were among the youngest presidential couples, and that they were the first to bring to the White House a child of their own who was under 10. Thomas, or "Tad," was 7, William 10, and their brother Robert, who would be off at college most of the time, 17, when Lincoln and his family arrived in Washington from Illinois, to be at the center of the nation's most tragic era.

Abraham and Mary Lincoln were loving and indulgent parents who often said, "Let the children have a good time." This the children did, and the president's friends and colleagues quite probably felt he was too permissive at times, as when he failed to punish Tad for bombarding the door with his toy cannon during a cabinet meeting or when the boy stopped his father's callers to sell refreshments and wheedle money for war charities at stands he set up at the mansion. But the president found Tad's pranks a welcome relief from sorrow and responsibility, and he took pride in Tad's generous nature, as well as in the talent that gentle, cheerful Willie revealed in the verses and short speeches he composed.

Lincoln thoroughly enjoyed, too, the physical activity of a good wrestling match with his boys, and he encouraged them in the fun of collecting and raising pets of various kinds, including dogs, ponies, and goats. Lincoln bought Tad a pair of goats at $5 each. He got his money's worth in amusement when the youngster hitched the animals to a kitchen chair and drove his unlikely rig through the East Room, to the consternation of a group of visiting ladies from Boston. When one of the goats disappeared, Lincoln wrote a whimsical letter saying "poor Nanny" had last been seen "chewing her little cud, on the middle of Tad's bed."

Ulysses and Julia Grant, the next couple to arrive at the Executive Mansion with young children of their own, were fortunate in leading one of the happiest and most normal of family lives in the history of the White House. Their affectionate and outgoing children—three sons and a daughter named Nellie—ranged in age from 11 to 18. The middle son, Ulysses Simpson Jr., was called "Buck" because he was born in the Buckeye State of Ohio. Both he and his older brother, Frederick, worked for the president as confidential secretaries during Grant's second term.

One of the liveliest and warmest accounts of the Grants comes from the fun-loving youngest son, Jesse. In his book of reminiscences, *In the Days of My Father, General Grant*, he told of his joy in the gift of a small but powerful telescope, which he used to study the heavens. He recalled the gatherings of neighborhood friends who "flocked to the White House . . . the largest and best playground available." The "lot was our playground, in good weather," he wrote, "the big, airy basement . . . was reserved for rain or storm."

Jesse also became an ardent stamp collector. In his impatience to receive an order that he had paid for with $5 out of his savings, he appealed to his father, suggesting that the secretary of state write to the dealer, or the secretary of war could write, or Kelly, a policeman on White House duty. The matter was solemnly debated at

Young Tad Lincoln, seen photographed in 1864 in a lieutenant's uniform, was given a courtesy commission by Secretary of War Edwin M. Stanton.

THE FIRST FAMILY AT HOME

Four generations of President Benjamin Harrison's family posed at the White House for this photograph in 1889: his wife Caroline Harrison, daughter Mary McKee, grandchildren Benjamin Harrison McKee (Baby McKee) and Mary L. McKee, along with Reverend Dr. Scott (Mrs. Harrison's father).

a cabinet meeting, with Jesse pleading his case. It was finally decided to have Kelly write the following: "I am a Capitol Policeman. I can arrest anybody, anywhere, at any time, for anything. I want you to send those stamps to Jesse Grant right at once." The stamps came. Wrote Jesse in memory of his family: "The love of my parents for each other and their devotion to us children made no impression on me then. I had never known anything different. Appreciation and understanding come to me now, filling me with content."

Following Grant, both Rutherford B. Hayes and James A. Garfield brought warmhearted, close-knit families to the Executive Mansion. Each included four boys and a girl. Moreover, the two families were old friends, linked by common Ohio origins and congressional service in Washington. Fanny Hayes and Mollie Garfield, both 14, sat together at Garfield's Inauguration, behind the mother of the president-elect—the first mother to see her son take the Oath of Office. Mollie continued her friendship with Fanny after the family, including Grandmother Garfield, moved into the mansion. When Mollie gave a luncheon for ten young girls, she remembered her obligations as a hostess in the White House and seated Fanny, as the daughter of a past president, on her right.

Garfield's two older sons, Harry and James, stayed at the White House with their family, studying there under a private tutor instead of completing the remaining months of their prep-school terms. Thus they, too, happened to be with the rest of the family, along with Mollie and the two younger boys, Irvin and Abram, during most of the last six months of their father's life. He was shot in 1881.

The most photographed presidential grandchild of the nineteenth century must have been "Baby McKee," who lived in the White House with

Baby McKee holds the reins of His Whiskers, a goat presented to him by his grandfather, President Benjamin Harrison, c. 1892.

grandfather Benjamin Harrison and his four-generation family during the early 1890s. Among the numerous family members, which included parents, grandparents, aunt, uncle, cousins, and great-grandfather, mischievous little Benjamin gained a reputation with the press as the president's favorite who could do no wrong.

Professional and amateur photographers were just then discovering George Eastman's new, easy-to-operate Kodak box camera—one of the first to use roll film—and they haunted the grounds, hoping to get pictures of little Benjamin. Published photographs soon showed the active and appealing youngster as he played with his dog, led the Marine Band, or drove his own goat cart about the grounds.

The goat, called His Whiskers by the coachman, once ran away with Baby McKee, giving reporters one of their best stories about him. As His Whiskers darted off with the boy down the White House driveway onto Pennsylvania Avenue, the portly president himself, dressed in top hat and frock coat, followed in hot pursuit.

With such a start in the 1890s, illustrated news coverage of the younger members of the chief executive's family has never slackened.

First Lady Frances Folsom Cleveland holds her daughter Esther, the only presidential child to be born in the White House, as her first daughter Ruth stands beside them. The sisters attracted the relentless attention of the press and the public during their years in the White House.

In 1893 Esther Cleveland, the second daughter of Grover and Frances Cleveland, was born in the mansion, the only president's child to have that distinction. Esther's sister Ruth, who had arrived during the interlude between Cleveland's two terms, was almost two years old at the time of Esther's birth. Before the president's second term ended, another little girl, Marion, was born at the Clevelands' summer home in Massachusetts.

"The Cleveland children were . . . much beloved by everyone around the place," wrote durable Chief Usher Ike Hoover, who would serve in ten administrations. "We often wished that more of them had been born in the White House." The public seemed to feel the same way about the three little girls. Gifts and advice on how to rear them poured into the White House from all over the country.

One Washington boy organized what he called an honor guard for Ruth. Marching his young company up to the door, he asked for, and received, an interview with the president. Cleveland regretted he was too busy to review the troops, but he delegated the role to Mrs. Cleveland, who complied with pleasure. Another, less pleasant, incident occurred when a group of curious visitors gathered around Ruth and her nurse during an outing on the Grounds. One of the women picked up the child

LIFE IN THE WHITE HOUSE

and passed her around to the accompaniment of pats and kisses. The episode so alarmed Mrs. Cleveland that from then on the gates to the South Lawn were closed to the public—an exclusion that resulted in cruel and baseless rumors about the child.

Four and a half years after the departure of the demure little Cleveland girls, the uninhibited children of Theodore Roosevelt came on with the force of a hurricane. "A nervous person had no business around the White House in those days," observed Ike Hoover in describing their behavior. "Places that had not seen a human being for years were now made alive with the howls and laughter of these new-comers. . . . Nothing was too sacred for their amusement and no place too good for a playroom."

Among other pranks, the five younger children—aged 3 to 14 when the Roosevelts arrived—slid down the stairways on trays stolen from the pantry, stalked the halls on stilts, and bicycled and skated on newly polished floors. Speeding in his toy wagon, Quentin, the youngest, rammed the full-length portrait of Lucy Webb Hayes, leaving a hole.

The boys' lovely, self-willed half sister, Alice, then 17, contributed to the uproar in her own way. She refused to go away to boarding school, but she later made trips around the country, as well as to Cuba, Puerto Rico, and Asia. From shipboard in the Pacific came the story that "Princess Alice" had jumped, fully dressed, into the ship's pool. "I can do one of two things," the president once said. "I can be President of the United States, or I can control Alice."

The Roosevelt children also kept a small zoo of pets. Underfoot, inside and out, were a badger, a bear, raccoons, rabbits, turtles, parrots, pigs, cats, dogs, rats, guinea pigs, snakes, and a calico pony named Algonquin. When Archie had the measles, his brothers entertained him by leading the pony into his Second Floor bedroom, after riding up in the president's elevator.

The children of President and Mrs. Roosevelt filled the White House with their boisterous activity and many pets. Theodore Roosevelt Jr. poses with Eli Yale, a pet macaw, one of many animals in the Roosevelt children's menagerie.

THE FIRST FAMILY AT HOME

President Theodore Roosevelt is joined by his sons (from left to right): Theodore Jr., Archibald, Quentin, and Kermit, 1904.

The Roosevelt children were often photographed during their White House years. *Opposite, clockwise from top left:* Archie Roosevelt with a White House policeman, c. 1902; First Lady Edith Roosevelt with daughter Ethel, c. 1904; Alice Roosevelt and her dog, 1902; and Quentin Roosevelt with his friend Roswell Newcomb Pinckney, the son of a White House steward, 1901.

When Quentin grew old enough, he was sent to a nearby public school, and he often brought his pals home to add to the commotion. One of these friends, Earle Looker, many years later wrote a book called *The White House Gang*. In it he described the hilarious adventures of the boys and the quick and just punishment meted out by the president after such antics as the spattering of Andrew Jackson's portrait with spitballs.

TR, as the gang called him—not disrespectfully but with a mixture of affection and awe—had an amazing knowledge of the interests and needs of active children. When official business was slow, he sometimes joined the youngsters for games in the White House attic. On one such occasion, as the president was about to catch up with a boy he was chasing, young Earle turned out the light. A crash followed, and when Earle found the switch again, he saw Roosevelt holding his head and leaning against a post, from which a nail protruded shockingly close to the height of his eyes. "I'm quite all right," he told the contrite boys, "but never, n-e-v-e-r, never again, turn off a light when anybody is near a post!"

Mrs. Roosevelt managed to preside with grace and calm over her large, boisterous group of children, and TR once summed up his feelings in a letter to their son Kermit: "I don't think that any family has ever enjoyed the White House more than we have."

THE FIRST FAMILY AT HOME

President William Howard Taft and his children, Charlie and Helen, on horseback, c. 1909.

When the Tafts moved into the White House in 1909, their daughter, Helen, 18 at the time, often assisted her mother as hostess, while her younger brother, Charles, 12, was as active as the Roosevelt children. Their older brother, Robert, was often away at school.

Next came the three daughters of Woodrow and Ellen Wilson—Margaret, Jessie, and Eleanor ("Nell"). Though Wilson often appeared to outsiders as the perfect example of the austere, erudite professor, in his close-knit and affectionate family circle he was a jaunty, fun-loving man who was fond of group singing, impersonations, and limericks. The Wilson daughters supported their ill mother, who died in the White House in 1914. A decade later, the two Coolidge sons, John and Calvin Jr., away at school most of the year, had a brief time together in the White House before Calvin Jr., 16, died of blood poisoning in 1924.

First Lady Ellen Wilson is joined by her daughters Jessie, Margaret, and Nell, on the South Portico (above), 1913. The spot is also enjoyed by President and Mrs. Calvin Coolidge and their sons, John and Calvin Jr. (left), 1924.

THE FIRST FAMILY AT HOME

LIFE IN THE WHITE HOUSE

Stories and pictures of Franklin D. Roosevelt's grandchildren Anna Eleanor and Curtis Dall made their nicknames, "Sistie" and "Buzzie," household words throughout the country during their stay in the White House. In January 1945, all thirteen of his grandchildren attended Roosevelt's historic fourth Inauguration—the largest group of grandchildren ever assembled at the Executive Mansion.

First Lady Lou Hoover (on the left) with grandchildren on the South Lawn, 1930 (opposite). President Franklin Roosevelt is joined by many of his grandchildren at Christmas (above).

THE FIRST FAMILY AT HOME

In their time, Dwight D. and Mamie Eisenhower delighted in the visits of their four grandchildren—David, Barbara Anne, Susan, and Mary Jean. Though none of these children of John and Barbara Eisenhower actually lived in the White House, the youngest, Mary Jean, was christened in the Blue Room, and all found plenty of toys and playground equipment on hand for their amusement. The children called their grandmother "Mimi," and a revealing story shows how they regarded Grandfather Eisenhower. Someone had asked small David his name. "Dwight David Eisenhower," he replied. "Then who's that?" probed the questioner, pointing to the president. "That's Ike," said the boy.

Ten administrations would follow that of Grover Cleveland before the cry of a president's infant was again heard inside the Executive Mansion. Then, early in 1961, came John and Jacqueline Kennedy with their two-month-old baby, John Jr., and his engaging sister, Caroline, three years old. Soon newspaper and magazine editors were publishing stories and pictures of the youngsters' Third Floor playroom, where the Eisenhower grandchildren had romped not long before. There were also stories about the new tree house, swings, and other playground equipment behind South Lawn shrubbery, and about Caroline's pet canary Robin, her pony Macaroni, and her dog Pushinka, the gift of Soviet Premier Nikita Khrushchev.

Fond anecdotes told how "John-John" had refused to greet the Grand Duchess of Luxembourg because he had not been given his usual cookie and ginger ale; how Caroline had presented India's Prime Minister Jawaharlal Nehru with a rose for his buttonhole; and what she said when reporters asked what her father was doing. "Oh, he's upstairs with his shoes and socks off," she said, "not doing anything." As a child of the Space Age, Caroline Kennedy made news again when she asked John Glenn not about his pioneering flight around the Earth but about another orbital test with chimpanzees. "Where's the monkey?" she asked the astronaut.

Opposite: **President Dwight D. Eisenhower's grandchildren Barbara Anne and David ride their tricycles outside the South Portico, 1953.**

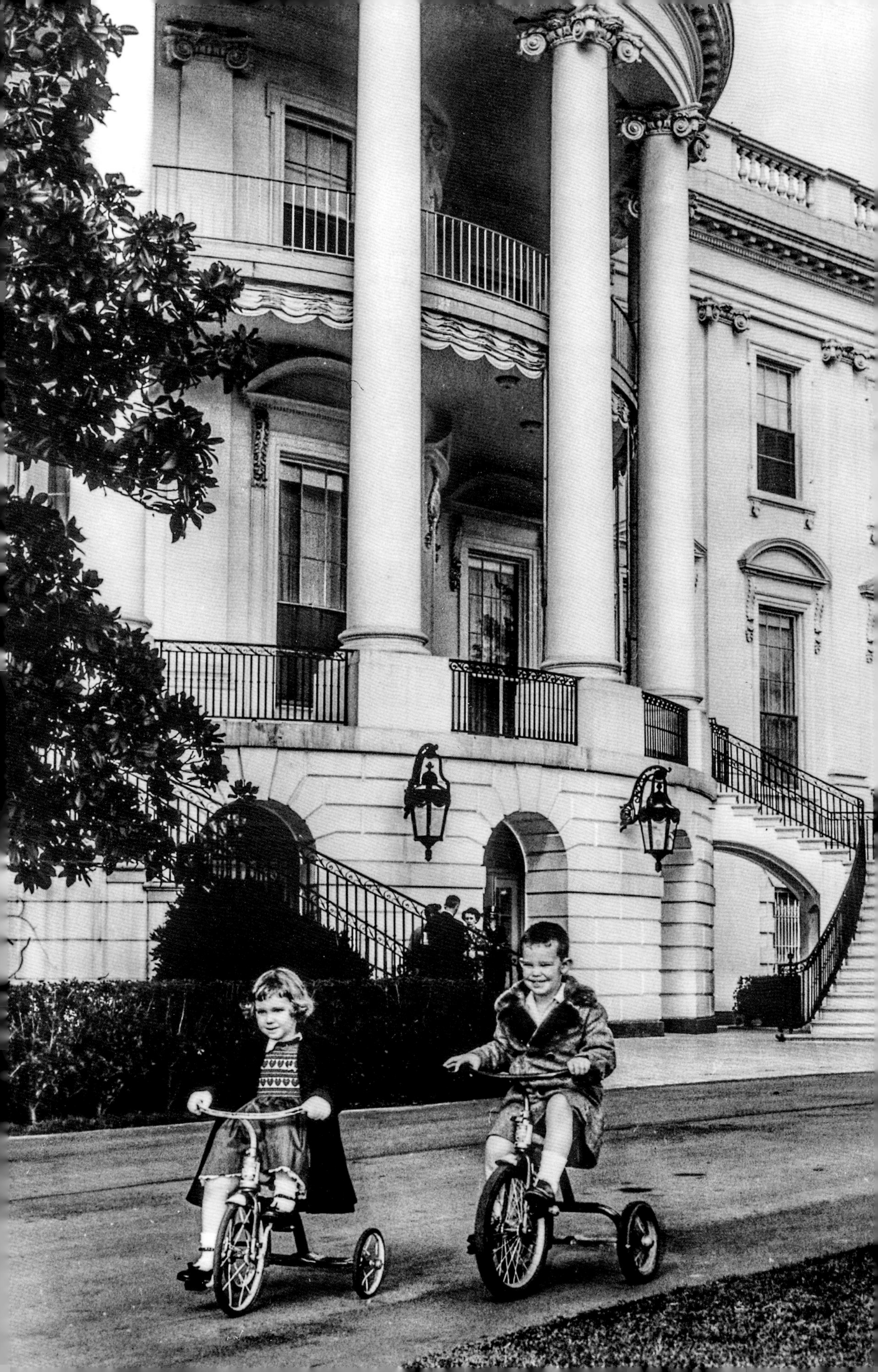

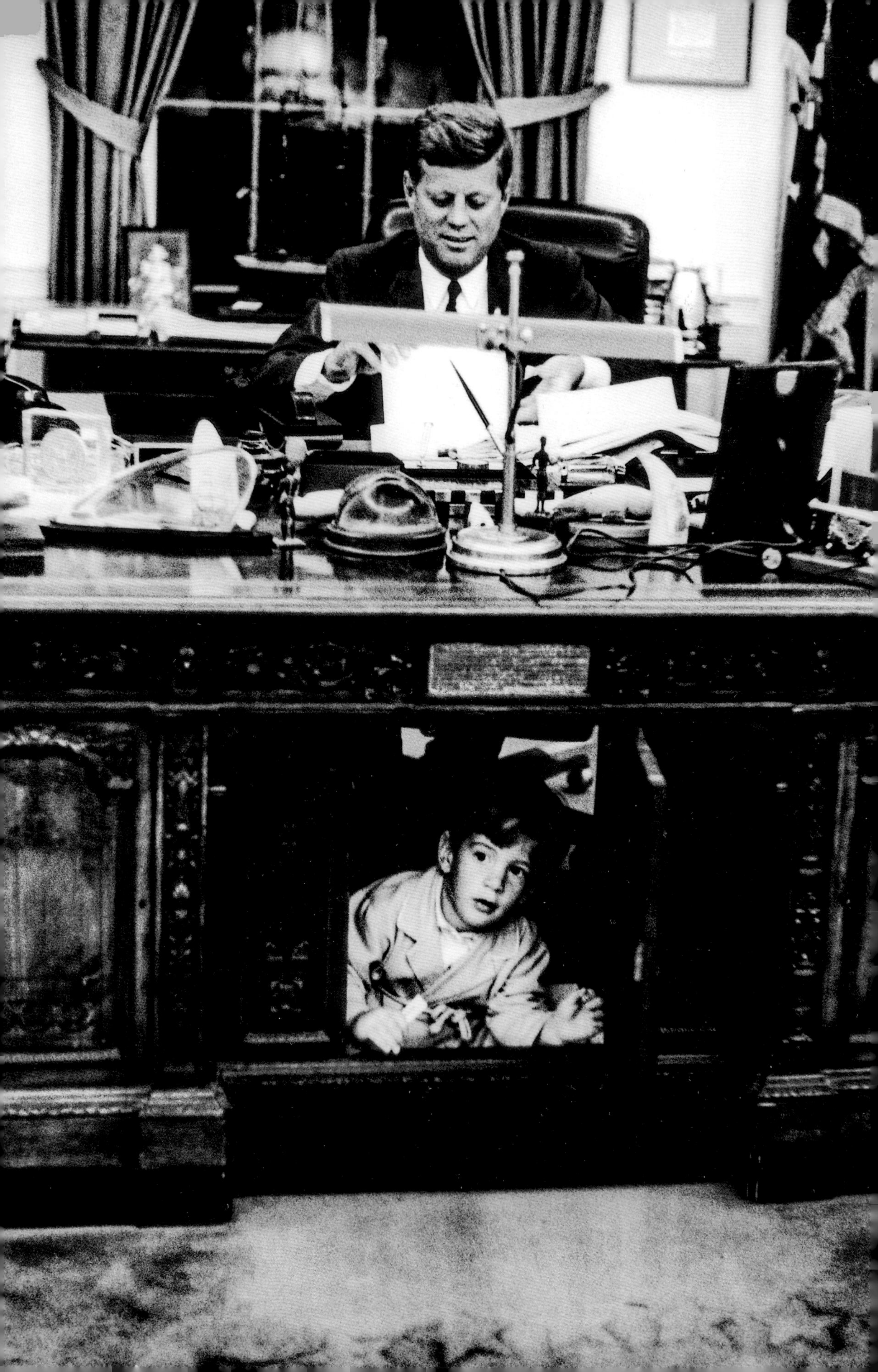

By restricting photographs and limiting access to her children, Mrs. Kennedy sought to protect them from the effects of so much concentrated attention. She established a kindergarten at home, as had Mrs. Cleveland, so that Caroline and little John could play with children of their own age, away from the public eye.

The two teenage daughters of President and Mrs. Lyndon B. Johnson, Luci, a high school student, and Lynda, a college student, brought a different liveliness to the Executive Mansion. Of dating age, they had to adjust to life in the public eye. Both married while in the White House. Of the same generation, Julie and Tricia Nixon, too, learned to live both private and public lives. Julie and her husband, David Eisenhower, the grandson of Ike, lived at the White House from time to time; she was an articulate defender of her father during the Watergate crisis. Tricia lived with her parents in the White House until her marriage in 1971.

The Gerald Fords had a teenage daughter, Susan, when they took up residence in 1974. In her last year of high school, she held her senior prom in the East Room. The three older sons—Michael, Jack, and Steven—with careers of their own, often spent time in the mansion.

Amy Carter, 10 years old when her father assumed office, captured the attention of the nation. The youngest of the Carter offspring, Amy was by far the best known. Her tree house in the gnarled old cedar on the South Lawn, her delight in reading, her violin lessons, pets, and school friends became part of the continuing White House chronicles that began with Susanna,

Opposite: "My house," John Kennedy Jr. called the president's massive desk. He liked to hide behind its secret door while his father worked, 1963.

Above left: President Richard Nixon's daughter Julie poses with her husband David, the grandson of President Dwight D. Eisenhower, on the South Portico, 1970.

Above right: First Lady Rosalynn Carter listens while daughter Amy practices the violin, 1979.

THE FIRST FAMILY AT HOME

granddaughter of John and Abigail Adams. Two of her older brothers, Chip and Jeff, lived with their families in Third Floor suites; the oldest son, Jack, and his family came for special occasions.

Ronald Reagan's oldest daughter, Maureen, a strong supporter of her father, stayed at the White House often while lending support to her father's agenda. Son Michael and his children, the president's grandchildren, came for special holidays and events, as did Patricia and Ron Jr.

In the late 1980s, George and Barbara Bush's extended family of four sons and a daughter, with their children, frequently spent time at the White House. They were active users of the White House swimming pool, tennis courts, and horseshoe pit.

A young teenager, Chelsea Clinton, 13, grew into a young woman during the eight years of her father's presidency. She studied ballet, attended high school, and led a normal life out of the spotlight. George W. and Laura Bush's twin daughters—Barbara and Jenna—entered their first year of college in 2000, months before their family moved into the White House. After their 2004 graduations, they joined their father at campaign events

President Donald J. Trump enjoys the Inaugural Parade from the reviewing stand with his son Barron by his side, 2017.

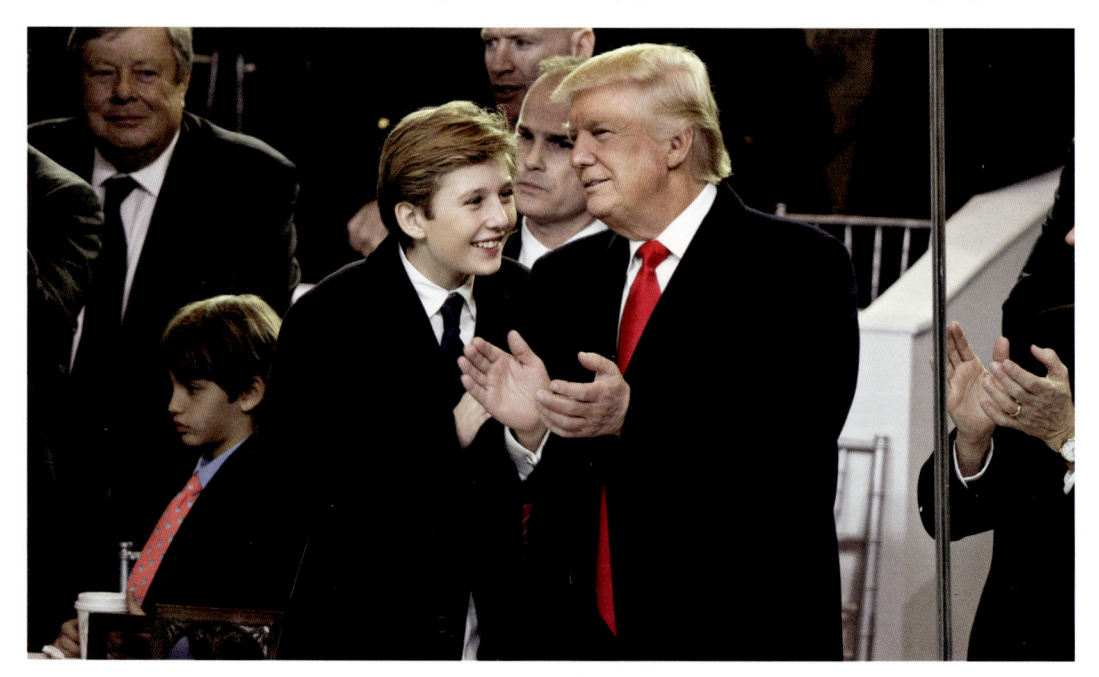

and accompanied their mother on foreign trips. Barack and Michelle Obama raised their young daughters, Malia and Sasha, away from the glare of the public. They attended local schools, played on sports teams, and occasionally participated in official White House events such as the arrival of the White House Christmas tree.

Donald and Melania Trump's son, Barron, lived in the White House. President Trump's four adult children, Don Jr., Ivanka, Eric, and Tiffany, were frequent visitors, as were his grandchildren.

President Joe Biden's children include three with his first wife Neilia, Beau who died in 2015, Hunter, and Naomi. Neilia and Naomi were killed in a car crash in 1971. He shares one daughter, Ashley, with First Lady Jill Biden. The Bidens' grandchildren often visit the White House.

First Lady Jill Biden is joined by her grandson Beau in the Reading Nook during the White House Easter Egg Roll, 2023.

THE FIRST FAMILY AT HOME

THE FIRST FAMILY AT HOME
WHITE HOUSE PETS

First Lady Grace Coolidge holds Rebecca, a pet raccoon, c. 1925.

President Lyndon B. Johnson and Yuki, a terrier mix, sing in the Oval Office, 1968.

Socks, the Clintons' cat, makes an appearance in the White House Press Room, 1993.

The Obama family's Portuguese water dogs relax in the West Garden Room, 2016.

Willow, the Bidens' tabby cat, plays with a toy outside the East Room, 2022.

Commander joins President Joe Biden on the steps outside of the Oval Office to celebrate National Pet Day, 2022.

THE FIRST FAMILY AT HOME

THE FIRST FAMILY AT HOME
WHITE HOUSE WEDDINGS

In 1812 Dolley Madison arranged the first nuptials held at the White House—the wedding of her widowed sister, Lucy Payne Washington, to "the estimable and amiable" Supreme Court Justice Thomas Todd. According to one observer, charming Dolley innocently held the spotlight, "looking every inch the queen."

When James and Elizabeth Monroe announced plans in 1820 for the first White House wedding for a presidential daughter, Maria Monroe, not yet 17, to her cousin and father's secretary, Samuel Laurence Gouverneur, a tempest brewed. The ceremony would be private, the family decreed. Foreign diplomats were pointedly advised "to take no notice" of the event. Afterward, Sarah Gales Seaton, wife of a prominent Washington newspaper editor, commented, "The New York style was adopted. . . . Only the attendants, the relations, and a few old friends of the bride and groom witnessed the ceremony."

The John Quincy Adams family also held a historic wedding. On February 25, 1828, young John Adams, grandson of one president and son of another, married his cousin Mary Catherine Hellen, who had lived with the family in the White House. The event marks the only time that a president's son has been wed in the mansion. The ceremony was held in the First Floor oval room—now the Blue Room—which was then decorated in crimson and gold. It was not an altogether happy occasion for the Adams family. The president had disapproved of the match, probably because Mary Catherine had flirted earlier with John's two brothers. But the reception provided a bright note to an otherwise gloomy election year. Even the reserved and formal president danced the Virginia reel.

Letitia Tyler, wife of John Tyler, appeared in company only once in the White House, at the wedding of her daughter, Elizabeth, to William Waller of Virginia in 1842. Wearing a simple gown and a soft lace cap that framed

White House bride Maria Monroe is believed to be wearing her white satin wedding dress in this portrait by Charles Bird King, 1820.

In the middle row of these Adams family silhouettes made in 1829 are John and Mary Catherine, who married at the White House in 1828, and their daughter, Mary Louisa.

her dark eyes, she sat quietly during the festivities. "Lizzie has had quite a grand wedding," sister-in-law Priscilla Cooper Tyler wrote of the event, which all Washington society attended. Dolley Madison, now 73 and popular as ever, was there, as well as the eloquent Daniel Webster, Tyler's secretary of state and a great friend of the family. In his deep, resonant voice, Webster quoted Sir Walter Scott when someone remarked that the president's daughter was giving up capital "belleship" to live in quiet Williamsburg. "Love rules the court, the camp, the grove," he said—and spoke more prophetically than he knew. In June 1844, almost two years after the death of Letitia Tyler and eight months before the end of his term, the widower president took a second wife, Julia Gardiner, in a private ceremony in New York City.

The highlight of the Grant presidency's social activity

Nellie Grant's East Room wedding to Algernon Sartoris as illustrated for the cover of *Frank Leslie's Illustrated Newspaper*, 1874.

came in 1874 when their idolized daughter, Nellie, wed a young Englishman, Algernon Charles Frederick Sartoris, whom she had met on a trip abroad. The 18-year-old bride, dressed in white satin trimmed with yards of Brussels lace, was married amid elaborate floral decorations in the East Room. The wedding breakfast included an awesome assortment of elegant dishes for the most fashionable event of the season. One participant at the festivities was plainly distraught, however. Tears filled the eyes of President Grant, who was losing his only daughter.

The Grants' son, Fred, a graduate of West Point, married Ida Maria Honoré later the same year, though the wedding was not held at the White House. Later the couple came to live with the family, and here a daughter was born and named Julia, after her grandmother.

The wedding of the only president to marry in the White House created a furor in 1886, when 49-year old Grover Cleveland took as his wife lovely 21-year-old Frances Folsom, daughter of his former law partner. The couple planned a private wedding; the bridegroom issued fewer than forty handwritten invitations to close friends and relatives. Cleveland had the Blue Room turned into a bower of flowers for the occasion, and church bells all over the city announced the end of the ceremony as a twenty-one-gun salute boomed from the Navy Yard.

Theodore Roosevelt's eldest daughter, Alice—by his first wife, who had died shortly after childbirth—set off

Frances Folsom on the day of her wedding to President Grover Cleveland, June 2, 1886.

Crowds waiting outside the White House for Alice Roosevelt's wedding, 1906.

social fireworks during his presidency. "Princess Alice," as the newspapers called her, became the most headlined debutante and bride of her generation. A thousand guests came to the White House wedding and reception when she married Congressman Nicholas Longworth of Ohio in 1906. Their gifts included rare silks and jade sent by the empress dowager of China, a pearl necklace presented by the Cuban government, a feather duster, and a hogshead of popcorn.

President Woodrow Wilson and his first wife, Ellen, launched two of their daughters into marriage in the White House. The wedding of their second daughter, Jessie, to law professor Francis B. Sayre in 1913, was the outstanding social event of the administration, though perhaps not so grandiose as one headline writer put it: "Nations of all the world do homage to White House bride as she takes solemn vows amid scenes of unequaled

President Theodore Roosevelt with his daughter Alice and her husband, Nicholas Longworth, on the day of their East Room wedding, February 17, 1906.

Above: The wedding party of Jessie Wilson and Francis Bowes Sayre pose in the East Sitting Hall on the Second Floor. President and Mrs. Wilson are in the back row, December 6, 1913.

Opposite: President Wilson's daughter Eleanor on the day of her marriage to Secretary of the Treasury William Gibbs McAdoo, 1914.

splendor." In contrast, the marriage of the Wilson's youngest daughter, Eleanor, to Secretary of the Treasury William Gibbs McAdoo six months later was held to a minimum of display because of the fast-failing health of her mother. In 1915, the widowed president quietly married his second wife, Edith Bolling Galt, at her Washington home.

More than fifty years later, the weddings of the two daughters of Lyndon and Lady Bird Johnson were highly publicized social events. Scores of reporters, photographers, and television crews recorded Luci's August 1966 church wedding to Patrick J. Nugent of Illinois and the reception that followed in the flower-adorned mansion. Sixteen months later, in December 1967, Lynda married Captain Charles S. Robb of the U.S. Marine Corps and a former White House social aide, in an elegant East Room ceremony decorated for the Christmas holidays.

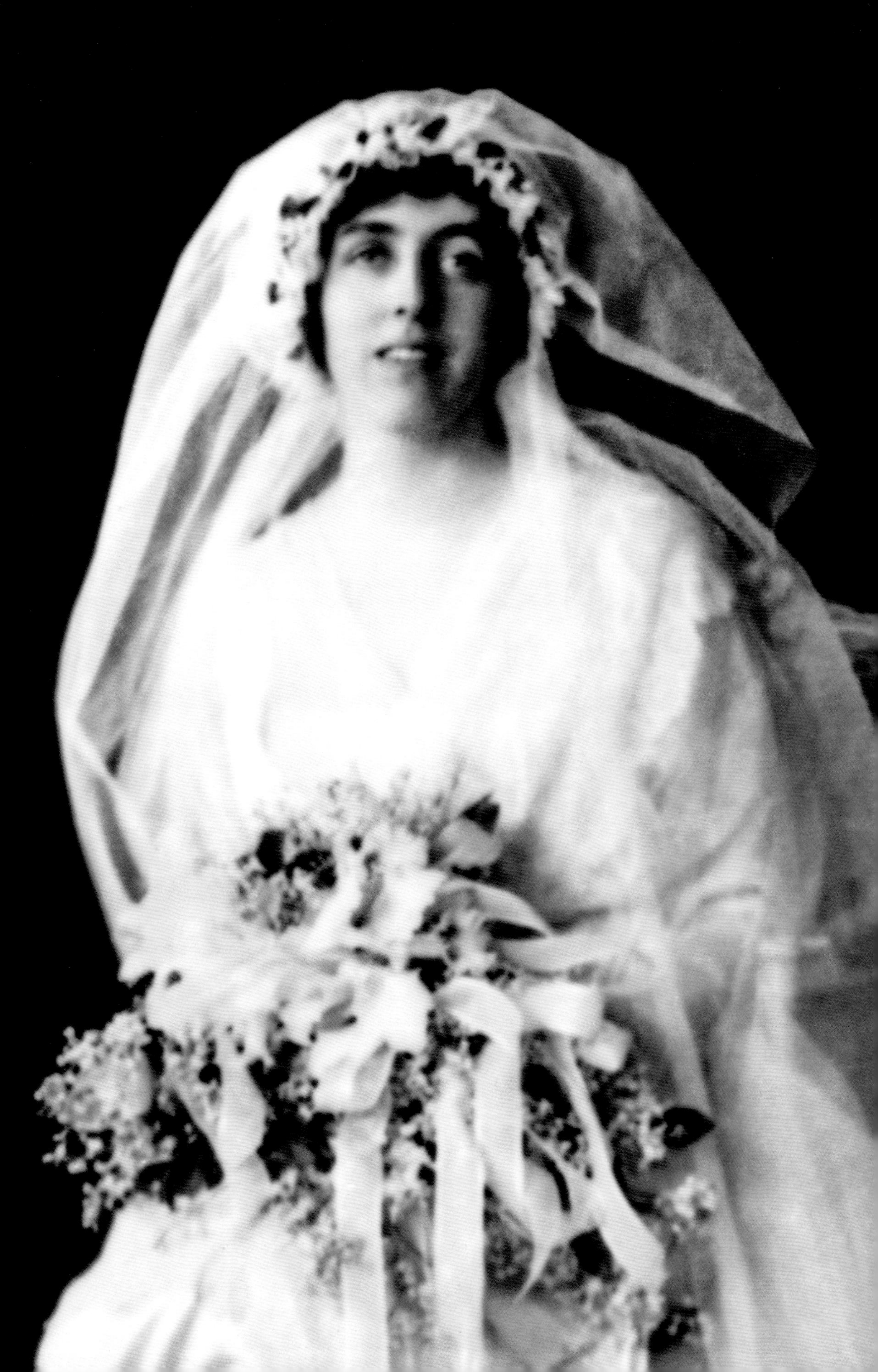

Newlyweds Chuck and Lynda Robb cross under the saber arch provided by Robb's fellow Marines as they exit the East Room after exchanging vows, 1967.

Richard and Pat Nixon's two daughters were also married in the midst of public attention. Julie missed most of the fanfare by marrying David Eisenhower, grandson of the former president, in New York City in 1968, shortly before her father was inaugurated. Tricia, however, chose the White House for her marriage to law student Edward Finch Cox of New York. Arranging for the ceremony to be performed in the famous Rose Garden, on June 12, 1971, she became the first president's daughter to have an outdoor wedding at the White House. Some four hundred guests were seated in the garden, which was decorated with masses of roses, lilies, and petunias. Afterward there was a reception in the mansion. Another family wedding took place in the Rose Garden in May 1994 when Hillary Clinton's brother, Tony Rodham, married Nicole Boxer.

The most recent outdoor wedding was held November 19, 2022, when President and Dr. Biden attended the wedding of their granddaughter Naomi Biden to Peter Neal on the South Lawn.

Edward and Tricia Cox recess down the aisle (above) following their wedding ceremony in the Rose Garden, 1971. Slightly more than a half century later, Naomi Biden, granddaughter of a president, also married on the White House Grounds. Following the ceremony on the South Lawn, she and her new husband Peter Neal were joined by President Joe Biden and First Lady Jill Biden (below) for a photograph outside the Oval Office, November 19, 2022.

THE FIRST FAMILY AT HOME

THE FIRST FAMILY AT HOME
PASSAGES

Behind the scenes, the men and women who have lived in the Executive Mansion have known the same happiness and frustration, pride, and misery that come to us all. Grief, both national and personal, has been too frequent a caller at the President's House. Eight chief executives have died in office, four of them by assassination.

Every night, the gruff and lonely Andrew Jackson performed a tender ritual. After removing the treasured miniature of his dead wife, Rachel, which he carried next to his heart, he would place it on the bedside table near her worn and faded Bible so that he might see her face first thing on awakening in the morning.

William Henry Harrison was, at 68, the oldest man to become president up to the time of his Inauguration in 1841. In an icy wind, he delivered the longest Inaugural Address in history. Other exposures to wintry weather followed, leading to a cold that turned into pneumonia. One month after his Inauguration, he was dead.

During the election year of 1848, Zachary Taylor told supporters that his wife prayed nightly for his defeat. If he were unlucky enough to win the office, she had declared, it would shorten his life. Margaret Taylor's dark prophecy came true a little more than a year after her husband's Inauguration. On July 4, 1850, the president sat for hours under the hot sun at a celebration on the grounds of the unfinished Washington Monument. Overheated and exhausted, he became ill of what was then called cholera morbus—the result, legend would say, of his having consumed too much iced milk and raw cherries. Five days later, Taylor was dead. His grieving widow, secluded in her apartment, could hear the sounds of his office staff making way for the next occupants, and she could feel the vibrations of hammering as workmen assembled a catafalque in the East Room. She could not bear to attend the ceremony, but she was forced to listen to its accompaniment, a sympathetic eyewitness reported, "as one band after another blared the funeral music . . . and the heavy guns boomed . . . to announce the final parting."

A devastating blow came to the Lincoln family when son Willie developed a severe fever and died soon

The Marine Band is pictured in procession on the sheet music for the funeral dirge for President William Henry Harrison, who died one month after his Inauguration in 1841.

An engraving depicting a crowd of mourners gathered around the black-draped catafalque in the East Room where President Abraham Lincoln lay in state, April 1865.

afterward, on February 20, 1862. The president shouldered his grief with his other burdens, but high-strung, erratic Mary Lincoln was inconsolable. She turned to spiritualism in the hope of receiving a message from beyond the grave and arranged at least one session with a popular medium of the day at the Soldiers' Home—the Lincolns' "summer White House"—and another in the Red Room. For a while Mrs. Lincoln believed her lost boy had returned. "He comes to me every night," she told her sister, "and stands at the foot of my bed, with the same sweet, adorable smile." Later she wrote, "The loved & idolized being, comes no more." Some insisted that Lincoln himself attended one of the spiritualist meetings, though it was never clear whether this was to please his wife, to satisfy his own curiosity, born of a streak of mysticism, or to show up the medium's tricks.

On the eve of Union victory in early April 1865,

Lincoln described a strange dream to his wife and a good friend. In the dream, he said, he was awakened from a deep sleep by a "pitiful sobbing." Getting up, he followed the wailing sound to the East Room, and there he found a catafalque surrounded by mourners. On it he saw a still figure shrouded in funeral garb, the face covered. "The President," one of the soldiers standing in the honor guard whispered to Lincoln, "killed by an assassin." Within two weeks, Abraham Lincoln had been shot by John Wilkes Booth in Ford's Theatre. In the East Room, Lincoln's body lay on a catafalque, surrounded by mourners as foretold by the dream. In her room above, Mary Lincoln lay prostrated by grief. While Tad and Robert sought to comfort her, they could hear the sound of weeping from long lines of people passing the bier to pay their last respects.

In one of the family rooms, frail Eliza Johnson, devoted wife of Andrew Johnson for forty-one years, rocked and sewed as she awaited word of the Senate vote at her husband's impeachment trial in 1868. "I knew he'd be acquitted," she said firmly, but with tears in her eyes, to the official who brought the good news. "I knew it."

For the rest of their lives, Harry and James Garfield would look back in horror upon the morning of July 2, 1881, when they and the president were planning to join his wife, Lucretia, who was then in Long Branch, New Jersey, recuperating from an illness. The two boys were in high spirits at the prospect of the trip, and President Garfield, a large and active man despite his bookish bent, joined them in a bit of horseplay before they all departed for the Washington depot of the Baltimore and Potomac Railway. Less than an hour later an office-seeking fanatic, Charles Guiteau, fired two shots at Garfield as he entered the waiting room. Garfield fell; physicians rushed to the scene, and a horse-drawn police ambulance soon returned the gravely wounded president to the White House.

For more than two months Garfield battled for his life in his Second Floor bedroom at the mansion, while his wife and children waited and prayed. Outside the gates, frequent bulletins kept the public informed of the condition of the man in the sickroom. A metal-detecting device developed by Alexander Graham Bell was used in an attempt to locate the bullet, but the effort failed because of interference from the bed's steel springs. In the hope that sea air might help cure the president, he was transferred by train—with every precaution taken to prevent jolting—to the ocean resort of Elberon at Long Branch. But no air could combat the infection that had developed. Garfield died on September 19, and his body was carried directly to the Capitol to lie in state in the Rotunda. It was the only time in history that a president who had died in office did not lie in state in the East Room.

Fashionable Chester A. Arthur, who succeeded Garfield as president, lived luxuriously in the White House but showed another side of his nature when he was alone. Like Jackson, he, too, was a recent widower and, like the earlier president, Arthur carried on a ritual of remembrance by ordering fresh roses to be placed daily next to the photograph of his dear Ellen, which was displayed on a little easel. He had been stunned by her sudden death from pneumonia in January 1880, at the age of 42, which left him alone with two children. He demonstrated his love and concern for their young daughter Nellie and their college-age son Alan by keeping them with him as much as possible.

Unlike the murders of Lincoln and Garfield, the third slaying was committed far from Washington. In September 1901, William McKinley was shaking hands with visitors at the Pan-American Exposition in Buffalo, New York, when a young man extended his left hand to the president, then shot him with a concealed revolver. The attack, by an anarchist named Leon Czolgosz, mortally wounded the president. McKinley died eight days later. The courage and

Mortally wounded by an assassin's bullet on July 2, 1881, President James A. Garfield lingered at the White House (opposite) until his death at the New Jersey shore on September 19, 1881. The White House (below) was draped in black in mourning for him, 1881.

LIFE IN THE WHITE HOUSE

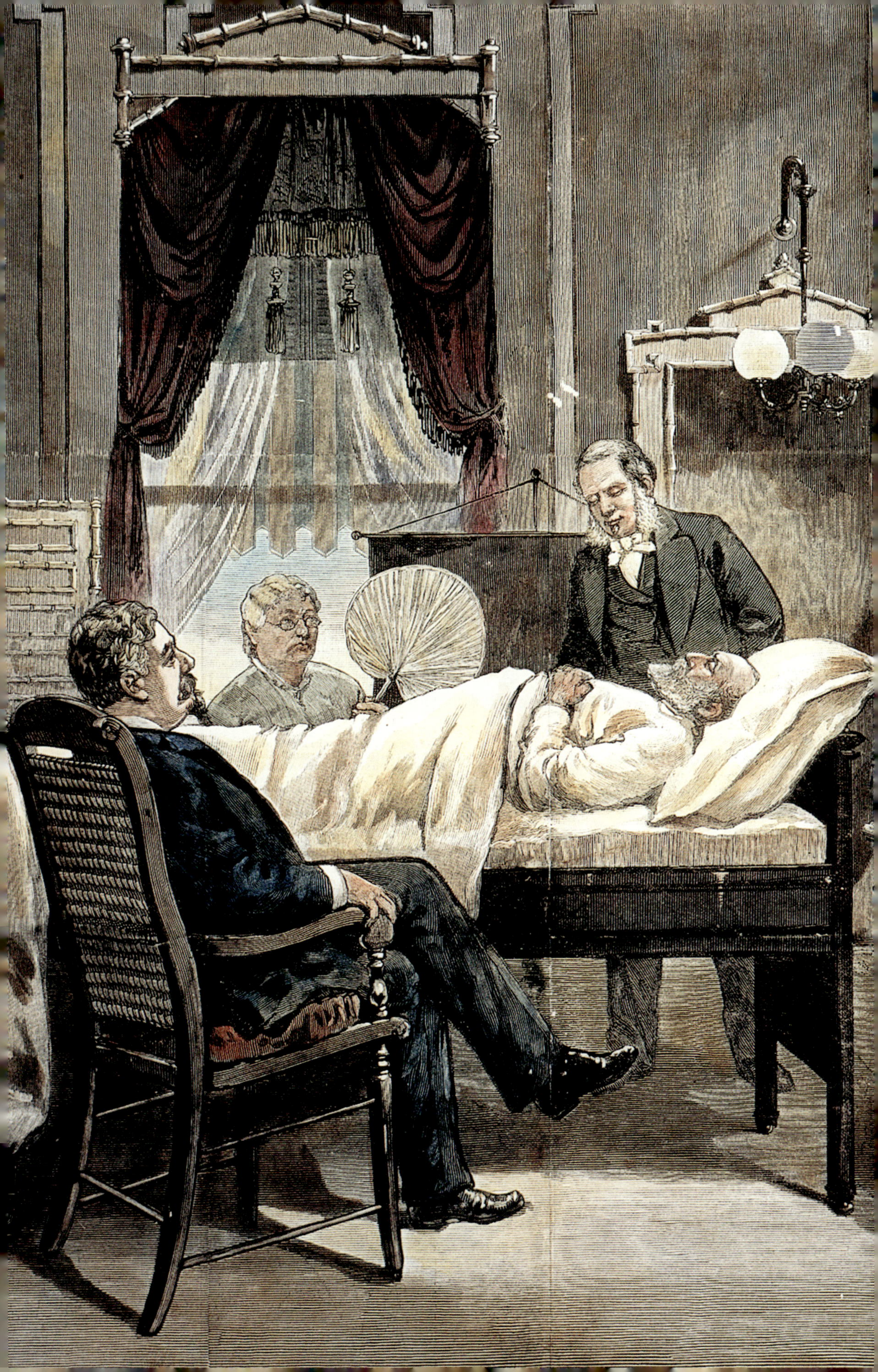

strength in adversity of his widow, Ida, would amaze all who had known her as almost helpless and ill.

Warren G. Harding, on a trip to the western states in the summer of 1923 and in the midst of increasing scandals of his administration, died of a heart attack in San Francisco. His body was borne by train back to Washington, where he lay in state in the East Room.

Calvin Coolidge Jr., then barely 16, died in the summer of 1924—the result of blood poisoning that had developed after he rubbed a blister on his toe while playing tennis on the South Grounds of the White House. "When he went," his father wrote in his autobiography, "the power and glory of the Presidency went with him."

A grieving figure, the stricken nation personified, appears atop William McKinley's mourning ribbon. McKinley was shot at the Pan-American Exposition in Buffalo, New York, on September 6, 1901, and died eight days later. He lay in state in the East Room (top), and then in the Capitol Building before he was taken to Canton, Ohio, for burial.

LIFE IN THE WHITE HOUSE

The body of President Warren G. Harding lies in state in the East Room of the White House, August 1923.

One of the most touching scenes in the history of the great changeovers that have come to this house occurred in Eleanor Roosevelt's study on the Second Floor, after the death of her husband. Vice President Harry Truman, summoned to the White House, arrived without knowing of the massive stroke that had ended the president's life at Warm Springs, Georgia. He heard the news from Mrs. Roosevelt. As Truman described the meeting in his memoirs, he asked Mrs. Roosevelt, "Is there anything I can do for you?" He would never forget her reply, he wrote. "Is there anything we can do for you?" she said. "For you are the one in trouble now."

Above: The body of President Franklin D. Roosevelt lies in state in the East Room, April 14, 1945.

Right: A crowd gathers to view the funeral procession of Franklin D. Roosevelt on Pennsylvania Avenue, April 1945.

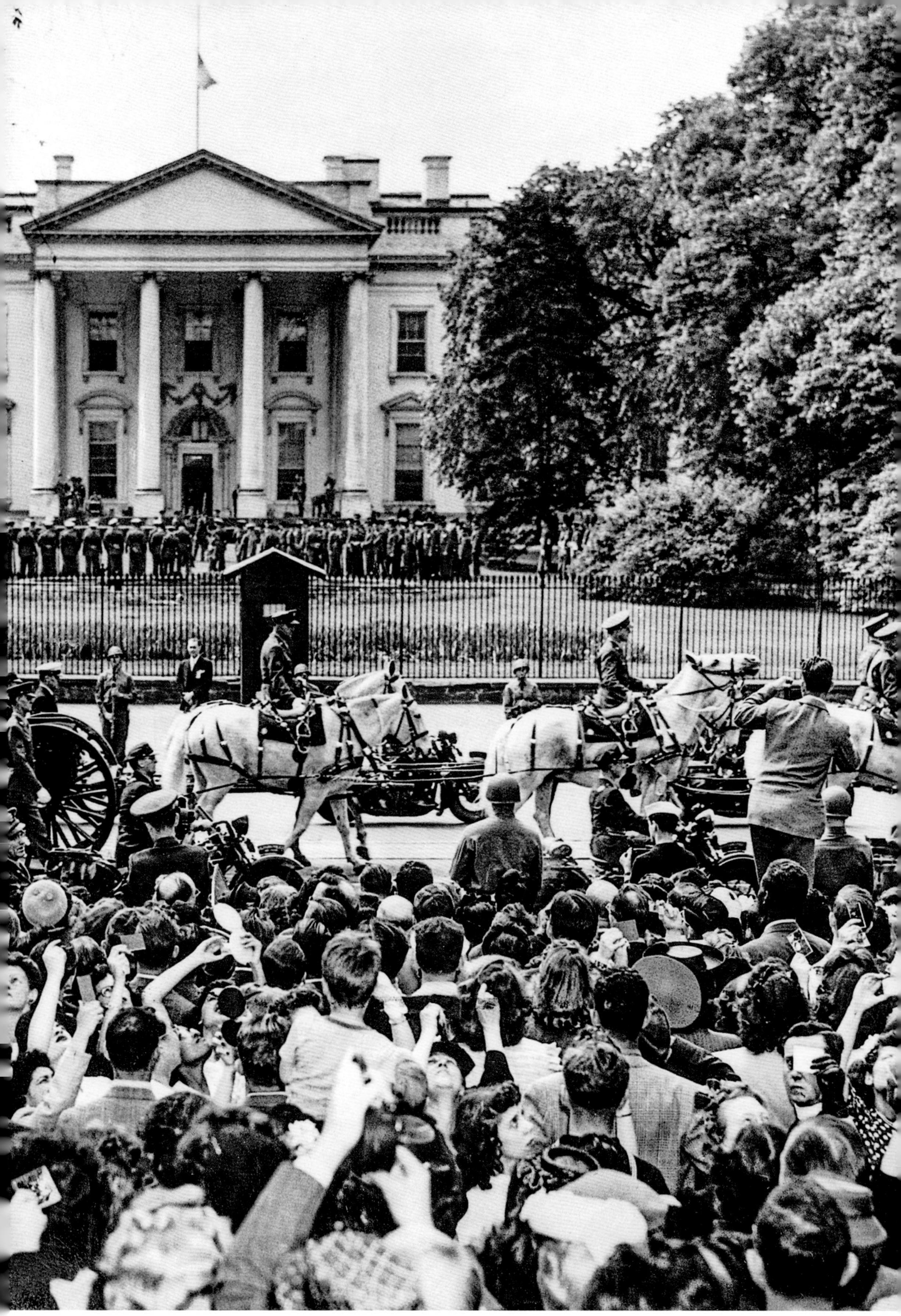

LIFE IN THE WHITE HOUSE

Sixty-two years after McKinley's death, another assassin pressed a trigger, in Dallas. As waves of shock spread from that Texas city, President John F. Kennedy lay dead in the prime of life. Then, once more, the casket of a chief executive rested in the black-draped East Room of the White House. From all over the globe came an extraordinary procession of the world's great—heads of state, prime ministers, and royalty—to pay their last respects and to share the grief of Kennedy's family, friends, and the nation.

Black bunting hangs from a chandelier in the East Room as the body of President John F. Kennedy lies in state (left) with military honor guard standing by, November 23, 1963. The president's family stands on the North Portico steps (above), preparing to follow his coffin to St. Matthew's Cathedral on November 25, 1963.

THE FIRST FAMILY AT HOME

A Uniformed Division officer stands vigilant at 1600 Pennsylvania Avenue.

THE FIRST FAMILY AT HOME
SECURITY

Today people are not permitted to get as close to the first family as they sometimes did in the past. Nor can individual members of the public enter the White House Grounds without an official pass or previous clearance by authorities. Armed, highly trained personnel of the Uniformed Division, U.S. Secret Service, are stationed in gatehouses along the high iron fence and closely check the identity of all callers. The Secret Service maintains various other security measures in carrying out its responsibility of guarding the president—a responsibility given to it in 1901, after William McKinley's assassination. Specific regulations followed; one of the most important requires Secret Service agents to remain near the chief executive at all times. The objective is to offer maximum safeguards with a minimum of interference, but many presidents have grown restive under the attention.

While William Howard Taft conceded that the record of assassinations was such that "Congress would be quite derelict" in disregarding it, he added that it was difficult for a chief executive "to avoid the feeling . . . that he was under surveillance rather than under protection." Theodore Roosevelt wrote to a friend: "The secret service men are a very small but very necessary thorn in the flesh." Then he went on to express his belief that no effort could prevent an assault upon his life, quoting Lincoln's remark that "though it would be safer for a President to live in a cage, it would interfere with his business." Since a 1917 law extended Secret Service protection to other family members, unmarried sons and daughters of presidents have faced the choice of giving up dates or accepting the company—however discreet—of an agent of the Secret Service. John Coolidge's classmates at Amherst joked that John would have to "elope from his agent" if he wanted to marry anyone. And Margaret Truman, in her book *Souvenir*, gives an account of the "handicap the Secret Service offers to escorts and beaus." She had made up her mind, she wrote, not to marry while she lived in the White House. But

A Secret Service officer keeps watch from the roof of the White House during the Congressional Picnic, 2019.

Following President McKinley's assassination, the director of the U.S. Secret Service immediately stationed two agents at the White House full time to protect President Roosevelt and his family. The White House Police (seen above with young Quentin and Archie Roosevelt) also protected the first family. First Lady Grace Coolidge was accompanied by Police Sergeant Alpheus Walter and Secret Service Operative James Haley as she hosted the Easter Egg Roll at the White House (right), 1925. The Secret Service agent detailed to protect the Kennedy children attracted the interest of the press with telephoto lenses as he accompanied Caroline Kennedy exercising her pony Macaroni on the South Lawn (opposite), 1962.

she asked the reader "to consider the effect of saying good night to a boy at the door ... in a blaze of floodlights, with a Secret Service man in attendance. There is not much you can do except shake hands, and that's no way to get engaged."

Subsequent legislation now requires the Secret Service to guard not only the president and his family but also the president-elect, the vice president, their families, as well as former presidents, their widows and minor children, presidential candidates, and top officials from abroad.

THE FIRST FAMILY AT HOME

Under the close watch of the Secret Service, White House visitors have occasionally been surprised by the unexpected opportunity to shake the president's hand.

President Herbert Hoover (left) is protected by Col. Richard Starling of the Secret Service as he approaches a crowd of visitors on the South Lawn in 1932, and President Lyndon B. Johnson (below) greets tourists at the White House gate in 1966. President Gerald R. Ford surprised crowds waiting in the White House tour line (opposite top) in 1977, and President Joe Biden stopped to greet guests at the Turkey Pardoning ceremony (opposite bottom) in 2022.

156 LIFE IN THE WHITE HOUSE

THE FIRST FAMILY AT HOME

THE FIRST FAMILY AT HOME
THE QUEST FOR PRIVACY

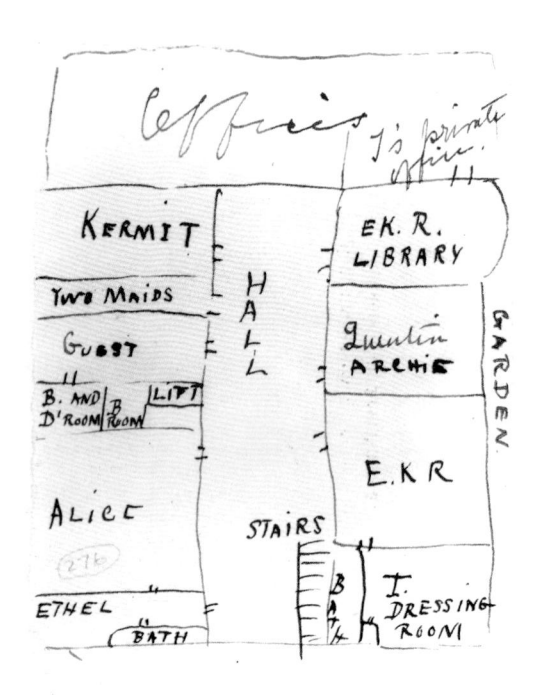

Above: This sketch made by First Lady Edith Roosevelt in 1901 shows the close proximity of the first family's crowded Private Quarters to the office spaces of the White House.

Opposite: First Lady Caroline Harrison's proposed expansion of the White House, shown in this c. 1891 plan drawn by architect Frederick Dale Owen, included the addition of a private central court enclosed by historic and official wings, as well as a series of greenhouses and conservatories.

Lack of personal privacy is a major concern of presidents and their wives and families, who are never prepared for the intense scrutiny residents of the White House receive. Certainly no couple suffered more from it than did the Clevelands. During the election campaign of 1888, scurrilous rumors of Cleveland's mistreatment of his young wife gained such wide circulation that Frances Cleveland issued an indignant denial. "I can wish the women of our Country no greater blessing," she said, "than that their homes and lives may be as happy, and their husbands may be as kind, attentive, considerate and affectionate as mine."

Despite whatever hazards and lack of privacy our modern presidents may endure, nothing could approach the conditions that prevailed in family living arrangements until the beginning of the twentieth century. Until Theodore Roosevelt moved to new offices in the West Wing, the executive offices and family apartment shared space in the mansion itself. For much of the time, these rooms occupied opposite ends of the same floor.

In those days, a multitude of callers, ranging from tradesmen and patronage seekers to cabinet officers and foreign dignitaries, streamed into and out of the North Entrance. Some lounged as they waited in rooms on the State Floor; others trudged up the public stairway to see the president or members of his staff. To avoid the often-rough crowds, some of the older and more delicate wives of presidents seldom ventured out of their west-side family quarters.

One of these was First Lady Letitia Tyler. Because of a stroke suffered before she came to the White House, she ran the household from her bedroom. This she did so efficiently and "so quietly," wrote her admiring daughter-in-law, Priscilla, "that you can't tell when she does it."

Margaret Taylor was a reluctant first lady and a White House homebody. She received visitors only in her own quarters and limited her guests almost entirely to close friends and to relatives from the South. The general, she felt, deserved a rest after forty years of active duty that included service in the War of 1812, in skirmishes with Indigenous peoples, and in the Mexican-American War.

In later years, as executive responsibilities grew heavier and the number of visitors increased, presidential families faced ever-greater inconveniences. A member of President Garfield's staff recalled in his memoirs that a mere acquaintance of the family "pushed himself in past the doors that marked the private domain ... and took his afternoon siesta upon the most comfortable sofa he could find."

Caroline Harrison, wife of President Benjamin Harrison, in an 1889 interview, complained that she was "being made a circus of.... I've been a show, the whole family's been a show since Mr. Harrison was elected," she said. "All last fall I sat in my sewing room and watched the procession of feet pass across the parlor floor wearing their path into the nap, and disappear like the trail of a caravan into the General's room beyond. Day by day, I watched the path grow wider and deeper.... But I don't propose to be made a circus of forever! If there's any privacy to be found in the White House, I propose to find it."

Mrs. Harrison's solution to the problem called for Congress to adopt one of three drastic measures, for which she presented detailed architectural plans. The simplest of these would have provided the president with a separate residence and remodeled the mansion for entertaining and executive business only. The second design proposed the addition of wings to be used for office and guest suites. The most elaborate of the suggestions was to extend the house into a fantastic four-sided palace enclosing a huge court and fountains. Though Congress rejected Mrs. Harrison's projects, it did appropriate $35,000 for essential housecleaning and repairs to the deteriorating old house. Moreover, airing the need for reasonable family privacy and adequate office space helped pave the way for the future construction of wings on the west and east sides of the mansion to serve as offices and accommodate service functions.

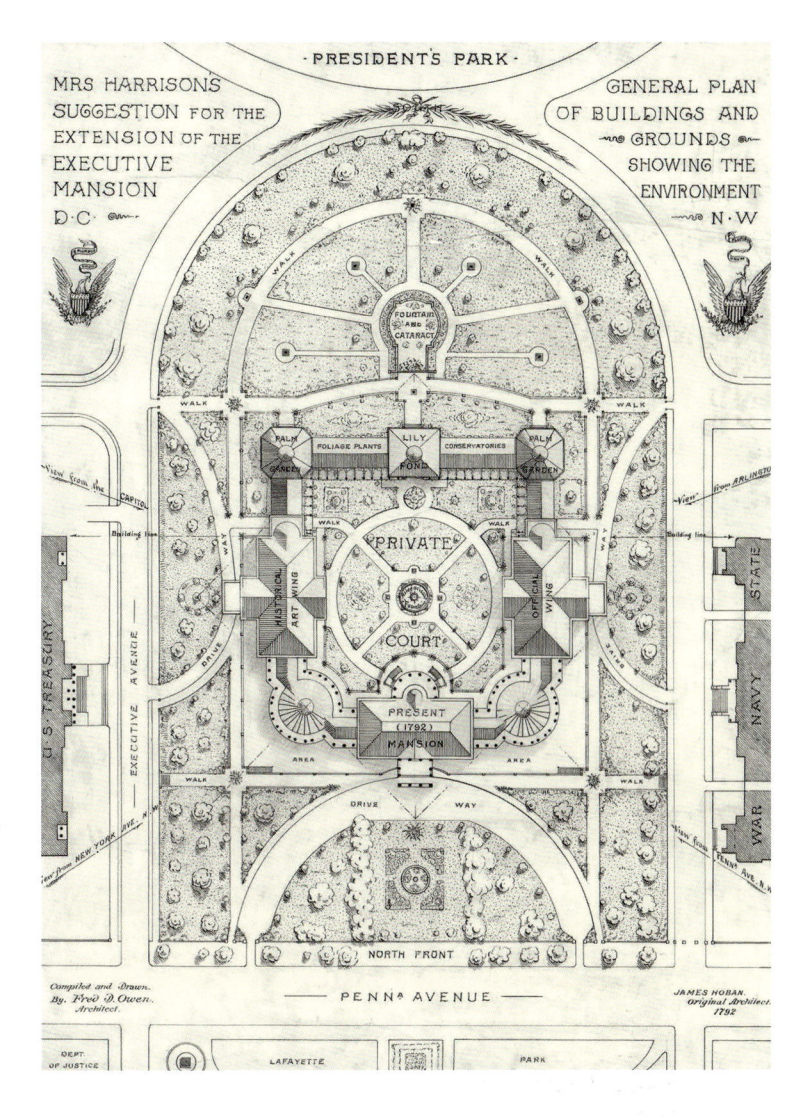

THE FIRST FAMILY AT HOME
MAKING AND FURNISHING A HOME

From the beginning, presidents and their families have created highly individual homes within the Executive Mansion by furnishing and embellishing it in their own taste. The White House occupies a unique place in American life. As the home of presidential families for more than two hundred years, it has represented, by democratic extension, the homes and families of all Americans. "I was always conscious of the character which a century of history had impressed upon the White House," wrote Helen Taft, but "it came...to feel as much like home as any house I have ever occupied." Similar thoughts were expressed by Grace Coolidge, who saw the house as a home "rich in tradition, mellow with years, hallowed with memories." The personal and family life in the White House has given to this center of national power

President Rutherford B. Hayes and his family often gathered with cabinet members in the Second Floor family library to sing hymns on Sunday nights, c. 1880.

LIFE IN THE WHITE HOUSE

and influence a warm, human note of common experience and understanding.

Since the early Federal period of John and Abigail Adams, this "First Home" has mirrored America's everyday domestic fashions and attitudes, household decor, furnishings and tableware, in ways that would have been unthinkable to the followers of social and political traditions practiced in Europe's great state residences. Beginning with John Adams, whose personal discomfort in the new White House was matched only by the political vicissitudes of his outgoing administration, succeeding presidents have led two lives while in office—their own and their country's.

President and Mrs. John Adams, for instance, were apprehensive in November 1800 when the time came to move into the damp and incomplete Executive Mansion being readied in the new capital city. In December they learned that Adams had lost his bid for reelection, so only a few months remained of what would be his single term. Mrs. Adams was increasingly dismayed at the condition of their temporary home and its grounds. The most famous housekeeping problem Mrs. Adams faced still makes an amusing subject for conversation at White House parties. Since there was, she said, "not the least fence, yard, or other convenience" available outside, she had a servant hang the presidential laundry to dry in the huge, unfinished East Room, destined to become the most elegant of the State Rooms used for entertaining.

Thomas Jefferson maintained an atmosphere of personal moderation and intellectual interests that belied the crude surroundings of the wilderness capital. To relax from the heavy responsibilities of leadership in a young republic starting out in a world of hostile monarchies, the long-widowed president turned to hobbies he had

Frances Folsom Cleveland sits by the fire, c. 1893.

enjoyed at his Monticello home. He played his violin, experimented with familiar and rare plants, and taught his pet mockingbird to peck food from his lips and to hop up the stairs after him.

The White House reflected the quiet happiness of James and Dolley Madison and the generous hospitality presided over by the genial first lady before they were burned out of the mansion in the War of 1812. Observers praised the couple's mutual admiration. Dolley Madison expressed her warm and vibrant personality in decorating her parlor (today's Red Room) with bright yellow draperies and upholstery.

Abigail Fillmore, a onetime schoolteacher, obtained congressional funds for the first official library in the Executive Mansion. With a dictionary, histories, sets of Charles Dickens, William Makepeace Thackeray, and other works, she filled the bookshelves installed in the upstairs oval sitting room. There she and President Millard Fillmore spent many quiet evenings reading and chatting, while their young daughter, Mary Abigail, played the piano or harp.

Sedate and proper Lucy Hayes had her bedroom walls "tinted pale blue, with panels of light gray and pink," as described by a woman correspondent permitted the rare privilege of seeing the Hayeses' private apartment in the 1870s.

Presidential families have the option of bringing their own furnishings and personal belongings to the residence, and personal possessions have moved in and out of the White House with each successive family. With the Tafts, for instance, came the president's many law books, recalling his long and distinguished legal career capped eventually by his appointment as chief justice of the United States. The erudite Hoovers brought many mementos from their world travels: South American rugs, Asian art, caged songbirds, and books in various languages,

Cartoonist Clifford Berryman depicts a Teddy Bear deciding whether to leave the White House with President Theodore Roosevelt's possessions on moving day in March 1909.

162 LIFE IN THE WHITE HOUSE

including their own translation from Latin of an important sixteenth-century volume on mining. All helped Lou Hoover transform the broad, bare hall on the Second Floor into an inviting reception area for guests.

To the White House from Hyde Park, New York, Franklin and Eleanor Roosevelt shipped a wheelchair to carry the president along the family corridor. They also brought sturdy handcrafted furniture that had been scratched during family pillow fights and wrestling matches in which "Pa," with his powerful shoulders, won as often as his sons. When Mrs. Roosevelt left the White House in 1945 after the death of the president, twelve years of accumulation required twenty big army trucks to transport the possessions back to Hyde Park.

Every president's family takes its place in the flow of historic continuity, finding its own uses for the many public and private spaces within the various levels of the White House. Before Theodore Roosevelt separated his office from his home, the basement of the mansion—now called the Ground Floor—served as a service and storage area, cluttered with buckets and lumber and defaced with pipes run through the walls. Today this wide corridor shows off nineteenth-century American furnishings and displays on its walls a gallery of first ladies' portraits,

A moving van parked at the South Portico delivers President and Mrs. Clinton's possessions to the White House on January 20, 1993.

THE FIRST FAMILY AT HOME

President Dwight Eisenhower enjoyed barbecuing outside the Third Floor Solarium.

Opposite: In preparation for the Nixon family's move into the White House, Lady Bird Johnson reviews floor plans with the incoming first lady, Pat Nixon, and Chief Usher J. B. West in the West Sitting Hall, in November 1968.

an idea first suggested by Edith Roosevelt in 1902. Off the corridor are several handsome rooms, including the Library, with its nineteenth-century portraits of Native Americans; the China Room, showcasing the varied presidential table services; and the Map Room, where FDR kept up with World War II's progress.

During the Trumans' time, the Second Floor held three pianos—appropriate symbols of the harmony that characterized the spunky, close-knit family from Independence, Missouri. One piano stood in the oval room that was then the president's study; daughter Margaret practiced on another in her sitting room, where she also kept her record collection; while a third—a spinet in the hall—was frequently used for duets. The Truman family often spent evenings together, reading, and playing or listening to music.

A few years later, when friends of President Eisenhower visited him in the upstairs oval room, which he, too, used as a study, they found displayed there a fascinating array of military and civilian awards, decorations, swords, and other gifts presented by world leaders. In his book *The White House Years*, the president wrote that he received visitors in the study "informally in the evening, whenever a somewhat homier atmosphere than could be obtained in my office was desirable." His "personal mementos of a fairly long life," he added, "were kept there for a temporary period only, and later were transferred to a suitable museum—the Smithsonian, the Library of Congress, or the museum which bears my name in Abilene, Kansas." For the Eisenhowers, the White House was the most permanent home they had known during the far-ranging career of the popular army general. "I have seen my grandchildren growing up in these historic rooms,"

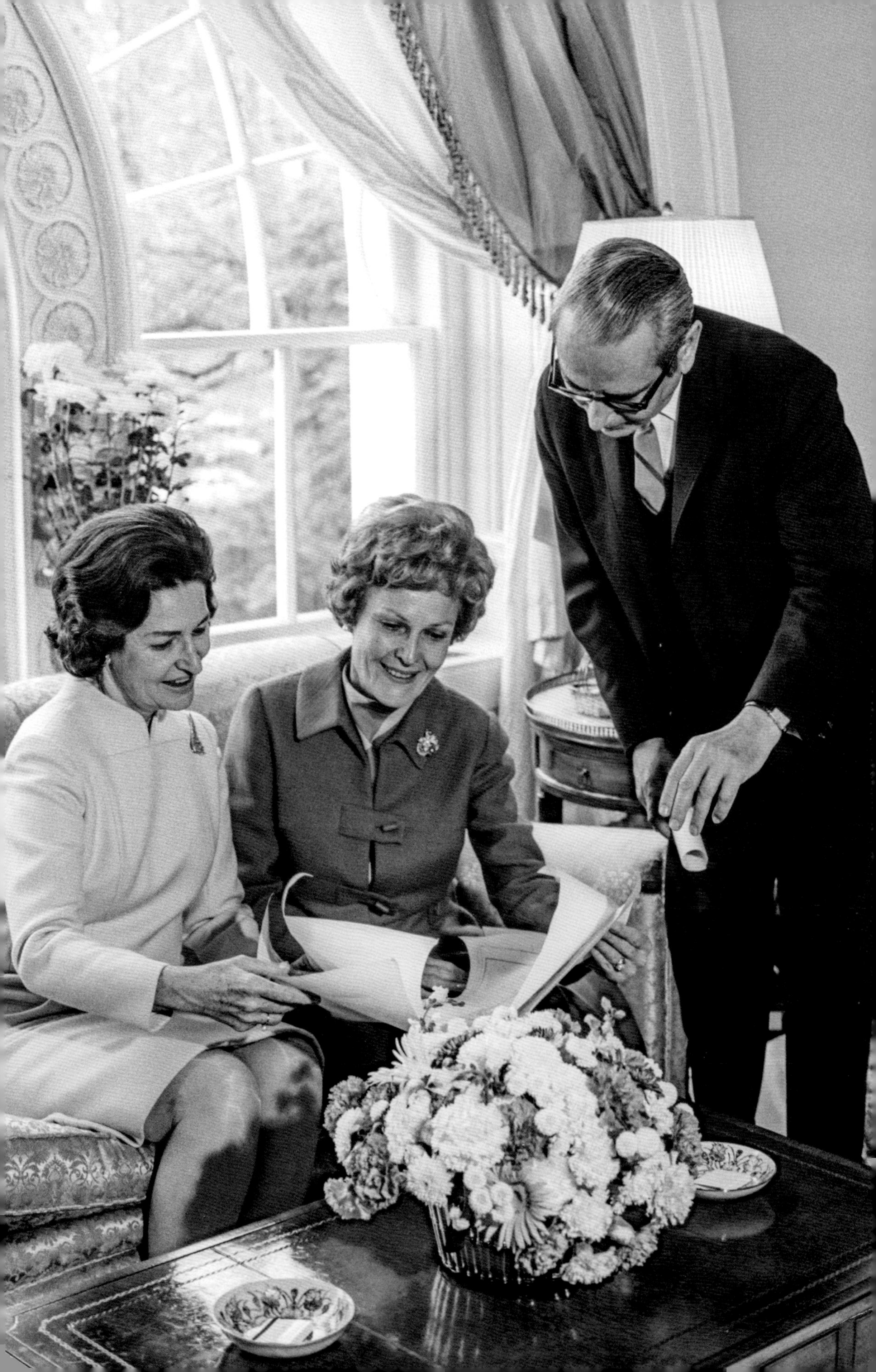

Mamie Eisenhower wrote. "Here my son and daughter-in-law have shared our family evenings."

The changing scenes on the family floor continued to mirror, in colors and furnishings, the tastes and activities of each new group of White House occupants. Mrs. Eisenhower's decor, with its "Mamie pink" accents, gave way to Mrs. Kennedy's light blue curtains and blue-and-white furnishings that showed to advantage against plain off-white walls in the private bedroom and sitting room areas. American period pieces, French antiques, and valuable art objects began to appear in various places: the sitting halls that share the wide corridor; the Queens' Bedroom and Lincoln Bedroom, where visiting royalty had slept; and what was called the Treaty Room, then decorated in Victorian style. They gave visible evidence of Jacqueline Kennedy's program to restore to the White House furnishings that awaken a feeling of the historic past of the nation and the house.

The Yellow Oval Room on the Second Floor has served the same function for the last twelve administrations. Mrs. Kennedy turned this room into a formal drawing room, and it has proved to be the most suitable place in the

President Jimmy Carter's family during a meal in the President's Dining Room on the Second Floor.

house to entertain state guests before dinners or luncheons given in their honor. Many families have placed their family Christmas tree here, where the first White House Christmas tree was displayed in 1889. With the arrival of the Johnson family, Lady Bird Johnson put her own signature on the look and use of the Second Floor apartments. In her mainly green-and-yellow bedroom, she set up a cozy working space in which she dictated letters and speeches, and planned and directed her many activities. Down the hall—in rooms that had lately known the toys of the Kennedy children—the Johnsons' teenage girls, Lynda and Luci, had their bedrooms. And when Richard Nixon brought his family to the White House in 1969, his daughter Tricia moved into the suite that had been used by Lynda and Luci. After the Carters moved in, 10-year-old Amy occupied the bedroom that had been Luci Johnson's, then Tricia Nixon's.

Life for President Jimmy Carter and his family reflected the easy atmosphere found in many small southern towns, such as their native Plains, Georgia. A story that made the capital rounds early in 1977 revealed something of their ways. Picking up a telephone soon after she arrived at the White House, Rosalynn Carter asked to be connected with Jimmy. "Jimmy who?" came the response from the operator.

Ronald and Nancy Reagan put their California-inspired stamp on the Second Floor Private Quarters as well as on the Solarium, the expanded living space that had been added as the Third Floor in 1927, during the Coolidge presidency. Most of the rest of this floor was then divided into bedroom, bath, and sitting room apartments, which are available today for family members and personal guests. The remaining areas serve as space for storage and housekeeping.

President and Mrs. Reagan often dined off tray tables in the Private Quarters while watching the evening news, 1981.

THE FIRST FAMILY AT HOME

The George H. W. Bushes created a warm family atmosphere in the White House. Family photographs were displayed throughout the Private Quarters, and stuffed toys were available for their grandchildren when they visited. The focal point of the family sitting room was a needlepoint rug with floral and animal motifs that Barbara Bush had worked on for many years.

Hillary and Bill Clinton instituted a casual life for their family, sharing family meals with their daughter in the Second Floor kitchen. On the Third Floor, a special music room for the president, with instruments and memorabilia, was created for him as a gift from Mrs. Clinton.

The White House has an extensive collection of furniture and art that reflects the changing styles of the times and the personalities of its inhabitants. Each first lady may make selections from furniture already in the mansion or from an off-site support facility containing pieces used by previous residents. And, of course, she may refurnish and redecorate the Second and Third Floor quarters as she chooses. The Ground Floor Corridor and principal public rooms on the State Floor, however, retain their museum character, in accordance with a law passed by Congress in 1961 to protect and continue the historical work begun by Jacqueline Kennedy. Major changes in these rooms must now be approved by the Committee for the Preservation of the White House, established in 1964 by executive order.

Before George W. and Laura Bush arrived at the White House, Mrs. Bush called her mother-in-law, Barbara Bush, to ask her what she should bring. "She told me there were already so many lovely and comfortable furnishings in the White House that we would need to bring very little." Michelle Obama made the Private Quarters of the White House a sanctuary for her family: "I thought initially that it would be like living in a museum . . . but there are a few different White Houses. The State Floor, the

First Lady Barbara Bush with a new grandchild, Charles Walker Bush, 1989.

Ground Floor are open to the public, then you go upstairs, and you reach the two residence floors. And the first time I entered that space, I thought, well, this feels like home." She selected several contemporary American artworks on loan from Washington museums to hang on the walls of the Private Quarters. "Every day, we feel the history that surrounds us," she said. President Obama, like George Bush, his father George H. W. Bush, and Bill Clinton, used as his private office the Second Floor room where presidents of the late nineteenth century convened their cabinet meetings. The impressive Victorian walnut table that served as a desk for President Obama was ordered by Ulysses S. Grant and has eight locking drawers—enough for Grant and each member of his cabinet. Jimmy Carter had this table placed on the North Grounds for the signing of the treaty between Egypt and Israel in March 1979. Then in September 1993, Bill Clinton had it moved to the South Lawn for the signing of the peace accord between the Israelis and the Palestine Liberation Organization, and again on July 25, 1994, for the declaration ending the state of war between Jordan and Israel.

The floral preferences of first ladies make a varied bouquet. Mamie Eisenhower, for example, showed a preference for sweetheart roses and carnations in her favorite color, pink. Jacqueline Kennedy experimented with mixed floral designs, and Lady Bird Johnson enjoyed each season's offerings—from spring pastels to deeper shades of fall. Nancy Reagan loved peonies and coral-colored arrangements in vermeil bowls. Hillary Clinton favored contemporary arrangements of warm-colored red and yellow flowers, as well as those using a variety of garden flowers.

Today, floral arrangements continue to be prepared by the White House floral designers.

A colorful arrangement created by the White House florist complements the portrait of First Lady Michelle Obama in the Ground Floor Corridor, 2022.

THE FIRST FAMILY AT HOME

A view across the South Lawn of the White House with the Washington Monument and Jefferson Memorial in the distance (above), 2019. Until 1872, much of the area was marshy, as envisioned by Peter Waddell in his painting *Tiber Creek* (opposite).

CHAPTER FOUR

IN THE PRESIDENT'S PARK

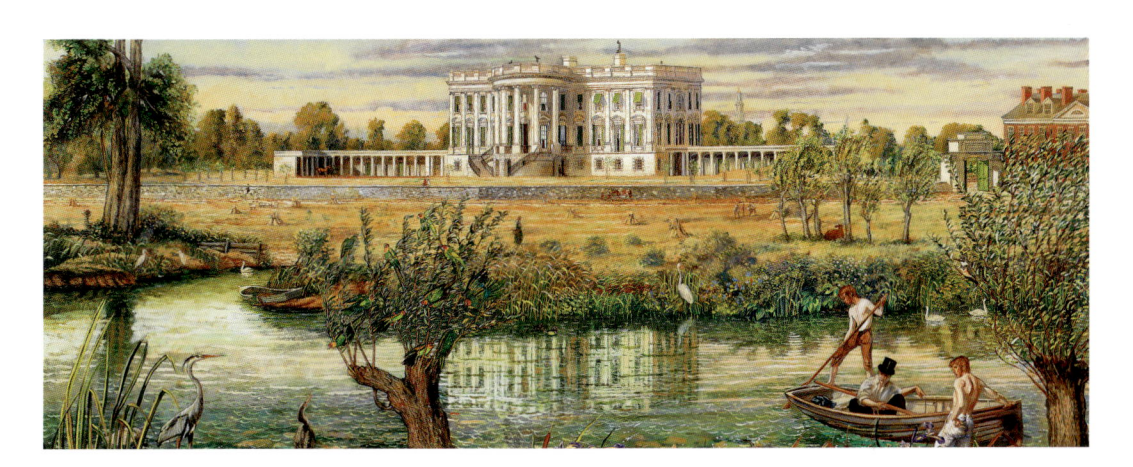

Few settings are lovelier than the rolling expanse of lawn to the south of the White House. Looking past a shimmering pool and fountains toward the Washington Monument and Jefferson Memorial, one would not suspect that the lawn once merged with malarial marshes along a creek, which by 1817 had been walled and deepened into a sluggish canal. Odorous with sewage and dead animals, alive with mosquitoes and flies, the canal was the bane of White House occupants. As a summer retreat, Martin Van Buren rented a house north of the White House. Later presidents, including Abraham Lincoln and Rutherford B. Hayes, were glad to go in the hot months to a cottage at the Soldiers' Home, 3 miles away. "I am alone in the White pest-house," a Lincoln secretary wrote a friend. "The ghosts of twenty thousand drowned cats come in at night through the south windows." In 1872 the canal-sewer was covered and the street above it named Constitution Avenue. With landscaping, the present Ellipse was completed by 1884.

Today the President's Park, with its well-kept gardens and grounds, is open to the public in the spring and fall, continuing a tradition begun by Pat Nixon in 1972.

IN THE PRESIDENT'S PARK
THE GROUNDS AND THE GARDENS EVOLVE

Over the years, the 18-acre estate that today surrounds the White House has shown many different faces. John and Abigail Adams found it a barren expanse littered with workmen's shacks and tools. The Grounds had appeared so grim before their arrival, in fact, that a member of the president's cabinet wrote to one of the District commissioners complaining that "a private gentleman preparing a residence for his Friend, would have done more than has been done." He suggested that the commissioners plant "something like a garden, at the North side of . . . [the] large, naked, ugly looking building" and provide a yard enclosure.

Thomas Jefferson obtained funds to build the first fence. For a few years, this rustic rail-and-post enclosure blended nicely into a village capital where "excellent snipe shooting and even partridge shooting was to be had on either side of the main avenue," as the secretary of the British Legation noted. Then Jefferson replaced the wood

The President's House, probably drawn by Benjamin Henry Latrobe in 1811, showing the North Front, or public side of the house.

The White House and Capitol in about 1827 during John Quincy Adams's presidency. President Jefferson's stone wall, open pastures, and the orchard and vegetable garden can be seen in this view of the southwest side of the house.

fence with a fieldstone wall and constructed an imposing arched gate, designed by architect Benjamin Henry Latrobe, over the driveway leading to the southeast entrance. Jefferson also devised an overall landscape plan that included grading and planting the South Grounds to provide more privacy, while leaving a central view toward the river.

It remained, however, for that austere New Englander and ardent gardener, John Quincy Adams, to devote the most lavish personal care of any president to the White House nurseries and gardens. His diaries from 1825 to 1829 tell of the happy hours he spent on this hobby. Entries reveal his enjoyment of pungent herbs—balm, rue, sage, tansy, and tarragon—and his delight in the "deep blood-colored beet, the white-flowered carrot and yellow-flowered parsnip." In this "small garden, of less than two acres," he wrote, there were "forest- and fruit-trees, shrubs, hedges, esculent vegetables, kitchen and medicinal herbs, hot-house plants, flowers and weeds, to the amount, I conjecture, of at least one thousand."

Adams planned to introduce useful crops to American farmers. On his rides about Washington and on travels to and from his Massachusetts home, he collected nuts, seeds, and seedlings, and he encouraged his friends to do the same when they went abroad. After Congress passed a resolution to encourage the growing of mulberry trees

IN THE PRESIDENT'S PARK

The North View of the White House seen from Lafayette Square, c. 1848.

to form a base for a silkworm industry in the United States, Adams added the white mulberry to his flourishing White House nurseries. With his wife, Louisa, he nurtured silkworms on the leaves, and in the evenings he would sit beside her, writing, as she unreeled and rewound the fragile silk filaments from the cocoons. Adams's dream of a silk industry in America never materialized.

With the arrival of Andrew Jackson and the building of the North Portico that completed construction of the mansion, the evolution of the Grounds entered a new phase. Instead of the rambling gardens of Adams, graveled footways appeared, along with a carriage house, driveway, stable for the president's favorite racing horses, and an orangery on the east side. As Washington grew less bucolic, the President's Park was enhanced with fountains and flower beds. In 1842, when Charles Dickens called at the White House to see President John Tyler, he found the "ornamental ground about it . . . laid out in garden walks; they are pretty and agreeable to the eye; though they have that uncomfortable air of having been made yesterday."

Time and professional landscape architects, including the talented Andrew Jackson Downing, would overcome the effect of newness that Dickens observed. Within fifteen years, the White House estate, particularly its tree-dotted South Lawn, had become part of "a scene of beauty and attractiveness," according to an article in an 1856 issue of *United States Magazine*. Open to the public on weekdays, the "agreeable promenades" drew "the elite of the city," said the author. "Usually the President, the Cabinet, and the Foreign Ministers and their wives may be seen here [with] thousands of ladies and pretty children, most bewitchingly dressed."

Visitors stroll on the South Grounds of the White House, c. 1867.

IN THE PRESIDENT'S PARK
THE ROSE GARDEN

Prior to the redesign of the Rose Garden during the John F. Kennedy presidency, long rows of privet divided the space and limited the number of guests that could be accommodated at events such as the one seen in the photograph below of President Harry S. Truman speaking to a group of journalists in May 1951.

Adjacent to the South Lawn and just outside the Oval Office, the Rose Garden has long been a favorite of presidents. Ellen Wilson planted the first roses here in 1913, replacing a colonial-style garden dating from 1902. In 1962, at the request of John Kennedy, Rachel Lambert Mellon supervised its redesign by the landscape architect Perry Wheeler. The garden's broad lawn, seasonal flower beds, and saucer magnolia trees provide a serene setting for the president as he walks to the Oval Office or looks out from his desk. They are also an attractive stage for official ceremonies such as bill signings, press conferences, presidential announcements, and elegant dinners.

Here President Kennedy greeted the early astronauts, and here, in 1971, Tricia Nixon was married. During the Bicentennial year, 1976, Gerald and Betty Ford hosted several State Dinners under a large tent covering the garden, including one for Queen Elizabeth II of Great Britain. In a ceremony on September 24, 1981, Ronald Reagan honored Sandra Day O'Connor—the first woman to be named to the U.S. Supreme Court. George H. W. Bush also held numerous official events in the Rose Garden, including a meeting with the Cincinnati Reds after their victory in the 1990 World Series. Bill Clinton held several press conferences in the garden, and it was here that he signed such historic legislation as the Family Leave Act in 1993. George W. Bush presented Teacher of the Year and Preserve America awards and announced major policy initiatives in the Rose Garden. Barack Obama used the historic space for press and policy announcements. With a reverence for the John F. Kennedy garden plan of 1962, Melania Trump oversaw a renovation of infrastructure and planting updates in 2020. Joe Biden continues to use the Rose Garden for press conferences, receptions, and events of many kinds.

A large Magnolia soulangeana tree is positioned in the Rose Garden in April 1962 during a redesign of the space that created the open lawn surrounded by flower beds, as we know it today.

As President John F. Kennedy envisioned, Rachel Lambert Mellon's redesign of the Rose Garden created a green theater just outside the Oval Office. The redesigned steps (above) continue to serve as a presidential stage today. Recent presidents have used the garden for press conferences, announcements, receptions, and even for State Dinners. The Rose Garden was the setting for a glamourous State Dinner in honor of Australia's Prime Minister Scott Morrison (left) during the Donald Trump presidency, 2019.

LIFE IN THE WHITE HOUSE

Right: In 2020, First Lady Melania Trump oversaw a renovation of the infrastructure of the garden, which included installation of a perimeter stone path as well as new plantings of boxwood and roses.

Below: President Joe Biden welcomes guests to a Rose Garden reception to mark Asian American, Native Hawaiian, and Pacific Islander Heritage Month, May 17, 2022.

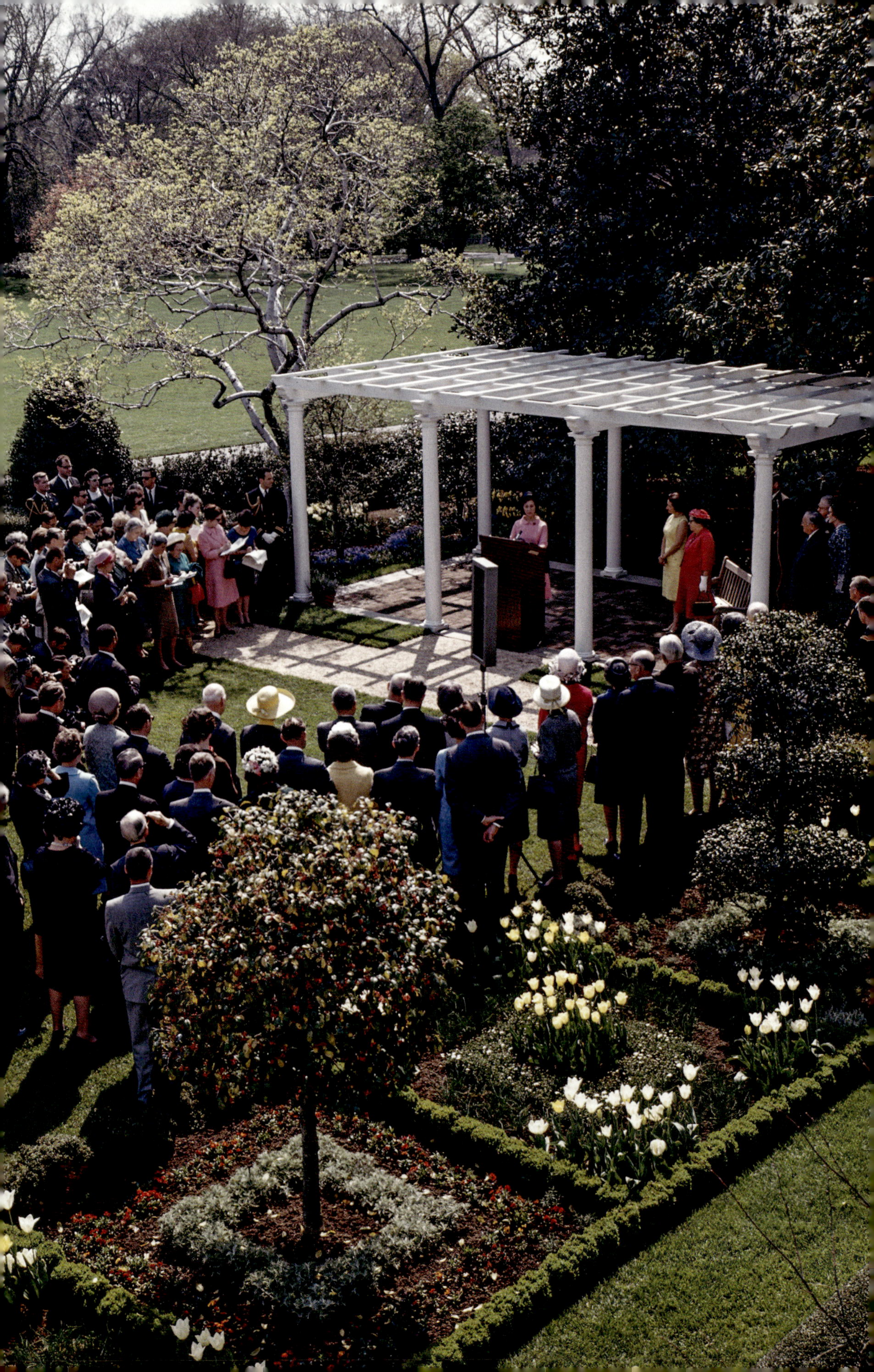

IN THE PRESIDENT'S PARK
THE JACQUELINE KENNEDY GARDEN

Variously named the East Garden and the First Lady's Garden, this intimate, quiet setting on the east side of the White House has always been a private garden and retreat for first families and their friends. In 1903, Edith Roosevelt, who had a strong interest in gardening, created a formal garden where, at spring garden parties, guests walked along the graveled paths to view the flower beds of roses and lilies outlined with boxwood and privet. Ten years later, another first lady with a love of gardens, Ellen Wilson, invited the highly respected landscape gardener Beatrix Jones Farrand to submit plans for the garden. The result was an expansive central green lawn with a lily pond in the center, surrounded by ivy plantings, evergreens, and four L-shaped flower beds in the corners. Changes made in 1952, at the end of the massive Truman renovation of the house, simplified the garden.

Shortly after moving into the White House in 1963, Lady Bird Johnson asked that the plans for the garden, begun by Rachel Lambert Mellon and approved by President and Mrs. Kennedy and the National Park Service, be continued. The plan retained a central grass panel in the center with the north and south sides framed by holly osmanthus hedges and square planting beds with clipped American holly trees. Also in the beds are herbs grown for the White House chefs. When Mrs. Johnson dedicated the garden to Jacqueline Kennedy in 1965 she stated, "I dedicate it to the enduring heritage she has given all of us."

Succeeding first ladies have held receptions and teas in this serene setting, and, in the 1990s, Hillary Rodham Clinton showcased eight exhibitions of contemporary American sculpture in the garden, organized by museums throughout the country. Barack and Michelle Obama hosted receptions in the garden, as did President and Mrs. Trump and most recently President and Dr. Biden.

Opposite: First Lady Lady Bird Johnson (near top in yellow) hosts a ceremony dedicating the East Garden to Jacqueline Kennedy, 1965.

Below: First Lady Hillary Clinton showcased in the East Garden a series of eight exhibitions celebrating contemporary American sculpture. *Vertical Void* by Carol Hepper is displayed on the right, May 15, 1995.

IN THE PRESIDENT'S PARK
GREENHOUSES

President James Buchanan's niece and official hostess, Harriet Lane, persuaded her uncle to build the first of several conservatories and greenhouses that would give much pleasure to future White House residents and visitors. In these steamy glass buildings, filled with the color and fragrance of exotic blossoms, fruits, and tangled tropical vines, Miss Lane became the first of many hostesses at the mansion to find a quiet haven away from the obligations of her official position.

The White House Conservatories as they appeared in the late nineteenth century, where the West Wing stands today.

The energetic First Lady Lucy Webb Hayes worked here with trowel and shears among her lilies and roses. Frances Cleveland spent pleasant hours wandering with her girls along the sweet-scented aisles of the greenhouses. Caroline Harrison, who was fond of orchids, had several rare varieties planted in the Conservatory, and she used the vivid, showy blooms as models for china she selected and painted.

From the time President Buchanan's Conservatory opened until all the "glass houses" were torn down to make way for the West Wing in 1902 during the presidency of Theodore Roosevelt, no first lady had far to go for flowers or potted plants to decorate her home. Today, all flowers for arrangements come from wholesale distributors. Off-site greenhouses run by the National Park Service, which is responsible for the care and upkeep of the Grounds, supply potted plants and azaleas, roses, hydrangeas, and orchids.

First Lady Lucy Webb Hayes and her children Fanny and Scott, with their playmate, in the Conservatory, c. 1879.

IN THE PRESIDENT'S PARK

IN THE PRESIDENT'S PARK
THE CHILDREN'S GARDEN

Lauren Bush, one of twelve grandchildren of President George H. W. Bush, sits in the Children's Garden beside her hand prints (above). The entrance to the garden bears a reminder that it was a gift from President and Mrs. Lyndon B. Johnson on Christmas, 1968. Hand prints of presidential grandchildren have been regularly added to the garden since it was created. The private garden is seen (opposite) in 2016.

Created in 1968 at the request of Lyndon and Lady Bird Johnson as a private place for children and grandchildren of presidential families, this garden on the South Grounds is a quiet, secluded spot. With its child-size garden furniture, small pool, and flagstone blocks with handprints of recent presidential grandchildren, it evokes the memory of all children who have resided at the White House.

IN THE PRESIDENT'S PARK

IN THE PRESIDENT'S PARK
ROOM TO PLAY

Children have long found the rolling acres of the South Lawn a great playground. With room for every favorite activity from organized sports to make-believe, children can explore hidden nooks in hedges and bushes, ride ponies, and raise pets of every description.

President Ulysses S. Grant's children enjoyed rolling a hoop and bicycle riding, while President Dwight D. Eisenhower's grandchildren took to their tricycles for trips around the South Drive.

Theodore Roosevelt's six energetic children pushed the limits with their escapades. Theodore Roosevelt once caught young Quentin walking on stilts through a flower bed. The boy obeyed Roosevelt's stern order to get out of the flowers but grumbled, "I don't see what good it does me for you to be President."

In 1933, President Franklin D. Roosevelt had a playground, complete with a swing set, jungle gym, and sandbox, erected for his grandchildren to enjoy. In later years the Obama children would also have a swing set built within view of the Oval Office.

Caroline Kennedy's pony was stabled on the far South Grounds, while a playground for her and her young brother, John, was closer to the house. Amy Carter enjoyed a tree house so famously built on the South Lawn with the help of her father, President Jimmy Carter.

President Bill Clinton's daughter Chelsea enjoyed practicing soccer on the lawn, as did Barron Trump, son of President Donald Trump, more recently.

Built for Sasha and Malia Obama in 2009, the play set on the South Lawn was in view of President Obama's Oval Office.

LIFE IN THE WHITE HOUSE

Above: Macaroni and the Kennedy children visit the president outside the Oval Office, 1962.

Left: President Jimmy Carter is seen with daughter Amy and a grandchild playing in the tree house he designed for them on the South Grounds, c. 1977.

Below: A soccer goal set up in the Jacqueline Kennedy Garden is ready for Barron Trump to practice his game, 2018.

IN THE PRESIDENT'S PARK

IN THE PRESIDENT'S PARK
THANKSGIVING PARDONS

Below: The recipient of President Bill Clinton's 1998 Thanksgiving pardon sets off to explore the Rose Garden.

Opposite: "Chocolate," a recipient of a presidential pardon granted ahead of Thanksgiving by Joe Biden, enjoys a sunny day on the South Lawn following the ceremony, November 21, 2022.

The Thanksgiving Turkey Pardon at the White House is a highly publicized annual ritual and signals the start of the holiday season. Little Tad Lincoln made a pet of a turkey that relatives sent for the family's Christmas dinner in 1863. He named it Jack. When the cook prepared to kill the turkey, Tad ran in tears to his father, who interrupted a cabinet meeting to write an official reprieve. The event became immortalized in the president's "pardoning" of a Thanksgiving turkey. The tradition has been carried on in the twenty-first century with President Joe Biden "pardoning" turkeys presented by the National Turkey Federation in Rose Garden ceremonies. In 2021, it was Peanut Butter and Jelly who received the presidential pardon; they were followed by Chocolate and Chip in 2022.

IN THE PRESIDENT'S PARK

The White House Kitchen Garden, 2021.

IN THE PRESIDENT'S PARK
THE KITCHEN GARDEN

Michelle Obama planted a White House Kitchen Garden to start a national conversation around the health of the nation's families, and she involved schoolchildren from Washington, D.C., and across the country in planting the garden in order to teach them about healthy eating. One section of the garden contained a variety of plants grown from heirloom seeds from Thomas Jefferson's Virginia home, Monticello. Annual planting has continued during the Trump and Biden presidencies, and the produce is used for the first family's meals and for official functions, including State Dinners.

Schoolchildren join Michelle Obama in harvesting vegetables in the fall, 2011.

IN THE PRESIDENT'S PARK
COMMEMORATIVE TREES

John Quincy Adams indulged in the hope, he confided to his diary, that a certain border of oaks, chestnuts, and other trees would "outlast many Presidents of the United States." In fact one of his shade trees—a great American elm—survived until 1990, spreading its branches over the South Lawn. In its place, Barbara Bush planted a new tree in 1991, one that had been propagated from the Adams elm.

Andrew Jackson was one of the first presidents to plant a memorial tree on the Grounds, a magnificent magnolia in memory of his beloved Rachel. It still stands beside the South Portico.

Beginning with Rutherford B. Hayes, all the presidents and some of their wives have planted trees in the President's Park. Jimmy Carter brought a red maple from his Georgia farm. He knew all the old trees by name and took a special interest in their care. Ronald Reagan planted three trees, the George H. W. Bushes, five. Bill and Hillary Clinton added more than half a dozen to the park, including a white dogwood planted in memory of the children who died in the April 1995 bombing of the Federal Building in Oklahoma City.

The twenty-first-century presidents and first ladies have continued the practice of planting commemorative trees, and in doing so have followed the Olmsted Plan of 1935, which ensures that the Grounds of the White House are historically maintained.

Children lend a hand as First Lady Lady Bird Johnson plants a tree on the White House Grounds in 1968.

Above: First Lady Melania Trump was joined by Mary Jean Eisenhower, granddaughter of President Eisenhower, and Richard Emory Gatchell Jr., a descendant of President Monroe, in planting an oak tree on the South Lawn marking the two hundredth anniversary of President James Monroe's return to the White House after the fire of 1814. The gathering of presidential descendants was part of the Presidential Sites Summit hosted by the White House Historical Association in 2018.

Right: President and Dr. Biden plant a magnolia tree as part of a ceremony with Gold Star family members on Memorial Day, 2022.

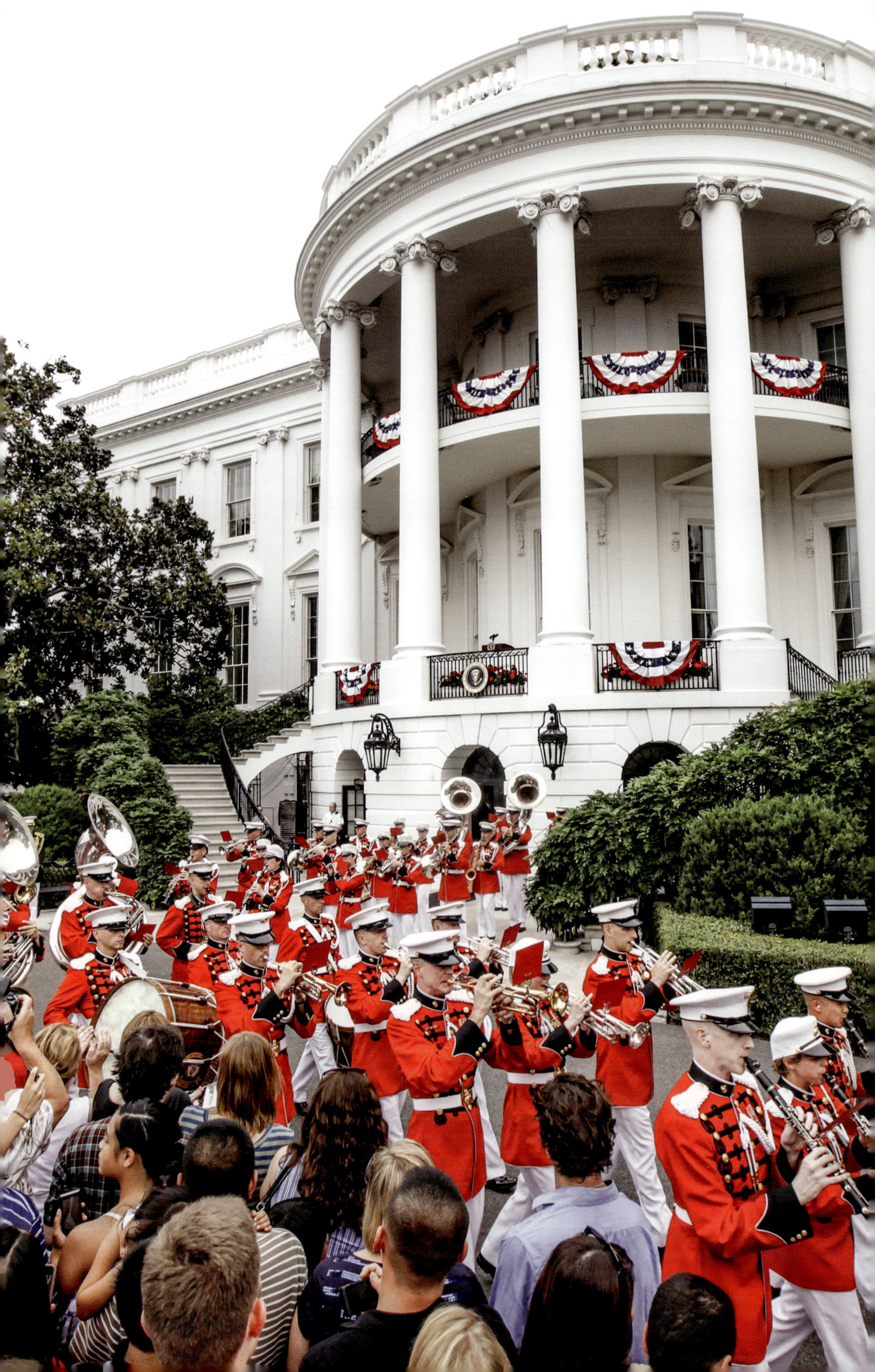

IN THE PRESIDENT'S PARK
MARINE BAND CONCERTS

From the beginning, the White House gardens and lawns have been settings for pageantry, entertainment, and the recreation of presidents. Thomas Jefferson's Fourth of July celebrations included reviews of the District of Columbia militia and other troops in the newly laid out "President's Park," with "their gay appearance and martial musick," wrote an eyewitness, "enlivening the scene, exhilarating the spirits of the throngs of people who poured in from the country and adjacent towns." In the mid-nineteenth century, several presidents invited Washingtonians to Marine Band concerts on the South Lawn on Saturday afternoons.

From the 1870s to the 1930s, large lawn parties regularly complemented the Marine Band concerts, with the band seated on the South Portico. In the summer of 1918, Woodrow and Edith Wilson invited war veterans to attend an annual garden fete. Warren and Florence Harding continued these parties for veterans with much enthusiasm.

Opposite: "The President's Own," the U.S. Marine Band, plays for military families at an Independence Day celebration on the South Lawn, July 4, 2011.

Below: President Abraham Lincoln towers over his guest Prince Napoleon on the South Portico, July 21, 1861. Beyond the flag-crowned Marine Band pavilion stands the unfinished Washington Monument.

IN THE PRESIDENT'S PARK
EVENTS ON THE SOUTH LAWN

Above: After learning to fly at the Wright Flying School in Huffman Prairie, Ohio, Harry Nelson Atwood completed the final leg of a fourteen-day flight from Boston to Washington, D.C., by landing his Wright Model B airplane on the South Lawn. President William Howard Taft was watching from the South Portico, 1911.

Opposite: The Black Watch performs a tattoo on the South Lawn, November 13, 1963, during the John F. Kennedy presidency.

When the Tafts celebrated their silver wedding anniversary in June 1911, they received more than three thousand guests on the South Grounds, where trees and bushes sparkled with tiny colored lights and strings of paper lanterns cast shadows on the lawn. That same year the broad South Grounds witnessed a prophetic and dramatic sight. A pioneering pilot, Harry Nelson Atwood, landed there in a Burgess-Wright biplane soon after completing a record-setting cross-country flight, and President Taft presented him with a gold medal for the feat.

On a cold day in January 1945, hundreds of guests (many were members of the armed forces) stood on the South Lawn to witness the fourth Inauguration of President Franklin D. Roosevelt on the South Portico. It was the only Inauguration to be held outdoors at the White House.

Summer after summer, the South Lawn has offered a perfect setting for large gatherings. The Eisenhowers, for example, held a reception there for more than four thousand members of the American Bar Association and counselors from the British Commonwealth. The

Kennedy children shared their playground with 1,700 youngsters from child-care agencies when the kilted Black Watch—the Royal Highland Regiment—paraded to the skirl of bagpipes. On a huge stage erected for the occasion, Lyndon B. Johnson presented awards to outstanding high school graduates who had won a place in his annual Presidential Scholar program, begun in 1964. Here in 1990 George H. W. Bush signed the Americans with Disabilities Act before a large crowd. Here Bill Clinton hosted the largest gathering of Native American tribal leaders to congregate at the White House and a dinner commemorating the fiftieth anniversary of North Atlantic Treaty Organization, attended by leaders of NATO countries.

During the George W. Bush presidency, moments of prayer and remembrance were observed for victims of the 2001 terrorist attacks, a tradition that has continued. In September 2005, President Bush awarded the 9/11 Medals of Valor in honor of the 442 firefighters, police officers, emergency medical technicians, and other public safety officers who gave their lives on September 11, 2001.

The South Lawn also is the setting for ceremonial occasions, such as the welcoming of a head of state for a State Visit. In 1993, in an event orchestrated by President Clinton, thousands gathered to witness the emotional signing of the Israeli-Palestinian peace agreement.

President Lyndon B. Johnson began the tradition of hosting a picnic on the South Lawn for members of Congress and their families, one of many annual traditions that Joe Biden continues. In May 2022, President Biden welcomed Team USA following the Winter Olympics in Beijing, China.

Right: The Johnson Country Fair brought a small amusement park to the White House Grounds and featured games, clowns, farm animals, and pony rides. Lynda Johnson, shown sitting on a lion, also attended the festivities, 1967.

Below: President Bill Clinton hosts Prime Minister Yitzhak Rabin of Israel and the Palestine Liberation Organization chairman, Yasser Arafat, for the Israeli-Palestinian treaty signing on the South Lawn of the White House, 1993.

Above: President and Mrs. George W. Bush lead the White House staff in a moment of silence on the first anniversary of the 9/11 terrorist attacks, September 11, 2002.

Right: President and Dr. Biden join a group photo with Team USA in celebration of their competition at the Winter Olympics in Beijing, China, 2022.

IN THE PRESIDENT'S PARK

199

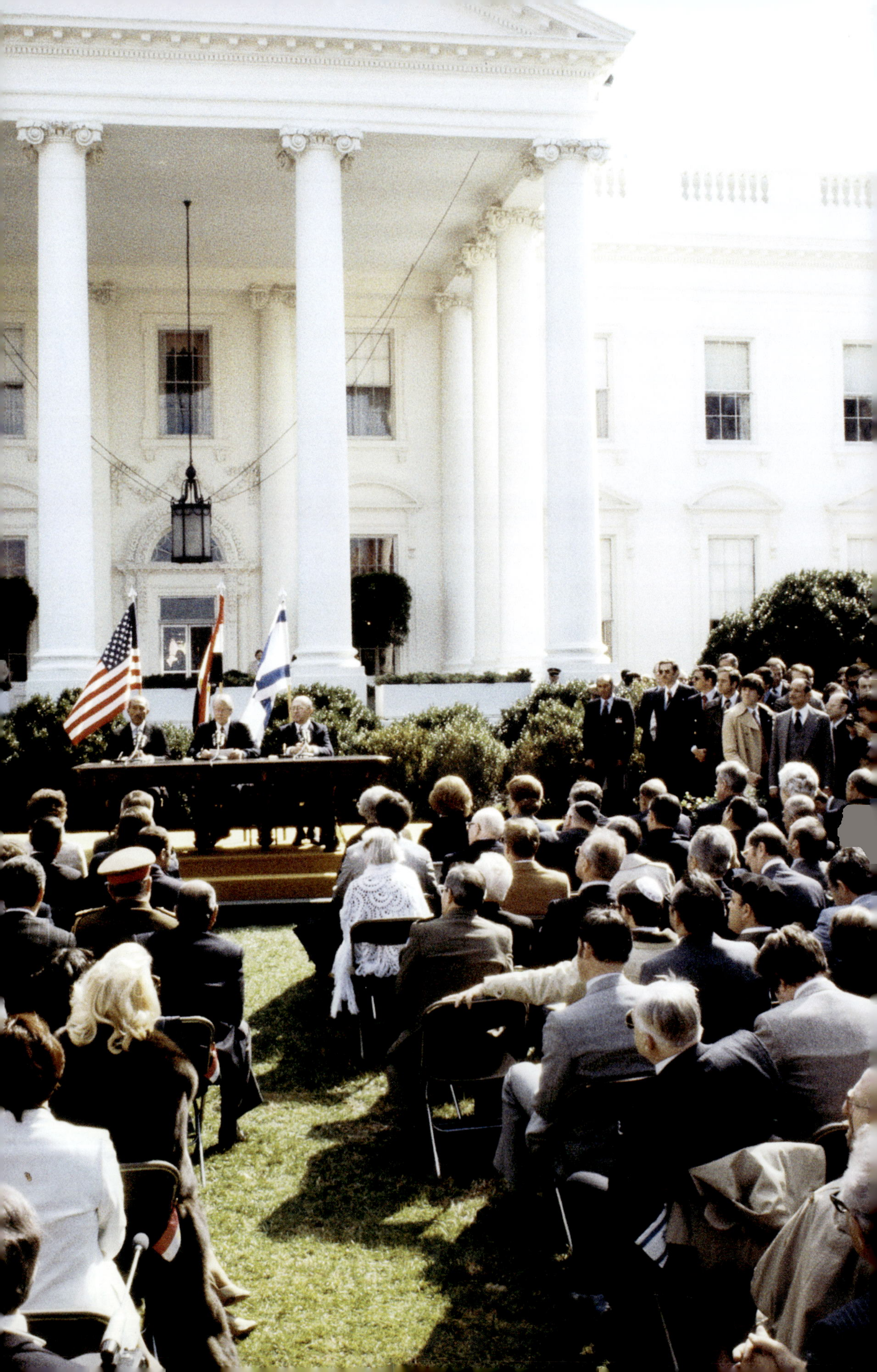

IN THE PRESIDENT'S PARK
EVENTS ON THE NORTH LAWN

On April 10, 1865, jubilant crowds surged across the North Lawn, singing and cheering the news of General Robert E. Lee's surrender at Appomattox Court House. Soon Abraham Lincoln came to a window in response to the cries of the people. He promised a victory speech later but meantime suggested that their enthusiastic band play "Dixie." It was one of the best tunes he had ever heard, he said, and he thought "we had fairly captured it."

Only a few ceremonies have been held on the North Lawn facing toward Pennsylvania Avenue. One that received worldwide attention was the 1979 signing of the Treaty of Peace between Prime Minister Menachem Begin of Israel and President Anwar el-Sadat of Egypt, which President Jimmy Carter had negotiated. That same year, President and Mrs. Carter welcomed Pope John Paul II, the first pontiff to meet with a president at the White House, at the North Entrance, followed by a large ceremony on the South Grounds.

The most dramatic and visible ceremonies on the North Grounds, however, take place during a change of administration when the outgoing president and first lady receive the incoming president and first lady at the North Portico. After a brief reception in the White House, they depart along the North Drive for the inaugural ceremony at the Capitol. The North Entrance was the only entrance to the White House for family, guests, staff, and visitors until 1902; today it is used most often when heads of state arrive for a State Dinner.

Pennsylvania Avenue in front of the White House, closed to traffic since the Oklahoma City bombing in 1995, was redesigned with new paving, lighting, tree plantings, and benches in 2004. Inaugural Parades continue to be reviewed by presidential families from a reviewing stand constructed in front of the North Fence every four years, and the American people continue to gather here to view the President's House and to express their political views.

Opposite: A ceremony on the North Lawn of the White House for the signing of the Egypt-Israel Peace Treaty in 1979. Seated at the table are Egyptian President Anwar el-Sadat, President Jimmy Carter, and Israeli Prime Minister Menachem Begin.

Below: First Lady Laura Bush speaks at a ceremony reopening Pennsylvania Avenue in front of the White House to foot traffic as Washington, D.C., Mayor Anthony Williams looks on, November 9, 2004.

IN THE PRESIDENT'S PARK
THE EASTER EGG ROLL

Once a year—on Easter Monday—youngsters are invited to an egg-rolling party on the South Lawn. It is the largest public event held annually on the White House Grounds. In 1878 this event, held on the Capitol grounds for many years, was moved to the White House at the invitation of President Rutherford B. Hayes. Since then, only war, inclement weather, and the COVID-19 pandemic have canceled the Easter Egg Roll. In recent decades, along with the Easter Bunny, cartoon characters and children's authors have participated.

In a competition first introduced during the Nixon presidency, children race to scoot hard-boiled eggs across the lawn with spoons. Thousands of real eggs are dyed for the races and for the egg hunts. Throughout the South Grounds there are live music performances, sports courts, cooking stations, and storytelling areas.

President and Dr. Biden welcomed children back to the White House for the annual egg-rolling festivities in 2022 following a two-year hiatus during the COVID-19 pandemic. Thirty thousand people participated in the 2023 Easter "EGGucation" Roll. Participants included thousands of military and veteran families, and caregivers as well as guests from across the country who received tickets through a free online lottery.

Right: A scene from the Easter Egg Roll held on the South Lawn in 1922 during the presidency of Warren G. Harding.

Opposite: New Easter Bunny costumes provided by the White House Historical Association were debuted at the 2023 Easter Egg Roll (top). Sharing their books with children in the Reading Nook are Rocco and Arioth Smirne (left) reading *Rocco at the White House Easter Egg Roll!*, and Gigi McBride (right) reading *Gigi at the White House!*.

IN THE PRESIDENT'S PARK

Above: President Herbert Hoover plays medicine ball with his "Medicine-Ball Cabinet," 1933.

Right: Pitching horseshoes has been a favorite sport of several presidents including President George H. W. Bush, c. 1991.

IN THE PRESIDENT'S PARK
PRESIDENTS AT PLAY

Many presidents have set up recreational facilities on the Grounds. Rutherford B. Hayes marked off a croquet court near the South Portico, where, a staff member wrote, clerks as well as the family "used to spend an hour now and then . . . over hard-fought games with mallet and ball."

There has been a tennis court on the South Lawn since the time of Theodore Roosevelt. The press called associates who joined him for a fast, tough game his "Tennis Cabinet." Warren G. Harding practiced golf shots on the lawn and trained his Airedale, Laddie Boy, to retrieve the balls. Herbert Hoover exercised with his "Medicine-Ball Cabinet" before breakfast conferences. Harry S. Truman pitched horseshoes; Dwight D. Eisenhower improved his golf on a presidential putting green.

The first outdoor swimming pool was installed near the Oval Office for Gerald Ford. The Carter family enjoyed the pool, the tennis courts, and the bowling alley under the North Portico. Ronald Reagan had no opportunity to enjoy his favorite exercise, horseback riding, on the White House Grounds. Both he and the first lady used exercise equipment installed in a Second Floor room. George H. W. Bush, an active president, added a horseshoe pit and a basketball half-court, and he pursued jogging, golf, tennis, and swimming. During the Clinton presidency, a quarter-mile jogging track was added, and the Eisenhower putting green was restored on the South Grounds.

In recent years, George W. Bush transformed a portion of the South Lawn into a baseball field for T-ball games for children each summer; Barack Obama frequently used the basketball court and gym; and Melania Trump added a new tennis pavilion, replacing a smaller structure on the South Grounds.

President Bill Clinton enjoys a run on the jogging track installed for him on the South Grounds. He is joined by South Korean President Kim Young-sam, 1995.

The outdoor swimming pool was installed for President Gerald R. Ford. Workers can be seen making progress on its construction, June 18, 1975 (above). Once completed, President Ford often went for a swim, as seen here (right).

206   LIFE IN THE WHITE HOUSE

Left and below: First Lady Melania Trump reviews plans for the new Tennis Pavilion in the tennis court area with Tham Kannalikham (left) and Peggy Marker (right), c. 2018. The neoclassical-style pavilion was completed in 2020.

IN THE PRESIDENT'S PARK

During a major cleaning and conservation of the exterior sandstone, the White House (opposite) was stripped of many layers of white paint, applied over more than 150 years. Painters are seen applying a coat of fresh paint to the cleaned stone around the North Front (above), 1980.

CHAPTER FIVE

A HOUSE FOR THE AGES

The President's House is the nation's house. It belongs to the people, and much care goes into its management. Over the years the house has been rebuilt, changed, expanded, and renovated, and those who have contributed to its permanency—its permanent place in the nation and in the hearts of the people—are many. They include builders and architects and stonemasons and engineers as well as housekeepers and chefs. As Calvin Coolidge observed, presidents come and go, but those who care for the White House stay on. At a dinner in honor of the White House's two hundredth birthday, Gerald Ford paid tribute to the permanent staff of the White House Residence: "To everyone who aids, comforts, and inspires a president and his loved ones," he said, and offered a toast "from our families to the White House family, to all you do to make this old house a home."

A HOUSE FOR THE AGES
STOCKING THE PANTRY

Until the early twentieth century, presidents had to pay for all of their family's daily needs, whether personal or in connection with official duties. Presidents even provided their own horses and carriages and were responsible for their upkeep. To be sure, Congress appropriated money for repairs and furnishings for the mansion, and to many the annual presidential salary of $25,000 must have seemed enough to take care of everything else. But the appropriations often varied with the whims of Congress, and the cost of maintaining a household that reflected the dignity of the nation worked a hardship on many presidents. Thomas Jefferson and James Monroe were later forced to sell land to pay debts accumulated during their White House years.

Jefferson's numerous and lavish gourmet dinners—the result of a habit he acquired in France of "mitigating business with dinner"—virtually ate up his salary. In eight years his bills for wine alone came to nearly $11,000. And he once noted that when Congress was in session he needed a great deal more wine, especially champagne. Washington food costs were higher, too, than elsewhere. Jefferson's grocery bill often amounted to $50 a day—at a time when 75 cents for a turkey and $3 for a hog were considered high prices. In William Henry Harrison's time, White House life was so casual that the president sometimes did his own marketing, carrying his groceries home in a basket. Helen Taft hired the first housekeeper in 1909, to supervise the food buying and the preparation of meals for both the president's family and guests. Previously a steward had seen to

First Lady Mamie Eisenhower, accompanied by butler John Ficklin, inspects a stock of canned goods in the White House Storeroom, 1958.

LIFE IN THE WHITE HOUSE

routine marketing, and caterers met special requirements. Today, a storekeeper takes care of the daily marketing needs, and the Secret Service checks the purchases before delivery.

It was not until the Taft presidency that Congress relieved presidents of having to pay the wages of house staff. Warren G. Harding was the first president for whom the government picked up the check for official entertaining. Congress also has recognized the advancing level of salaries in the United States, though the sums paid the chief executive have lagged behind those received by many corporation presidents. In 1873, effective with Ulysses S. Grant's second term, Congress raised the president's salary from $25,000 a year to $50,000. William Howard Taft, in 1909, became the first chief executive to earn $75,000. In 1949, Harry S. Truman was the first to receive $100,000. The annual salary is now $400,000. The president still must defray the first family's living expenses and is responsible for the cost of food, laundry, and dry cleaning, for their personal telephone calls, and for all their private parties.

White House Storeroom Chief Bill Hamilton at work, c. 2002.

Above: Paul Jennings, an enslaved worker in the White House during the presidencies of James Madison and James K. Polk, eventually purchased his freedom and became a property owner. He documented his experiences in a memoir, *A Colored Man's Reminiscences of James Madison*.

Opposite: Hired as a messenger by Abraham Lincoln, William Slade became the first official steward of the White House under Andrew Johnson.

A HOUSE FOR THE AGES
EARLY HOUSEHOLDS AND ENSLAVED WORKERS

Today most members of the White House household staff are salaried federal employees who hold their jobs from one presidency to the next, but the early presidents were responsible for the costs of running the house, including the wages of the servants. John and Abigail Adams, the first White House residents, brought their own servants with them to the house in 1800. Nine of the presidents who followed before the Civil War either brought enslaved workers with them or relied on enslaved labor at the White House. These presidents—Thomas Jefferson, James Madison, James Monroe, John Quincy Adams, Andrew Jackson, Martin Van Buren, John Tyler, James K. Polk, and Zachary Taylor—also often hired French or Belgian stewards or maîtres d'hôtel to arrange dinners and receptions.

Servants and enslaved individuals worked in the president's household as chefs, gardeners, stable hands, maids, butlers, lady's maids, valets, and in other positions. Their living conditions varied by presidency but were often difficult, with sleeping arrangements in the attic or Ground Floor where temperatures were extreme and dampness and vermin were common. Although little is known of their life stories, much has been learned from the memoir by Paul Jennings.

Born into slavery on President James Madison's estate at Montpelier, Jennings served as a valet to Madison at Montpelier and at the White House. After James Madison's death, Dolley Madison took Jennings with her when she left Montpelier for Washington and hired him out to serve in James K. Polk's White House. Then she sold Jennings. A few months later Daniel Webster purchased Jennings with the intent of allowing him to purchase his freedom, which, by 1847, he did. In 1865, he published *A Colored Man's Reminiscences of James Madison*, a memoir that includes his White House experiences.

After the Civil War, the first official steward, hired by Andrew Johnson in 1866, was William Slade, an African American. Slade, who had been a messenger for Abraham Lincoln, was put in charge of the domestic management of the house. African Americans have continued to work in the White House, to the present.

Late nineteenth-century photographs provide a glimpse of members of the White House domestic staff from the Rutherford B. Hayes presidency, c. 1880 (left). A cook poses in the smaller of two White House Kitchens (above), c. 1888–90; and housekeeper Jerry Smith wields a feather duster on the North Portico (opposite), c. 1900.

LIFE IN THE WHITE HOUSE

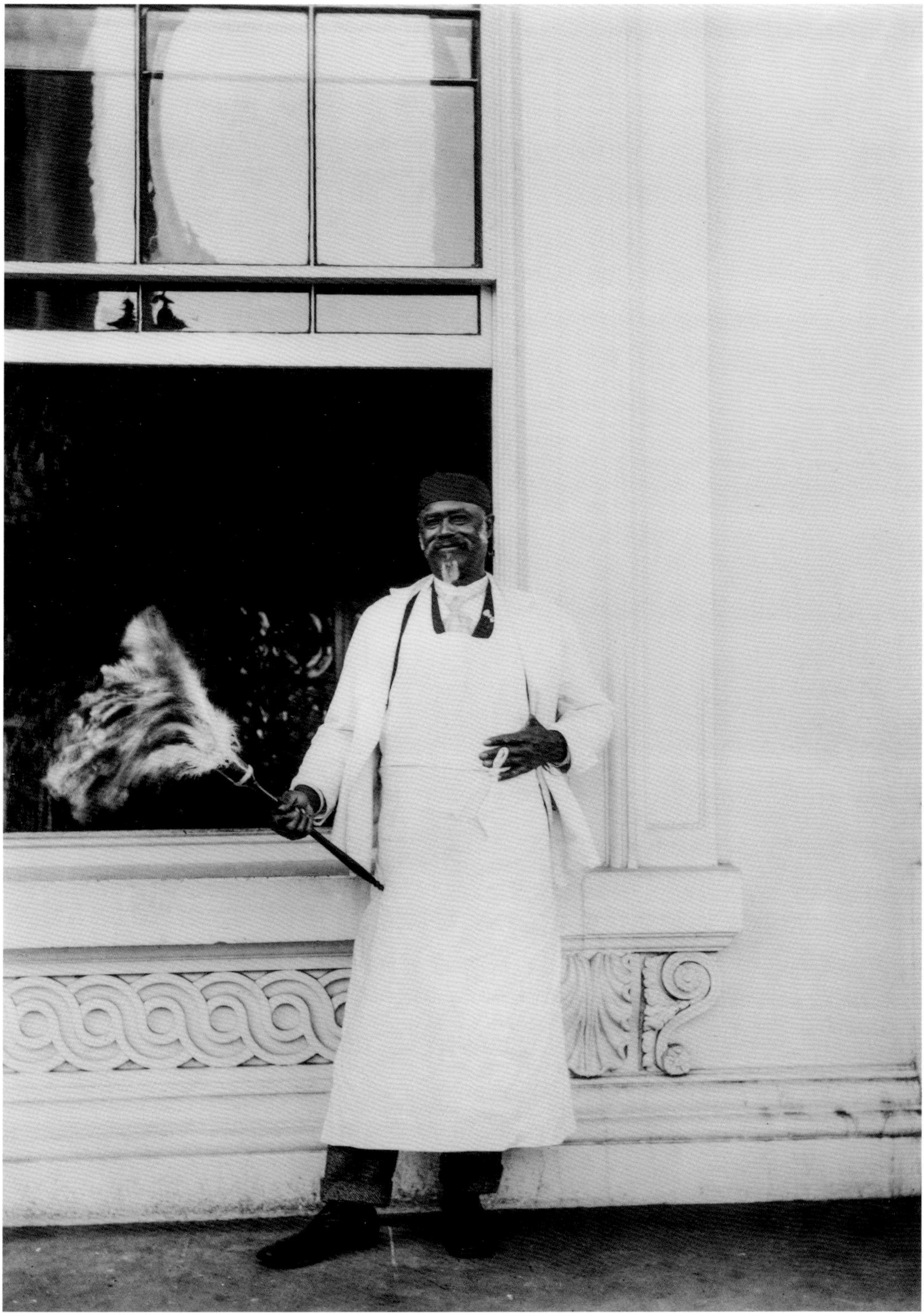

Daniel Shanks, the first food and beverage usher at the White House, is seen finalizing the table settings in the State Dining Room ahead of an annual Governors' Dinner, 1999.

A HOUSE FOR THE AGES
THE RESIDENCE STAFF

The first families who arrive at the White House today find a trained permanent staff ready to help manage what has now become a highly complex organization. In many ways the house resembles a small, well-run hotel. Furniture, works of art, bed and table linens, glasses, silverware, and china—state and informal—are all provided. Dedicated workers have assisted, and will continue to assist, each first family in making their home a comfortable one. Today the combined domestic and maintenance staffs—most of whom carry on from one presidency to another—number about one hundred employees: florists, curators, housekeepers, chefs, butlers, carpenters, painters, and plumbers. At the head of these workers stands the chief usher, whose job is to coordinate and manage the manifold activities of just about everything but ushering. If such a force seems large, consider how prodigious are the tasks for official events and how great the responsibility that comes with handling some of the nation's most valuable possessions. Consider, too, the normal wear and tear involved, and the cleaning needed after thousands of visitors pass through the State Rooms. The staff must keep the White House presentable and ready for the functions held there.

White House Butler James Ramsey was one of many long-serving members of the Residence staff, c. 2002.

LIFE IN THE WHITE HOUSE

Overseeing behind-the-scenes activity in the Blue Room, Gary Walters, chief usher from 1986 to 2007, looks on (far left) as plates are prepared to be carried into a State Dinner, 1994. Seen at his desk in the White House in 1962 (above), J. B. West, chief usher from 1957 to 1968, documented his experiences with the book *Upstairs at the White House*. The first woman to hold the position of chief usher was Angella Reid (left), who served from 2011 to 2017.

A HOUSE FOR THE AGES

A HOUSE FOR THE AGES
THE KITCHEN

The White House Kitchen opening off the arched Ground Floor Corridor is any chef's dream of equipment and efficient working space. In this gleaming white and stainless steel domain are grinders, slicers, choppers, mixers, electric ovens, and walk-in freezers. They help Executive Chef Cristeta Comerford, the first woman named to that position, and her assistants prepare State Dinners for as many as 140 guests, and hors d'oeuvres for a thousand or more.

Such expert aid and equipment would have appeared nothing short of miraculous to Abigail Adams, who wrote to her sister that she would have been pleased to have enough candles "lighting the apartments, from the kitchen to parlors and chambers." "The house was made habitable," she wrote to her daughter, but the main stairs were not yet up, not a single apartment had been finished, and bells for summoning servants were "wholly wanting to assist us in this great castle."

Other first ladies also struggled with managing the house. Dolley Madison, a biographer noted, "superintended all her domestic arrangements before breakfast." And in the 1860s, an admiring woman correspondent described a morning chore performed by capable Martha Patterson, daughter of President Andrew Johnson, who would "don a calico dress and spotless apron, and then descend to skim the milk and attend the dairy." As recently as the Taft presidency, a cow named Pauline Wayne supplied milk for the household and grazed on the White House lawn.

An engraving published in 1889 (right) depicts a chef and his assistants at work in an early White House Kitchen. An image of the kitchen in the 1830s is inset, as is a portrait of Hugo Ziemann, a chef in the 1880s. Today, the modernized White House Kitchen (opposite in 2022) is fully equipped for the preparation of everything from quick snacks to elaborate State Dinners. Executive Chef Cristeta Comerford and her assistants are seen at work in the Kitchen (below) preparing a dinner for Charles, Prince of Wales, in 2005.

A HOUSE FOR THE AGES

221

At the end of the administration, on their last morning in the White House, each president and first lady bid farewell to the household staff, who queue to shake hands. Clockwise from above, President and Mrs. Eisenhower, 1961; President and Mrs. George H. W. Bush, 1993; and President Bill Clinton, 2001.

A HOUSE FOR THE AGES

A HOUSE FOR THE AGES
IMPROVING THE WHITE HOUSE

Through the years, the latest home conveniences have added to the comfort in the President's House.

The building Jefferson moved into in 1801 may have been "big enough for two emperors, one pope, and the grand lama," as a satirist observed, but it lacked practical arrangements for the everyday management of a home. So the president added colonnaded wings on either side of the mansion; they contained servants' quarters, storage and laundry areas, an icehouse, a meat house, a wine cellar, and a henhouse. Inside, the inventive Mr. Jefferson devised a set of revolving trays, called a dumbwaiter, built into the walls of his dining room. With this contrivance, guests could be served from outside the room without having butlers close enough to overhear their private conversations. "You need not speak so low," Jefferson once assured a nervous guest. "Our walls have no ears."

Probably the greatest inconvenience of the early White House was the lack of running water. In the few months John and Abigail Adams lived there, servants had to haul water from nearly half a mile away. Jefferson set up an attic cistern with a system of wooden pipes reaching through the floors for water closets. But it was not until 1833, in Andrew Jackson's second term, that a system of iron pipes brought in spring water to the east terrace and permitted the general from the West to enjoy hot and cold showers.

Martin Van Buren put in a basement "reservoir" with a "double-forcing pump" to supply water for kitchen and bathing needs. He thereby added fuel to the political fires stoked by

In 1950 two workmen begin the process of gutting a White House bathroom to make way for more modern facilities during the Truman renovation.

224 LIFE IN THE WHITE HOUSE

Congressman Charles Ogle. In the "Gold Spoon Oration" that accused the president of living in decadent luxury, Ogle ridiculed him as one who indulged in the Grecian and Roman "pleasures of the warm or tepid bath."

The precise date of the introduction of modern plumbing in the White House is not known, but records show that in 1853 the Private Quarters had central plumbing and bathtubs with hot and cold running water. By 1876, water to several tubs and water closets was supplied by pipes connected to a 2,000-gallon tank in the attic.

The chronology of other improvements is clearer. In December 1848 the Polks became the first presidential couple to exchange oil lamps and candlelight for gas illumination. At a reception given soon after, the "brilliant jets suddenly vanished," leaving the guests in darkness—except in the Blue Room. There, Sarah Polk said with satisfaction, she had had the foresight to retain the "elegant chandelier," whose "wax candles were shedding their soft radiance." The Fillmores introduced a cookstove in the 1850s, new technology for the cook who had been preparing even the most lavish meals at a big, open fireplace filled with kettles, pots, skillets, hooks, and cranes.

From the start, the big rooms have been hard to heat. In the cold winter of 1800–1801, the chill in the house was caused by a scarcity of logs for the many fireplaces. "Shiver, shiver," Abigail Adams wrote, "surrounded with forests, can you believe that wood is not to be had, because people cannot be found to cut and cart it." "Hell itself couldn't warm that corner," Jackson later complained. A hot-air furnace was installed in the Ground Floor oval room in 1840 to heat the State Floor and Second Floor

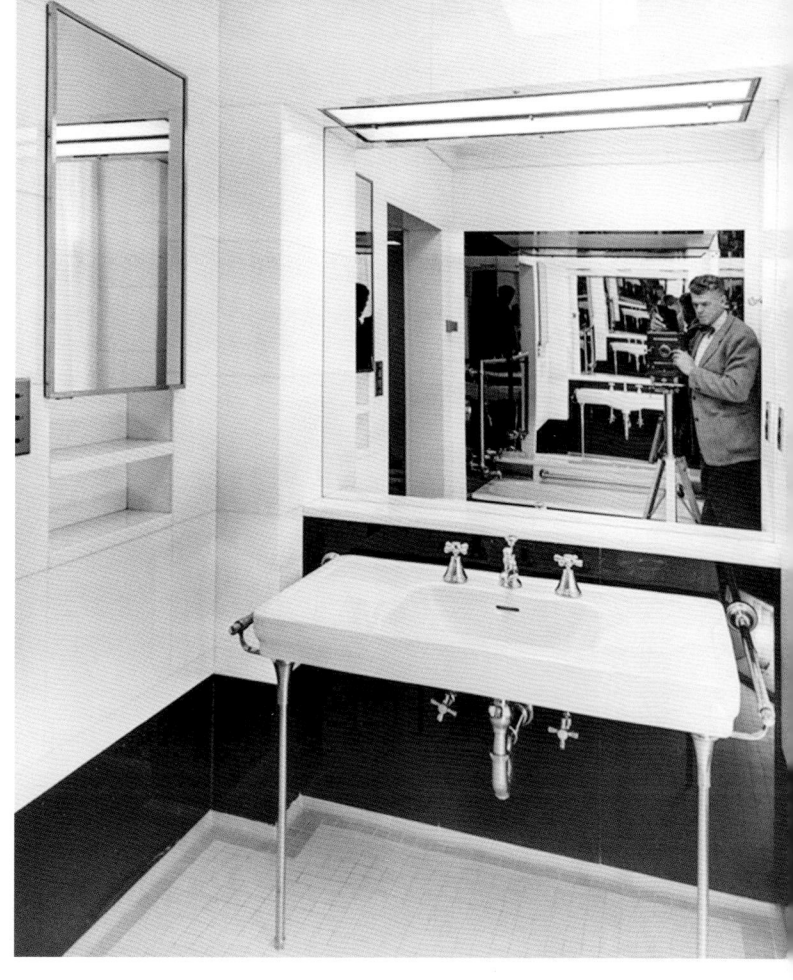

Abbie Rowe, a principal photographer of the Truman renovation, captures his reflection as he documents a newly installed bathroom, 1952. Today the White House has approximately thirty-five bathrooms.

hall. The mansion's first central furnace—a coal-fueled, hot water and forced-air system—was installed in 1853, after Franklin Pierce moved in.

Accustomed to the fine surroundings of his Tennessee plantation, Andrew Jackson immediately sought appropriations from Congress to improve the mansion, which the legislators had allowed to fall into a shabby state during the John Quincy Adams presidency. Throughout Jackson's two terms, a willing Congress provided him with nearly $50,000 to refurbish the house and to build the massive, rectangular North Portico to complement the gracefully curving South Portico added by Monroe. Before the end of Jackson's first year, the great East Room was at last completely and handsomely furnished to permit the ceremonial use for which it was originally planned. The president was particularly interested in having the Monroe chairs made for

226 LIFE IN THE WHITE HOUSE

the room in 1817 repaired and reupholstered, according to one account, so that people would not be kept "standing upon their legs as they do before kings and emperors."

When former Vice President Chester A. Arthur took office after the death of James Garfield in 1881, he began making some of the most drastic changes yet seen in the appearance of the mansion. "I will not live in a house like this," he said after inspecting the accumulation of mixed and battered furniture and ornaments. Nor did he. Arthur sold at public auction thirty barrels of china and twenty-four wagonloads of discards and turned to Louis Comfort Tiffany to lavishly redecorate the mansion, including the famous Tiffany stained-glass screen on the formal State Floor.

President and Mrs. Benjamin Harrison introduced electric lighting but were timid about using it. Ike Hoover, who became chief usher during the Taft presidency, began his forty-two-year White House career in 1891 by setting up the novel system. He wrote later that the Harrisons "were afraid to turn the lights on and off for fear of getting a shock."

Above: President Chester A. Arthur made many changes to the White House decor, including the transformation of the Entrance Hall with the installation of a stained-glass screen created by Louis Comfort Tiffany, c. 1882.

Opposite: As electricity was installed in the White House, some gas fixtures were replaced with electric light bulbs. The Family Dining Room is pictured (above) in 1892 with a new chandelier in place of the gas fixture pictured in 1889 (below).

A HOUSE FOR THE AGES

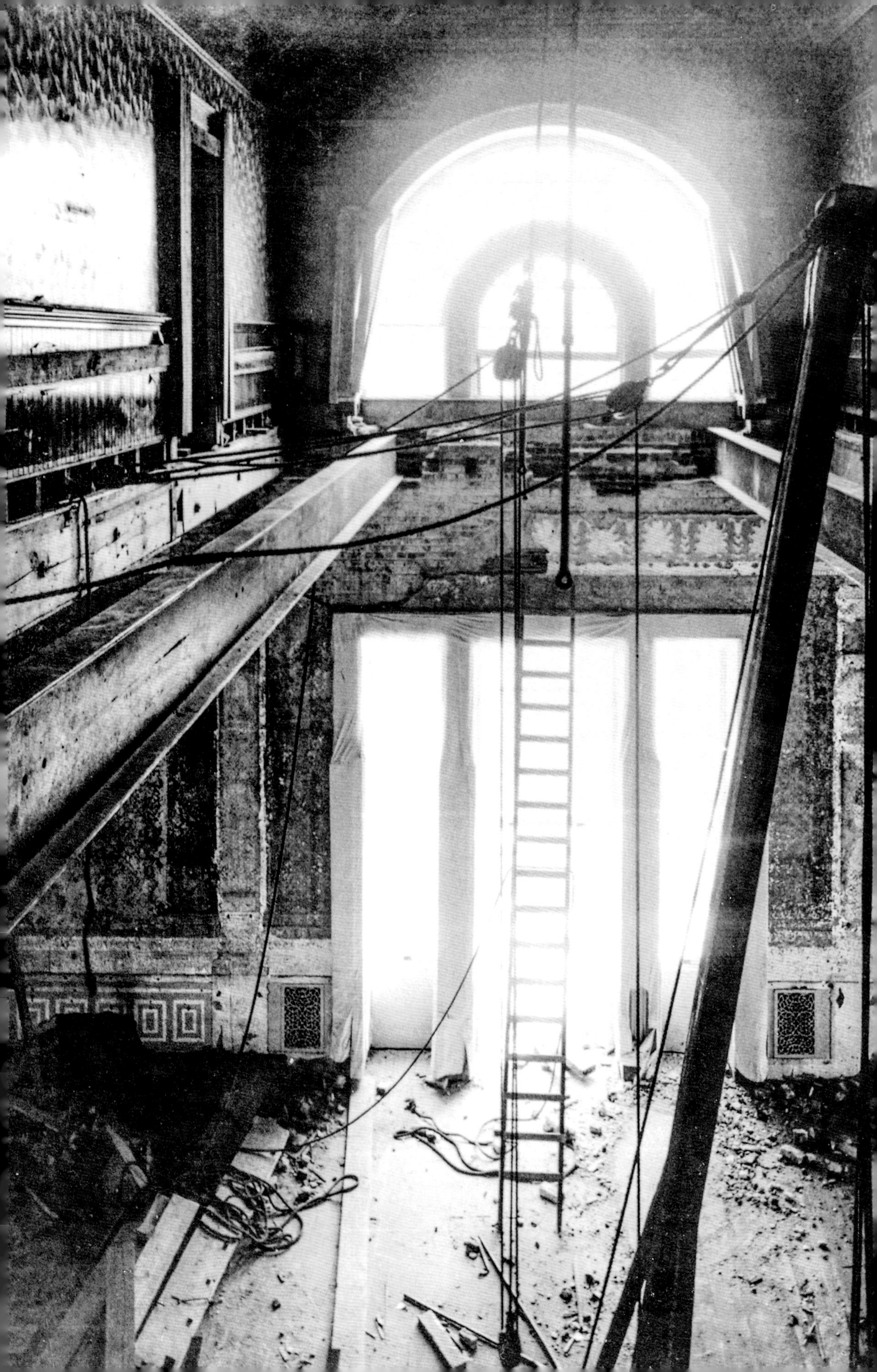

A HOUSE FOR THE AGES
THE ROOSEVELT RENOVATION

When Theodore Roosevelt and his large family moved into the White House in 1901, following the death of William McKinley, the house was still also the office of the president and an ever expanding staff. It was now more crowded than ever. Edith Roosevelt asked the distinguished architect Charles McKim for his advice, and his recommendations for a complete renovation led to major changes in the interior and the functioning of the house. The Roosevelt renovation doubled the space allocated to the Private Quarters by providing a new wing for the president and his staff, and a new area on the east for receiving guests. A rearrangement of the Grand Staircase enlarged the State Dining Room, and new steel beams girded the floors.

Then, in 1927, the Coolidges turned the attic into a full Third Floor, with guest rooms and a "Sky Parlor," a sleeping porch and sunroom.

The renovations made during President Theodore Roosevelt's presidency included the introduction of steel beams to support the floors (opposite) and the addition of the West Wing (below), 1902.

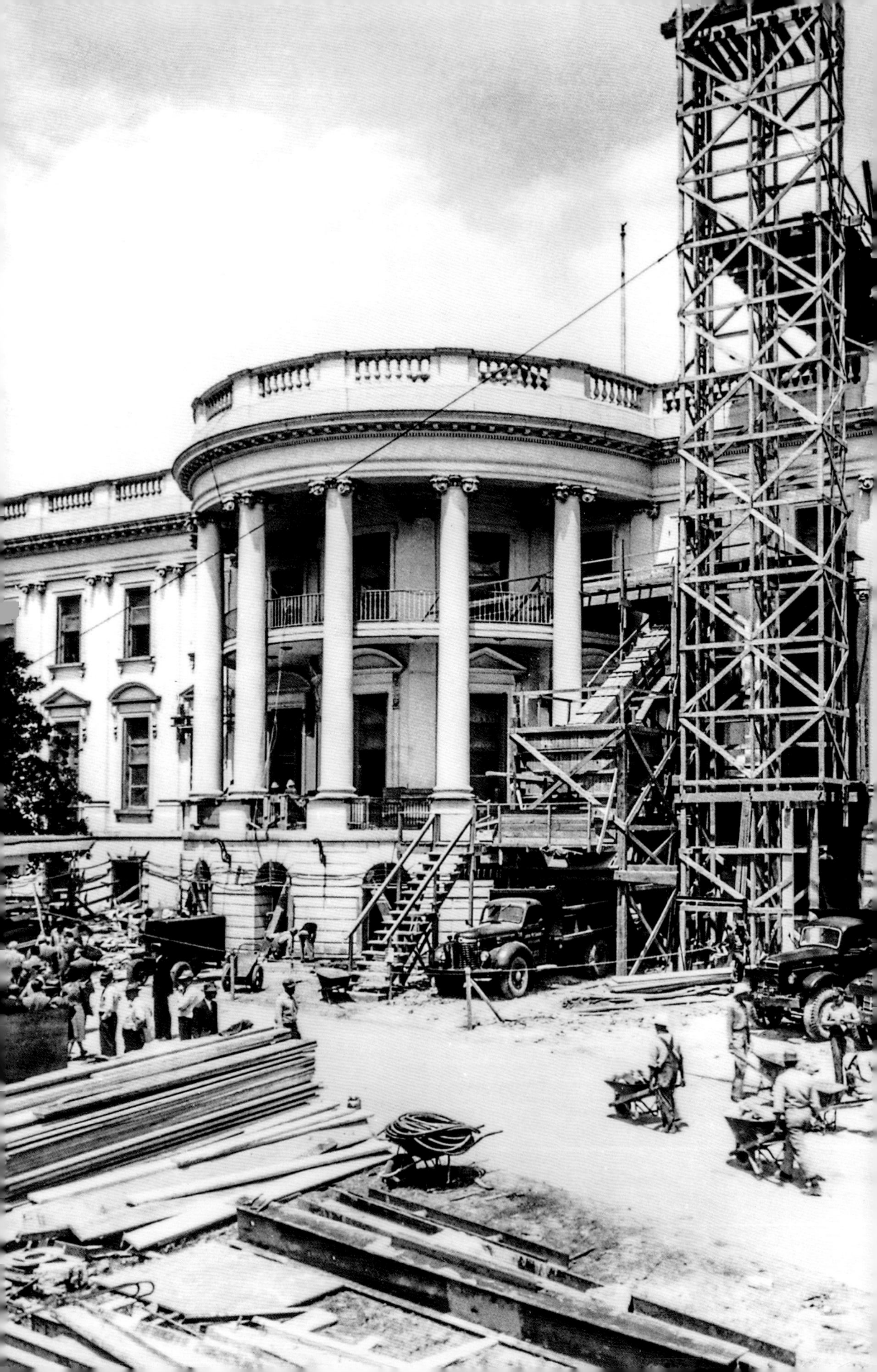

A HOUSE FOR THE AGES
THE TRUMAN RENOVATION

Each renovation and improvement brought in more wires, pipes, and flues, walls, and structural supports. The 1902 renovations had put severe stress on the building's structure, as had the weight of the raised roof that created the Coolidges' Third Floor. The creaking noises that had bred ghost stories for years finally forced an engineering survey in 1948. The report disclosed that the structure "was standing up," as one investigator put it, "purely from habit." The alternatives: renovate it or tear it down.

Backed by public pleas to save the White House in 1948, Congress provided funds to remove the interiors and reinstall them within the original shell. Inside, a skeleton of steel structural beams on a new concrete foundation assured the future of the house. In the end, many architectural modifications were made and little of the nineteenth-century or early twentieth-century interiors remained. Two levels of subbasements and service areas under the North Portico were constructed, and the Grand Staircase was substantially changed again to open into the Entrance Hall. One of the first central air-conditioning systems in the country was installed to provide relief from Washington summers. When the work was completed in 1952, the house at last was "built for ages to come," as Abigail Adams had seen it in 1800. It also was supplied with comforts that would have startled Millard Fillmore, who called it his "temple of inconveniences." The most radical renovation in White House history would provide a home for future presidents and their families.

The South Front during the Truman renovation (opposite), as demolition progresses inside the house, 1950. As the interior is reconstructed in 1952, carpenters lay a new wooden floor in the State Dining Room.

During the twentieth century, the Third Floor sunroom evolved from a screened sleeping porch into a comfortable, sun-filled family retreat now known as the Solarium, with sweeping views of the city across the South Grounds. It was refurnished following the Truman renovation, 1952.

A HOUSE FOR THE AGES
THE SOLARIUM

In the 1920s, the attic where Abraham Lincoln's and Theodore Roosevelt's children played had been transformed into guest rooms and a "Sky Parlor," with a magnificent view to the south. In the Truman renovation, it became a Solarium. Presidents and their families have found this bright room a pleasant spot for informal entertaining, or a place to relax and read, to listen to music, or to watch television. Children and adolescents have turned the room into a busy and happy place. Here was the Kennedy kindergarten; here Luci Johnson, surrounded by furniture she had painted, had her teenage hideaway. And here first family youngsters have exchanged news and confidences with their friends. In recent decades, the Ford, Carter, and Clinton families used the Solarium as a kind of second living room, more casual than the Second Floor sitting halls.

Caroline Kennedy's kindergarten class met in the Solarium (top), 1963. And President Lyndon Johnson's teenage daughters used the Solarium as a private retreat. In 1966, the room—its window decorated by Luci Johnson with a smiley face—was set for a buffet prior to her wedding to Patrick Nugent (above).

A HOUSE FOR THE AGES

233

A HOUSE FOR THE AGES
RENOVATIONS CONTINUE

Of all the additions to the mansion's facilities, one of the most useful was the Second Floor dining room—the President's Dining Room—with its pantry and kitchen. By converting one of the bedroom suites of the Second Floor apartment into a dining room and kitchen, the Kennedys made it possible for the family to enjoy meals with guests in a homelike atmosphere instead of having to use the State Dining Room or the smaller original Family Dining Room on the State Floor. At one of the Nixons' dinner parties in this room, Alice Roosevelt Longworth surprised and amused her hosts and other guests when she suddenly exclaimed, "My goodness . . . this is the room where I had my appendix out." Studying wallpaper in the room that depicted scenes of the American Revolution during a small dinner in May 1981, Great Britain's Prince Charles good-naturedly chided President Ronald Reagan for seating him where he had to look at Lord Cornwallis's surrender at Yorktown.

Stonemasons repair the walls of the South Portico prior to painting in 1997.

Work on the White House is never truly finished. Renovation of the exterior stone walls, begun during the Carter years, was completed in 1996. It included the removal of some forty coats of paint, repair of the stone, and repainting. The Reagan years saw an improved security system and the addition of a special visitors' entrance. Outside this entrance, East Executive Avenue was transformed into a tree-lined pedestrian mall.

In the 1990s, an effort to make the White House more energy efficient included the most extensive overhaul of the mansion's heating, ventilating, and air-conditioning system since the Truman presidency. A new roof was added, too. Hillary Clinton, with the advice of the Committee for the Preservation of the White House, oversaw the refurbishing of several of the formal spaces on the State Floor: the Blue Room, East Room, State Dining Room, Entrance Hall, and Cross Hall. Worn, faded fabrics in the Blue Room were replaced with brilliant sapphire ones, while the walls were repapered in a gold pattern with a blue-and-gold swag border. The East Room, used for press conferences, bill signings, concerts, and receptions, had long been uncarpeted. Three pale green-and-gold woven rugs were installed to soften the appearance of the room and to provide better acoustics for special events. This effort was part of the continuous change that goes on in and around this house.

In 1945, President Truman placed pieces associated with President Lincoln in the room that had served as Lincoln's office and cabinet room, later renamed the Lincoln Bedroom. Among the objects installed by President Truman is the massive carved rosewood bed

New wallpaper is installed in the Blue Room, 1996.

Among the many twenty-first-century refurbishments are the Lincoln Bedroom, a project overseen by First Lady Laura Bush in 2005 (above) and the Bowling Alley, overseen by First Lady Melania Trump in 2018 (opposite top).

President Barack Obama speaks to guests at an East Room ceremony held to unveil the new official portraits of himself and First Lady Michelle Obama, September 7, 2022 (opposite bottom).

purchased by Mary Todd Lincoln for the state guest room, and in which the Lincolns' third son, Willie, died in 1862. Little changed in the sixty years following the Truman renovation, and by 2002, the room showed its wear. Mrs. Bush requested the advice of the Committee for the Preservation of the White House for changes to the Lincoln Bedroom that would reflect the historic record and the styles of the 1860s. Replicas of the Lincoln-era marble mantel, draperies, and a carpet were created, based on historic photographs and sketches drawn by the artist Francis B. Carpenter, who spent hours in the room in Lincoln's time when he was preparing studies for his work *The First Reading of the Emancipation Proclamation Before the Cabinet*.

Throughout the White House, the walls of State Rooms, corridors, and both public and private spaces are hung with portraits of the nation's presidents and first ladies. In recent years the collection has been built with the support of the White House Historical Association, which commissions portraits of each outgoing president and first lady to be given to the permanent collection of the White House. In keeping with tradition, the Association commissioned portraits of Barack and Michelle Obama. The two portraits were unveiled during an East Room ceremony in 2022.

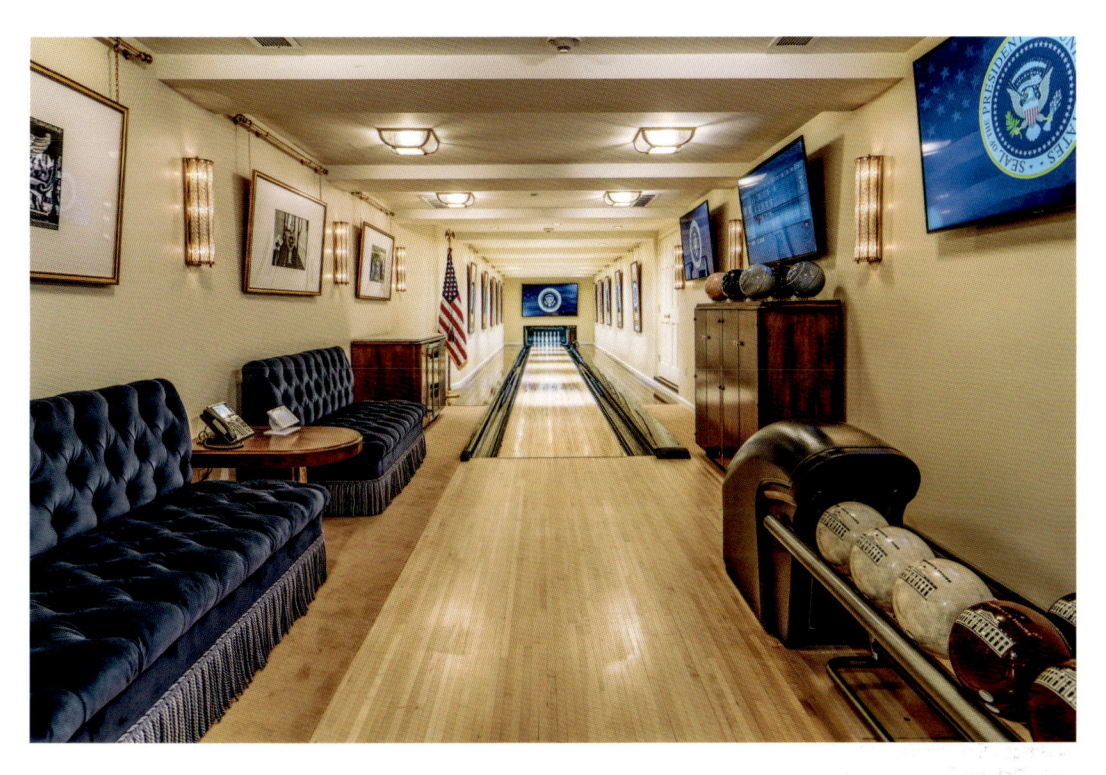

A HOUSE FOR THE AGES

A HOUSE FOR THE AGES
TOURS AND TALES

Whatever fate befalls the president, the presidency never dies. Perhaps that is why Americans never tire of stories about those who have held this office and the historic building in which they work and live with their families.

Visitors to the White House are always curious about the life-size Gilbert Stuart portrait of George Washington that dominates the East Room. It is the only object that has remained in the White House since before the British torched the building in 1814. That afternoon, as British troops approached Washington, Dolley Madison saved the portrait before she fled. James Madison had already left the city, to join the defending forces in Maryland. Mrs. Madison, in a letter to her sister, explained how she saved the painting. "Our kind friend, Mr. Carroll, has come to hasten my departure," she wrote, "and is in a very bad humor with me, because I insist on waiting until the large picture of Gen. Washington is secured, and it requires to be unscrewed from the wall. This process was found too tedious. . . . I have ordered the frame to be broken and the canvas taken out; it is done."

Mamie Eisenhower led one of the most unusual tours in 1959. Her guests were all children or descendants of former presidents, beginning with John Adams. Eight were sons and daughters of chief executives from Grover Cleveland to Dwight D. Eisenhower. History traveled with the party as past residents of the house moved upstairs and down, swapping anecdotes about how it was when they knew "life with father" here.

Alice Roosevelt Longworth, daughter of Theodore Roosevelt, recalled the three circular Victorian ottomans, crowned by potted palms, that once stood in the East Room. "The tops in the center came off," she said, "and my brothers and sister would hide there." Helen Taft Manning, daughter of William Howard Taft, remembered that her mother found the huge Lincoln Bed too depressing a symbol for sleep; she relegated it to the attic.

Gilbert Stuart's portrait of President George Washington is placed in a new frame in the East Room, 2004. It is the only object that has been in the White House Collection since before the fire of 1814.

LIFE IN THE WHITE HOUSE

Eleanor Wilson McAdoo, daughter of Woodrow Wilson, wanted to quash the myth that pictured her father as "an intellectual snob" and "a grim old Presbyterian." In fact, she said, he was "our most amusing and gay companion."

All of the homecomers but one received a surprise when the group made its way down the Center Hall to the Monroe Room that contained copies of President James Monroe's furniture, including a replica of the desk on which he signed his famous Monroe Doctrine. Pausing before this desk, Laurence Gouverneur Hoes, Monroe's great-great-grandson, pressed a panel that opened to reveal a secret compartment even Mrs. Eisenhower had not known about. Such a compartment, it turned out, had been discovered in the original desk in 1906, and young Hoes had been indirectly responsible for the find. As a small boy, he had somehow damaged this treasured family possession, and its repair had disclosed the hidden space. In it lay priceless letters written by Thomas Jefferson, James Madison, John Marshall, and the Marquis de Lafayette.

First Lady Mamie Eisenhower poses with her guests on a tour of the White House, 1959. Pictured are, from left: Alice Roosevelt Longworth, daughter of Theodore Roosevelt; Helen Taft Manning, daughter of William Howard Taft; John Eisenhower, son of Dwight Eisenhower; Marion Cleveland Amen, daughter of Grover Cleveland; John Coolidge, son of Calvin Coolidge; First Lady Mamie Eisenhower; James Roosevelt, son of Franklin Roosevelt; Eleanor Wilson McAdoo, daughter of Woodrow Wilson; and Richard Cleveland, son of Grover Cleveland.

A HOUSE FOR THE AGES

A HOUSE FOR THE AGES
TELEVISED TOURS

Millions turned on their television sets to follow the White House tours conducted by President Truman after the building's renovation in 1952, by Jacqueline Kennedy when she discussed her vision for a historical restoration and highlighted antiques and artwork acquired through her project in 1962, and by Tricia Nixon when she took television viewers on the first public showing of rooms in the family Private Quarters. Included were glimpses of the family dining and sitting rooms, her mother's sitting room, in which she read and answered her mail, and the piano her father liked to play. She also described an incident in which Nixon built the flames so high in the fireplace of his private study adjoining the Lincoln Bedroom that an alarm sent White House firefighters rushing to the scene. There they found him placidly writing a speech before the open fire, which, Tricia explained, was one of his great pleasures.

In September 1989, George H. W. and Barbara Bush gave television viewers another personal tour of their Private Quarters. Then, in 1995, the Clintons treated millions of viewers with a look at the freshly refurbished Blue Room and East Room. After the President's House was closed to tours following the tragic events of September 11, 2001, Laura Bush led a special television program of the White House Christmas decorations and did so each year thereafter.

President Truman (below) makes a point to Walter Cronkite, CBS commentator, during the the first televised tour of the White House, 1952. First Lady Jacqueline Kennedy checks a table set in the State Dining Room in preparation for her televised tour, which was aired by CBS in 1962 (opposite top). Tricia Nixon is interviewed by Mike Wallace and Harry Reasoner on the Truman Balcony (opposite bottom left) during a televised tour of the Private Quarters, 1970. And First Lady Laura Bush presents the 2007 White House Christmas decorations (opposite bottom right).

A HOUSE FOR THE AGES

241

In 2015, the White House lifted a forty-year ban on photography during public tours (above). Continuing a tradition begun during the Nixon presidency, the public is often welcomed to enjoy tours of the White House gardens in the spring and the fall. During the 2014 spring Garden Tour (opposite) visitors enjoy a view of the Rose Garden.

LIFE IN THE WHITE HOUSE

A HOUSE FOR THE AGES
THE PUBLIC TOURS TODAY

First ladies have long wanted White House visitors to feel welcome and regularly open the doors to the house to tourists. It was First Lady Jacqueline Kennedy who recognized the need for a guidebook to inform visitors about the history of the house and its collection. Under her direction, the White House Historical Association released *The White House: An Historic Guide* in 1962. Now in its twenty-sixth edition, the Historic Guide continues to enrich in-person tours with room-by-room illustrated accounts of the public spaces and Private Quarters.

Recognizing the public's enthusiasm for documenting their White House experiences, First Lady Michelle Obama lifted the ban on photography during tours in 2015. Most recently First Lady Jill Biden worked with the White House Historical Association to develop a free visitors' brochure with floor plans and interesting facts. The White House gardens and South Lawn are also open to the public one weekend each spring and fall, on a first-come, first-served basis.

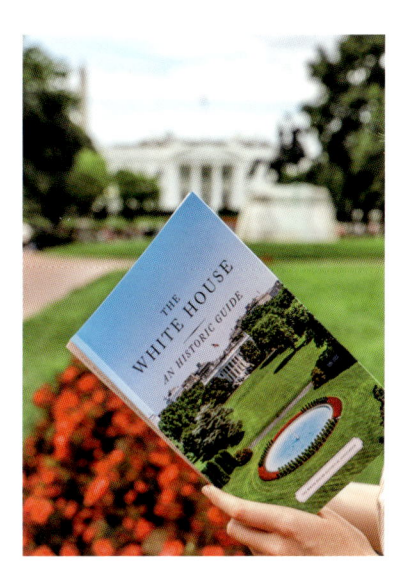

First published in 1962 at the request of First Lady Jacqueline Kennedy, who had felt a need for such a book since her childhood, *The White House: An Historic Guide* has been a resource for visitors for more than sixty years.

LIFE IN THE WHITE HOUSE

CONCLUSION
THE BEST OF BLESSINGS ON THIS HOUSE

Portraits of those whose lives are forever interwoven with memories of the White House hang throughout the State Rooms. Their attire, from knee breeches to modern dress, recalls the many eras the house has known, as presidents moved to shape and be shaped by events, and to leave on the American character the imprint of their philosophy and words. Thomas Jefferson wrote, "Our liberty can never be safe but in the hands of the people themselves." Abraham Lincoln said, "With malice toward none" and showed compassion that might have helped heal the wounds after the fratricidal war, had he survived. "Speak softly and carry a big stick" was a favorite motto of Theodore Roosevelt, who launched the building of the Panama Canal, won a formidable reputation for "trust-busting," and sent sixteen battleships of the United States Navy on parade around the world. A long list of memorable phrases emerged during the White House years of Franklin D. Roosevelt, the only president elected to four terms. Best remembered, perhaps, are, "The only thing we have to fear is fear itself," "New Deal," and "The Four Freedoms."

In reflecting on his years in the presidency, Harry S. Truman spoke to the American people in his farewell address in 1953. "So, as I empty the drawers of this desk, and as Mrs. Truman and I leave the White House, we have no regret. We feel we have done our best in the public service. I hope and believe we have contributed

President Barack Obama returns home to the White House through the South Portico, 2012.

to the welfare of this Nation and to the peace of the world." John F. Kennedy eloquently expressed the symbolic meaning of the White House in American history. "I consider history—our history—to be a source of strength to us here in the White House and to all the American people. Anything which dramatizes the great story of the United States—as I think the White House does—is worthy of the closest attention and respect by Americans who live here and who visit here and who are part of our citizenry."

Whether they come for social occasions, work, or sightseeing, visitors find inscribed on the mantel of the State Dining Room a benediction and an expression of hope from the earliest days of the republic. The words were taken from a letter written by President John Adams in 1800, on his second night in the new mansion. Franklin Roosevelt had them cut into the mantel.

I Pray Heaven *To Bestow*
THE BEST OF BLESSINGS ON
This House
And All that shall hereafter Inhabit *it.*
May none but Honest *and* Wise Men *ever rule*
under This Roof.

> I Pray Heaven To Bestow
> THE BEST OF BLESSINGS ON
> This House
> And All that shall hereafter Inhabit it
> May none but Honest and Wise Men ever rule
> under This Roof.
>
> From a Letter of JOHN ADAMS
>
> November MDCCC

CONCLUSION

ILLUSTRATION CREDITS

All images are held or copyrighted as listed below:

Illustration credits key:

AP	Associated Press
Bush Library	George H. W. Bush Presidential Library and Museum
Carter Library	Jimmy Carter Presidential Library and Museum
Eisenhower Library	Dwight D. Eisenhower Presidential Library, Museum, & Boyhood Home
FDR Library	Franklin D. Roosevelt Presidential Library and Museum
Ford Library	Gerald R. Ford Presidential Library and Museum
George W. Bush Library	George W. Bush Presidential Library and Museum
LBJ Library	Lyndon B. Johnson Presidential Library
LOC	Library of Congress
NARA	National Archives and Records Administration
Reagan Library	Ronald Reagan Presidential Library and Museum
Truman Library	Harry S. Truman Presidential Library and Museum
WH	Official White House Photo
WH Collection	White House Collection
WHHA	White House Historical Association

ii	Erin Scott, WH
v	Bruce M. White for WHHA
vi	Cameron Smith, WH
viii	WH Collection
x	Getty Images
xi	WHHA
xii	Hannah Foslien, WH
2	Adam Schultz, WH
3	Courtesy of Blair House, The President's Guest House, U.S. Department of State
4	WHHA, WH Collection
5	WHHA
6	© Ross Rossin, *A Meeting in Time II*, 2019, oil, 157.5" x 288.75" Collection of Brenda Patterson
7	© Ross Rossin, *A Meeting in Time I*, 2004, oil, 153.25" x 244.5" Collection of Brenda Patterson
8	Top: Rutherford B. Hayes Presidential Center Bottom: Truman Library
9	Top: Gerald Ford Foundation Bottom: Reagan Library
11	LOC
12	WHHA
13	LOC
14	Top: North Wind Picture Archives / Alamy Stock Photo Bottom: Carter Library
15	Pete Souza, WH
16	Top left and top right: LOC Bottom: Smithsonian Institution
17	Top: Wikiwand Bottom: Eisenhower Library
18	LOC
19	Top: Bettmann / Getty Images Bottom: Adam Schultz, WH
20	Bettmann Archive / Getty Images
21	Top: AP Photo / WOA Bottom: George W. Bush Library
22	Harvard College Library
23	Top left: Getty Images / Cynthia Johnson; Top right: Mark Wilson / Getty Images; Bottom right: Samantha Appleton, WH; Bottom left: Erin Scott, WH
24	LOC
25	Reuters / Jonathan Ernst
26	Top: LOC; Bottom: Alpha Stock / Alamy Stock Photo
27	Top: Shealah Craighead, WH Bottom: Adam Schultz, WH
28	Oliver Contreras, WH
30	Top: FDR Library Bottom: Pete Souza, WH
31	Top: Tia Dufour, WH Bottom: Erin Scott, WH
33	Fotosearch / Stringer / Getty Images
34	Photo by ©Corbis / Corbis via Getty Images
35	Reagan Library
36	Erin Scott, WH
37	Reagan Library
38	*Perley's Reminiscences*
39	WHHA
40	Top: Shutterstock; Bottom: LOC
41	WHHA
42	WHHA
43	WHHA, WH Collection
44	Genealogy Bank
45	Smithsonian American Art Museum
46	*Perley's Reminiscences*
47	WHHA, WH Collection
48	WHHA, WH Collection
49	George Eastman House
51	LOC
52–53	WH Collection
55	WHHA, WH Collection
56	WHHA, WH Collection
57	WHHA, WH Collection
58	New York Historical Society
59	LOC
60	NARA
61	LOC
62	LOC
63	Top: FDR Library Bottom: Wide World
64	Truman Library
65	WHHA
66	JFK Library
67	Top: Bettmann / Corbis Images Bottom: Ford Library
68	WHHA
69	WHHA
70	Top: Reagan Library Bottom: Bush Library
71	Clinton Library
72	Adam Schultz, WH
73	Adam Schultz, WH
74	LBJ Library
75	Top: Courtesy Betty C. Monkman Bottom: Ford Library
76	Top: Carter Library Bottom: Reagan Library
77	Top left: Luke Frazza / AFP via Getty Images; Top right: Clinton Library; Bottom left: Luke Frazza / AFP via Getty Images; Bottom right: AP Photo / Charles Dharapak
78	AP Photo / Andrew Harnik
79	Top: AP Photo / Susan Walsh Bottom: AP Photo / Patrick Semansky
80	Zuma Press, Inc. / Alamy Stock Photo
81	Top: Manny Ceneta / Getty Images; Bottom: Abaca Press / Alamy Stock Photo
82–83	Sipa USA / Alamy Stock Photo
84	Cameron Smith, WH
85	Carlos Fyfe, WH
86	Top: Adam Schultz, WH Bottom: Saul Loeb / AFP via Getty Images
87	Kent Nishimura / *Los Angeles Times* via Getty Images
88	Stefani Reynolds / AFP via Getty Images
89	Top and bottom: AP Photo / Jacquelyn Martin
90	JFK Library
91	Clinton Library
92	Nixon Presidential Materials
93	Kennedy Library
94	Top: George W. Bush Library Bottom: WH
95	Demetrius Freeman / *Washington Post* via Getty Images
96	WHHA, WH Collection
97	Erin Scott, WH
98	LOC
99	FDR library
100	LBJ Library
101	Nixon Presidential Materials
102	Top: Ford Library Bottom: Carter Library
103	Top: Reagan Library Bottom: Clinton Library
104	AP Photo / Pablo Martinez Monsivais

Page	Credit
105	WH
106	Cameron Smith, WH
107	AP Photo / Carolyn Kaster
108	*Harper's Bazaar*
109	LOC
111	NARA
112	LOC
113	LOC
114	WHHA
115	LOC
116	Photo by Arthur Hewitt / Archive Photos / Getty Images
117	Top left: Getty Images; Top right: LOC; Bottom right: Photo by Heritage Art / Heritage Images via Getty Images; Bottom left: Photo by Library of Congress / Corbis / VCG via Getty Images
118	LOC
119	Top and bottom: LOC
120	WHHA
121	NARA
123	Eisenhower Library
124	Corbis Images
125	Left: Nixon Presidential Materials Right: Carter Library
126	Daniel Acker / Bloomberg via Getty Images
127	AP Photo / Susan Walsh
128	Left: LOC; Right: LBJ Library Bottom: Smith Collection / Gado / Getty
129	Top: Bruce M. White for WHHA; Bottom left: Erin Scott / The White House via AP; Bottom right: Adam Schultz, WH
130	Courtesy Mary Fairfax Kirk Pickle
131	Massachusetts Historical Society
132	WHHA, WH Collection
133	LOC
134	WHHA
135	LOC
136	LOC
137	LOC
138	WHHA
139	Top: NARA Bottom: Adam Schultz, WH
141	Kiplinger Washington Collection
142	*Harper's Weekly*
144	Rutherford B. Hayes Presidential Center
145	Kiplinger Washington Collection
146	Top: LOC; Bottom: Ralph E. Becker Collection of Political Americana, Smithsonian Institution
147	LOC
148	NARA
148–49	Bettmann / Corbis Images
150–51	Bettmann / Corbis Images
151	Corbis Images
152	U.S. Secret Service Archives
153	Photo by Saul Loeb / AFP via Getty Images
154	Top: © Corbis / Corbis via Getty Images; Bottom: LOC
155	Bettmann / Getty Images
156	Top: AP Photo; Bottom: LBJ Library
157	Top: WHHA; Bottom: Photo by Saul Loeb / AFP via Getty Images
158	Theodore Roosevelt Collection, Houghton Library, Harvard University
159	NARA
160	LOC
161	Culver Service Photograph
162	NARA
163	Photo by Ron Sachs / Consolidated News Pictures / Getty Images
164	Eisenhower Library
165	LBJ Library
166	Carter Library
167	Reagan Library
168	Bush Library
169	Bruce M. White for WHHA
170	WHHA
171	WHHA
172	Mrs. John M. Scott, Jr.
173	Huntington Library
174	WHHA, WH Collection
175	Historical Society of Washington, D.C.
176	Truman Library
177	Bruce M. White for WHHA, Oak Spring Garden Library Collection
178	Top: Bruce M. White for WHHA Bottom: Keegan Barber, WH
179	Top: Martin Radigan for WHHA Bottom: Adam Schultz, WH
180	Bettmann / Corbis / Getty Images
181	AP Photo / Charles Tasnadi
182	LOC
183	Rutherford B. Hayes Presidential Center
184	Top: Courtesy of Lauren Bush Lauren Bottom: Bruce M. White for WHHA
185	Bruce M. White for WHHA
186	Zuma Press, Inc. / Alamy Stock Photo
187	Top: JFK Library; Bottom left: Carter Library; Bottom right: AP Photo / Alex Brandon
188	AP Photo / Doug Mills
189	Adam Schultz, WH
190	Bruce M. White for WHHA
191	Chuck Kennedy, WH
192	LBJ Library
193	Top: WHHA Bottom: Adam Schultz, WH
194	AP Photo / Charles Dharapak
195	LOC
196	Photo by LOC / Corbis / VCG via Getty Images
197	WHHA
198	Top: Photo by Pix / Michael Ochs Archives / Getty Images Bottom: Cameron Smith, WH
199	Top: Photo by Alex Wong / Getty Images; Bottom: Cameron Smith, WH
200	Wally McNamee / Corbis Images
201	AP Images / Charles Dharapak
202	Universal History Archive / Universal Images Group via Getty Images
203	Top: Cameron Smith, WH Bottom left: WHHA Bottom right: Hannah Foslien, WH
204	Top: Harper & Row Bottom: Bush Library
205	AP Photo / Wilfredo Lee
206	Top: WHHA; Bottom: George Tames / *New York Times* / Redux
207	Top: Image courtesy of Kannalikham Designs, all rights reserved; Bottom: Bruce M. White, 2021. Architecture by Steven W. Spandle and interior design by Kannalikham Designs. Image courtesy of Kannalikham Designs, all rights reserved.
208	WHHA, WH Collection
209	Jack E. Boucher, Historic American Buildings Survey, LOC
210	Getty Images
211	WH Collection
212	Courtesy of the Sylvia Jennings Alexander Estate
213	Abraham Lincoln Presidential Library and Museum
214	Top: WHH, WH Collection Bottom: Rutherford B. Hayes Presidential Center
215	LOC
216	WH Collection
217	Tina Hager, NARA
218	Collection of Gary Walters
219	Top: Kennedy Library Bottom: AP Photo / Carolyn Kaster
220	Bruce M. White for WHHA
221	Top: WH Collection; Bottom: WH
222	Edward Clark
223	Top: Bush Library; Bottom: WHHA
224	NARA
225	Truman Library
226	Top and bottom: LOC
227	LOC
228	Sagamore Hill National Historic Site
229	Sagamore Hill National Historic Site
230	Truman Library
231	Truman Library
232	WHHA
233	Top: Kennedy Library; Bottom: LOC, *Look* Magazine Photograph Collection
234	WHHA
235	WHHA
236	Bruce M. White for WHHA
237	Top: Bruce M. White for WHHA; Bottom: Tom Williams / CQ-Roll Call, Inc. via Getty Images
238	WHHA
239	Photo by PhotoQuest / Getty Image
240	Bettmann / Contributor
241	Top: AP Images; Bottom left: Nixon Presidential Materials; Bottom right: UPI Photo / Kevin Dietsch
242	Doug Mills / *New York Times* / Redux
243	Top: Garrett Goltermann for WHHA Bottom: AP Photo / Manuel Balce Ceneta
244–45	Pete Souza, WH
246–47	Bruce M. White for WHHA
Cover	Front: Tasos Katopodis / Getty Images Back: See credits for pages 221 (bottom), 188, 75 (bottom), 86 (bottom), 85, 138, 36, 203 (top), and viii.

ILLUSTRATION CREDITS

INDEX

Page numbers in bold indicate illustrations.

A

Adams, Abigail
 criticism of, 99
 grandchildren, 109
 hospitality, 38, 91
 making the White House a home, 161
 musical entertainment, 91
 President's Park, 172
 staff, 213, 224
 on White House conditions, 161, 220, 225, 231
Adams, Abigail S. (granddaughter), **131**
Adams, John
 on accountability to Americans, 1
 Clinton's commemoration ceremony for, 71
 descendants touring White House, 238
 grandchildren, 109
 hospitality, 38, **39**, 91
 making the White House a home, 161
 musical entertainment, 91
 office seekers and, 12
 on presidential duties, 10
 President's Park, 172
 protocol for foreign diplomats, 44
 staff, 213, 224
 White House blessing, 246, **246–47**
Adams, John (grandson), 130, **131**
Adams, John Quincy
 commemorative trees, 192
 enslaved workers, 213
 hospitality, 44–45
 presidential duties, 10
 President's Park, 173, **173**, 175
 road to the White House, 45
 as Secretary of State, 24
 silhouette, **131**
 son's wedding, 130
 White House conditions, 226
 on White House years as miserable, 32
Adams, Louisa Catherine, 44–45, **45**, 91, **131**, 175
Adams, Mary Catherine Hellen, 130, **131**
Adams, Mary Louisa, **131**
Adams, Susanna, 109
Afghanistan, war in, 34–35
Aikman, Lonnelle, 1
Air Force One, **23**
Aldrin, Edwin "Buzz," 26
Alexis, Grand Duke (Russia), 54–55
Algonquin (Roosevelts' pony), 115
Alpheus, Walter, **154**
Amen, Marion Cleveland, **239**
American Red Cross Comfort Kit program, 105
Americans with Disabilities Act (1990), 197
Anderson, Marian, 92
Apollo 11, 26
Arafat, Yasser, **198**
Armstrong, Neil, 26
Army and Navy Reception (1888), **57**
Arthur, Alan, 144
Arthur, Chester A., 55, 91, 144, 227, **227**
Arthur, Ellen, 144
Arthur, Nellie, 144
Asian American, Native Hawaiian, and Pacific Islander Heritage Month, **179**
Atwood, Harry Nelson, 196, **196**

B

Baryshnikov, Mikhail, 95
Batiste, Jon, **86**, 95
"Be Best" initiative, 104, **105**
Begin, Menachem, **200**, 201
Beirut, Marine barracks bombed, 34
Bell, Alexander Graham, 19, 144
Bell, Joshua, 95
Bell H-13J (helicopter), 17
Benham, Edith, 60
Berlin Wall, fall of, 34
Bernhard, Prince (Netherlands), 64
Berryman, Clifford, cartoon by, **162**
Beyoncé, 95
Bicentennial celebrations (1976), 69, 177
Biden, Ashley, 127
Biden, Beau (grandson), **127**
Biden, Beau (son), 127
Biden, Hunter, 127
Biden, Jill
 "Cancer Moonshot," 106
 charitable works and issues, 104, 106, **106**, 107
 commemorative trees, **193**
 Diwali reception, **36**
 Easter Egg Roll, **127**, 202
 family life, 127, **127**
 granddaughter's wedding, 139, **139**
 holiday traditions, 78, **79**, **81**
 hospitality, 73
 Jacqueline Kennedy Garden events, 181
 musical entertainment, 95
 South Lawn events, **199**
 State Dinners, **86**, **87**, 88, 95
 State Visits, **84**
 teaching career, 106
 visitors' brochure, 243
Biden, Joe
 boarding *Marine One*, **23**
 with cabinet, **25**
 commemorative trees, **193**
 Diwali reception, **36**
 Easter Egg Roll, 202
 family life, **97**, 127, 127
 foreign policy challenges, 35
 granddaughter's wedding, 139, **139**
 greeting tourists, **157**
 hospitality, **72**, 73, **73**
 Jacqueline Kennedy Garden events, 181
 Kitchen Garden, 191
 Medal of Honor presentation, 73, **73**
 musical entertainment, 95
 in Oval Office, **2**, **19**, **27**
 pets, 129
 press conferences, **28**, **31**
 Rose Garden events, 177, **179**
 South Lawn events, 197, **199**
 State Dinners, ii, **86**, **87**, **88**, 95
 State Visits, **84**
 Thanksgiving Turkey Pardon, **157**, 188, **189**
 as vice president, 106
Biden, Naomi, 127, 139, **139**
Biden, Neilia, 127
Black Watch, 197, **197**
Blair House, 64, **64**
Blake, Eubie, **68**
Bliss, Betty, 50
Blue Room
 chandelier, 225
 Christmas trees, 74, 75, 76, **76**, **78**
 Clinton refurbishing, 235, **235**
 Eisenhower, Mary Jean, christening of, 122
 as Elliptical Saloon, **41**
 Hayes hospitality, **56**
 as Oval Room, **39**, 130
 staff, **218–19**
 Truman reception, 64
 Tyler hospitality, 48–49
 weddings, 130, 133
Blue Room Balcony, **84**
Booth, John Wilkes, 143
Bowling Alley, 205, **237**
Boxer, Nicole, 139
Boy Scouts of America, 73
Brown, Mr. (V. M. Molotov), 62
Brumby, Grace, 92
Buchanan, James, 10, **49**, 50, **51**, 53, 182
Building the First White House (Wyeth), **4**
Bush, Barbara (First Lady), 71, **77**, 101, 126, 168, **168**, 192
Bush, Barbara (granddaughter), 126–27
Bush, Charles Walker, **168**
Bush, George H. W.
 commemorative trees, 192
 family, 126, **184**
 foreign policy challenges, 34
 hospitality, **70**, 71
 making the White House a home, 168
 recreation, **204**, 205
 Rose Garden events, 177
 Second Floor private office, 169
 South Lawn events, 197
 staff farewell, **223**
 State Dinners, **70**
 two-hundredth anniversary of the White House, 71, **71**
Bush, George W.
 boarding *Marine One*, **23**
 daughters, 126–27
 foreign and domestic policy challenges, 34
 holiday traditions, **81**
 hospitality, 73
 in Oval Office, **21**
 Rose Garden events, 177
 Second Floor private office, 169
 September 11 terrorist attacks, **21**, 34, 197, **199**
 South Lawn events, 197, **199**, 205
Bush, Jenna, 126–27
Bush, Laura
 charitable works and issues, 104
 china, 85
 daughters, 126–27
 holiday traditions, 76, **77**, 80, **81**, **241**
 hospitality, 73
 making the White House a home, 168
 North Lawn events, **201**
 White House refurbishing, 236, **236**
Bush, Lauren, **184**
Butt, Archie, 58

C

Cabinet Room, **8**
Camilla, Duchess of Cornwall, **94**
Camp David, 17
"Cancer Moonshot," 106, **106**
Carpenter, Francis Bicknell, 96, 236

Carpentry Shop, 80
Carroll, Mr., 238
Carter, Amy, 76, **125**, 125–26, 167, 186, **187**
Carter, Chip, 126
Carter, Jack, 126
Carter, Jeff, 126
Carter, Jimmy
 commemorative trees, 192
 computers, **14**, 15
 Egypt-Israel Peace Treaty, 169, **200**, 201
 family life, **125**, 125–26, **166**, 186, **187**
 foreign and domestic policy challenges, 34
 holiday traditions, 76
 hospitality, **68**, 69, **69**
 making the White House a home, 167
 musical entertainment, **68**, 92, 95
 North Lawn events, 201
 recreation, 205
 Solarium, 233
 State Arrival Ceremony, 84
 two-hundredth anniversary of the White House, 71, **71**
 White House improvements, 235
Carter, Rosalynn
 charitable works and issues, 101, **102**
 children, **125**, 125–26
 clothes and style, 99
 holiday traditions, 76
 hospitality, **68**, 69, **69**
 making the White House a home, 167
 musical entertainment, **68**, 92, 95
 North Lawn events, 201
 Solarium, 233
 two-hundredth anniversary of the White House, 71, **71**
Casals, Pablo, 91, **93**
Charles, Prince of Wales, **94**, 221, 234
Charlotte, Grand Duchess (Luxembourg), 66
Children's Garden, 184, **184**, 185
china, 57, 85
China Room, 164
Christmas. *See* holiday traditions
Churchill, Winston, 62, **63**
Cincinnati Reds, 177
Civil War, 6, 10–11, **52–53**, 53
Cleveland, Esther, 114, **114**
Cleveland, Frances Folsom
 family life, **109**, **114**, 114–15, 125
 greenhouses, 182
 hospitality, 57, **57**
 making the White House a home, **161**
 rumors about, 158
 wedding, 133, **133**
Cleveland, Grover
 children, **114**, 114–15, 238, **239**
 communications, **14**, 15
 hospitality, 57, **57**
 office seekers and, **13**
 rumors about, 158
 wedding, 133, **133**

Cleveland, Marion, **108**, 114
Cleveland, Richard, **239**
Cleveland, Ruth, **114**, 114–15
Clinton, Bill
 china, 85
 commemorative trees, 192
 daughter, 126, 186
 foreign policy challenges, 34
 holiday traditions, 77, **188**
 hospitality, 71, **71**
 Israeli-Palestinian treaty, **198**
 jogging track, 205, **205**
 making the White House a home, 168
 moving day (1993), **163**
 music, 91
 pets, **128**
 Rose Garden events, 177
 Second Floor private office, 169
 Solarium, 233
 South Lawn events, 197, **198**
 staff farewell, **223**
 treaty-signings, 169
 two-hundredth anniversary of the White House, 71, **71**, 85
 website, 20
Clinton, Chelsea, 77, 126, 186
Clinton, Hillary Rodham
 brother's wedding, 139
 charitable works and issues, 101, **103**, 104
 china, 85
 commemorative trees, 192
 daughter, 126
 floral preferences, 169
 holiday traditions, 77
 hospitality, 71, **71**
 Jacqueline Kennedy Garden events, 181, **181**
 making the White House a home, 168
 moving day (1993), **163**
 political offices held by, 104
 Solarium, 233
 two hundredth anniversary of the White House, 71, **71**, 85
 White House improvements, 235, **235**
A Colored Man's Reminiscences of James Madison (Jennings), 212, 213
Comerford, Cristeta, 88, **89**, 220, **221**
Commander (Bidens' dog), **2**, **129**
Commanders in Chief (Rossin), **6**, 7
Committee for a More Beautiful Capital, **100**
Committee for the Preservation of the White House, 168, 235, 236
Congressional Picnic, **153**, 197
Connick, Harry, Jr., **94**
Conservatory, 182, **182**, **183**
Constitution Avenue, 171
Coolidge, Calvin
 after-dinner porch-sitting, 97
 character traits, 61
 children, 118, **119**, 146, **239**
 hospitality, 40, **40**, 61, **61**
 Oval Office, in, **26**
 radio addresses, 20
 road to the White House, 7
 Solarium, 167

Third Floor renovations, 229
 on White House staff, 209
Coolidge, Calvin, Jr., 118, **119**, 146
Coolidge, Grace, 61, **61**, 100, **119**, **128**, **154**, 160, 229
Coolidge, John, 118, **119**, 153, **239**
COVID-19 pandemic, **31**, 35, 78, 202
Cox, Edward Finch, 139, **139**
Cox, Tricia. *See* Nixon, Tricia
Cronkite, Walter, **240**
Cross Hall, 235
Crow Tribe, **60**
Cuba, U.S. naval blockade of, 21, 33
Czolgosz, Leon, 144

D

Dall, Anna Eleanor "Sistie," 121
Dall, Curtis "Buzzie," 121
David Kalakaua, King (Sandwich Islands), 54, **55**
Davis, Paris, **73**
Depression era, 20, 61–62, **62**
Diana, Princess of Wales, **37**
Dickens, Charles, 162, 175
Diplomatic Corps, 44, 71
Diwali reception (2022), **36**
Donelson, Andrew Jackson, 110
Donelson, Emily, 110
Donelson, Mary Emily, 110
Douglas VC-54C Skymaster, **17**
Downing, Andrew Jackson, 175

E

Earhart, Amelia, **62**
East Garden, **180**, 180–81, **181**, **187**
East Room
 funerals
  Harding, Warren G., 146, **147**
  Kennedy, John F., **150–51**
  Lincoln, Abraham, **142**, 143
  McKinley, William, **146**
  Roosevelt, Franklin D., **148**
  Taylor, Zachary, 140
 furnishings, 226–27
 holiday traditions, 75, 76
 musical performances, 91, 92, **93**, **94**, 95
 press conferences, 29
 portrait unveiling, 236, **236**
 renovations, 226–27, 235
 State Dinners, **ii**, 85
 use by presidents and first families
  Adams (John), 161
  Biden, **ii**, 28, **36**, 73, **73**, 95, **106**, 129
  Buchanan, 50, **51**
  Bush, George W., 76
  Bush (George H. W.), 71
  Carter, 69, 92
  Eisenhower, 75
  Ford, **9**
  Jackson, 226–27
  Kennedy, **66**, **93**

Lincoln, 111
 Nixon, 67
 Obama, **94**
 Reagan, **35**, **103**
 Roosevelt (Theodore), 58, **58**, 238
 Truman, **90**
 Tyler, 49
 Washington portrait, **238**
 weddings
  Grant, Nellie, **132**, 133
  Johnson, Lynda, 136, **138**
  Roosevelt, Alice, **135**
East Sitting Hall, **136**
East Wing, 10, 80, 84
Easter Egg Roll, **127**, **154**, 202, **202**, **203**
Eastman, George, 113
Edward, Prince of Wales, 50, 53
Egypt-Israel Peace Treaty, 169, **200**, 201
Eisenhower, Barbara Anne (daughter), 122, **123**
Eisenhower, Barbara (mother), 122
Eisenhower, David, 122, **123**, 125, **125**, 139
Eisenhower, Dwight D.
 barbecuing, **164**
 on decision-making responsibilities, 32
 golf, 205
 grandchildren, 122, **123**, 125, **125**, 139, 186, **193**
 holiday traditions, 80
 hospitality, 64, **65**, 66
 jets and helicopters, 16, **17**
 oval room study, 164
 press conferences, 29
 road to the White House, 7
 son touring White House, 238, **239**
 South Lawn events, 196
 staff farewell, **222**
 The White House Years, 164
Eisenhower, John, 122, 238, **239**
Eisenhower, Mamie
 floral preferences, 169
 grandchildren, 122, 125, **125**
 holiday traditions, 75, 80
 hospitality, **65**, 66
 making the White House a home, 164, 166
 South Lawn events, 196
 staff farewell, **222**
 in Storeroom, **210**
 White House tour for children and descendants of presidents, 238–39, **239**
Eisenhower, Mary Jean, 122, **193**
Eisenhower, Susan, 122
Eli Yale (Roosevelts' macaw), **115**
Elizabeth, Queen Mother (Great Britain), 64, 66, 91–92
Elizabeth II, Queen (Great Britain), 64, **65**, 66, **70**, 177
Ellington, Duke, 92, **92**
Ellipse, 171
Elliptical Saloon (now Blue Room), **41**
Emancipation Proclamation, 39–40
enslaved workers, 109, **212**, 213
Entrance Hall
 Clinton refurbishing, 235

Ford's hospitality, 69
holiday traditions, **75**, **81**, **82–83**
Jackson's hospitality, **46**, 46–47
Nixon (Pat) and staff, **75**
Reagan's Oath of Office, **9**
Tiffany screen, **227**
Truman renovation, 231
Eppes, Maria, 109
Executive Office Building, 29

F

Family Dining Room, **226**, 234
Family Leave Act (1993), 177
Farrand, Beatrix Jones, 181
Ficklin, John, **210**
Fillmore, Abigail, 50, 162, 225
Fillmore, Mary Abigail, 50, 162
Fillmore, Millard, 32, 50, 162, 225, 231
First Lady's Garden. *See* Jacqueline Kennedy Garden
Fisk Jubilee Singers, 91
Folsom, Frances. *See* Cleveland, Frances Folsom
Ford, Betty
Bicentennial events, 177
charitable works and issues, 101, **102**
children, 125
clothes and style, 99
dance studies, 69
holiday traditions, **75**
hospitality, **67**, 69
Solarium, 233
State Dinners, 177
two-hundredth anniversary of the White House, 71, **71**
Ford, Gerald R.
Bicentennial events, 177
children, 125
greeting tourists, **157**
hospitality, **67**, 69
Oath of Office, **9**
pardon of Nixon, 34
road to the White House, 7
Rose Garden events, 177
Solarium, 233
State Arrival Ceremony, 84
State Dinners, 177
swimming pool, 205, **206**
two-hundredth anniversary of the White House, 71, **71**, 209
on White House staff, 209
Ford, Jack, 125
Ford, Michael, 125
Ford, Steven, 125
Ford, Susan, **75**, 125
Fourth of July, 38, 47, **97**, **194**, 195
Frank Leslie's Illustrated Newspaper, **132**
Fraser, Malcolm, xi

G

Gadsby's Hotel, 46
Galt, Edith Bolling. *See* Wilson, Edith Bolling Galt
Gardens. *See* President's Park

Garfield, Abram, 112
Garfield, Grandmother, 112
Garfield, Harry, 97, 112, 143
Garfield, Irvin, 112
Garfield, James A.
assassination, 13, 32, 55, 112, 143–44, **145**
family life, 97, 112
hospitality, 55
Inauguration, 112
Oath of Office, 112
office seekers and, 13, 32
privacy, quest for, 159
Garfield, James (son), 112, 143
Garfield, Lucretia, 55, 143
Garfield, Mollie, 112
Gatchell, Richard Emory, Jr., **193**
George VI, King (Great Britain), 64, 66, 91–92
gingerbread house, **77**, 78, **79**
Girl Scouts, 100
Glenn, John, 122
"Gold Spoon Oration" (Ogle), 47, 225
Gold Star family members, **193**
Gorbachev, Mikhail, 34, **35**, 69
Gouverneur, Samuel Laurence, 44, 130
Governors Ball, **94**
Governors' Dinner, **216**
Grand Staircase, **9**, 85, 229, 231
Grant, Frederick, 111, 133
Grant, Jesse, 111–12
Grant, Julia (First Lady), 54, 111–12
Grant, Julia (granddaughter), 133
Grant, Nellie, 111, **132**, 132–33
Grant, Ulysses S., 54, **55**, 111–12, **132**, 132–33, 169, 186, 211
Grant, Ulysses Simpson, Jr. "Buck," 111
Great Depression, 20, 61–62, **62**
greenhouses, **182**, 182–83, **183**
Ground Floor, 163–64, 169, 213, 225
Ground Floor Corridor, 168, 169, **169**. *See also* Kitchen
Guinness World Record, **104**
Guiteau, Charles, 143

H

Haley, James, **154**
Hamilton, Bill, **211**
Hanukkah, 80, **81**
Harding, Florence, 60, 100, 195
Harding, Warren G.
death, 60, 146, **147**
Easter Egg Roll, **202**
entertainment budget, 211
hospitality, 60, **60**, 195
recreation, 205
road to the White House, 7
staff, 15
Taft appointment to Supreme Court, 7
Harrison, Anna, 48
Harrison, Benjamin
family, **112**, 112–13
holiday traditions, 74
office seekers and, **13**
pets, 113, **113**
on public opinion, 24
road to the White House, 48

White House improvements, 227
Harrison, Caroline Scott
expansion proposal, 159, **159**
family, **112**
greenhouses, 182
holiday traditions, 74
hospitality, 57
music, 91
privacy, quest for, 159
White House improvements, 227
Harrison, William Henry, 6, 13, 48, **48**, **140**, **141**, 210
Hay, Eliza, 44
Hay, John, 11, **11**
Hayes, Fanny, 112, **183**
Hayes, Lucy Webb, 54–55, **56**, 115, 162, 182, **183**
Hayes, Rutherford B.
commemorative trees, 192
croquet court, 205
Easter Egg Roll, 202
family life, 112, **160**
hospitality, 54–55
Oath of Office, 8, **8**
Soldiers' Home cottage, 171
staff, **214**
telephone, 19
Hayes, Scott, **183**
Hellen, Mary Catherine, 130, **131**
Helm, Edith, **99**
Henry, Prince (Prussia), 58, **58**
Hepper, Carol, **181**
His Whiskers (Harrisons' goat), 113, **113**
Hoban, James, **4**, 5, **5**
Hoes, Laurence Gouverneur, 239
holiday traditions, 74–83. *See also* New Year's Day Reception
Christmas cards, 80, **80**
Christmas cookies, **75**, **77**
Christmas decorations, **241**
Christmas trees, 74, 74–76, **76**, **77**, **78**, 127, 167
decorating themes, 75–76, 78, **79**
Easter Egg Roll, **127**, **154**, 202, **202**, **203**
Fourth of July, 38, 47, **97**, **194**, 195
gingerbread house, **77**, 78, **79**
Hanukkah, 80, **81**
Official White House Christmas Ornament, **76**
Roosevelt (Franklin D.), with grandchildren, **121**
Thanksgiving Turkey Pardons, **157**, **188**, **188**, **189**
Trump's Christmas video conference with military members, **27**
Honoré, Ida Maria, 133
Hoover, Herbert
domestic policy challenges, 61–62
hospitality, 41, 61–62, **62**
making the White House a home, 162–63
"Medicine-Ball Cabinet," **204**, 205
road to the White House, 7
Secret Service detail, **156**
telephone use, **19**

Hoover, Ike, 61, 114, 115, 227
Hoover, Lou, 41, 61–62, 99, 100, **120**, 162–63
Horowitz, Vladimir, 95
Hudson, Jennifer, 95
Hughes, Ursula, 109
Hutchinson family singers, 91

I

"In Performance at the White House" (concert series), 92, 95
In the Days of My Father, General Grant (Jesse Grant), 111
Inauguration Day
date, 8
Garfield, 112
Harrison (William Henry), 140
parades, **126**, 192
Roosevelt (Franklin D.), 121, 196
Taylor, 140
Trump, **126**
Independence Day, 38, 47, **97**, **194**, 195
Intermediate Range Nuclear Forces (INF) Treaty, 34, **35**
Iraq, war in, 34–35
Irving, Washington, 41
Israel, peace treaties, 168, 197, **198**, **200**, 201

J

Jackson, Andrew
children and, 109–10
in *Commanders in Chief* (Rossin painting), **6**
commemorative trees, 192
enslaved workers, 213
hospitality, **46**, 46–47
inaugural ceremonies, 45–46
"kitchen cabinet," 25
portrait, 116
President's Park, 175
road to the White House, 6
spoils system, 12–13
on White House conditions, 225
White House improvements, 175, 224, 226–27
widowhood, 140, 144, 192
Jackson, Rachel, 109–10, 140, 192
Jacqueline Kennedy Garden, **180**, 180–81, **181**, **187**
James, Harry, **67**
James S. Brady Press Briefing Room, **30**
Janson, Charles William, 5
Japan
envoys from Imperial Japan, 50, **51**
jujitsu exhibition, 58
prime minister's visit (1979), **69**
World War II, 33
Jefferson, Thomas
correspondence, 239
enslaved workers, 109, 213
food and wine bills, 210
Fourth of July celebrations, 38, 195

grandchildren, 109
hospitality, 38–39, 41
learning and accomplishments, 39
Louisiana Purchase, 5
making the White House a home, 161–62
Monticello, 191
music, 91
philosophy, 245
on presidency as "a splendid misery," 32
President's Park, 172–73
White House improvements, 224
Jefferson Memorial, **170**, 171
Jennings, Paul, **212**, 213
Jérôme Bonaparte, King (Westphalia), 38
John Paul II, Pope, 201
Johnson, Andrew, 54, 143, 213, 220
Johnson, Cave, **49**
Johnson, Claudia "Lady Bird"
charitable works and issues, **100**, 101
Children's Garden, 184
commemorative trees, **192**
daughters, 125, 136
floral preferences, 169
hospitality, 67
Jacqueline Kennedy Garden, **180**, 181
with Nixon (Pat), **165**
Second Floor apartments, 167
two-hundredth anniversary of the White House, 71, **71**
Johnson, Dolly, **214**
Johnson, Eliza, 143
Johnson, Luci, 125, 136, 167, 233
Johnson, Lynda, 125, 136, 167, **198**
Johnson, Lyndon B.
Children's Garden, 184
china, 85
daughters, 125, 136, **138**
holiday traditions, **74**
hospitality, 67, **156**
road to the White House, 7
South Lawn events, 197
State Arrival Ceremony, 84
State Dinners and news media, 85, 88
Vietnam War, 34, **34**
with Yuki (dog), **128**
Johnson Country Fair, **198**
"Joining Forces" initiative, 104, 106, **107**
Joinville, Prince de, 48
Juan Carlos I, King (Spain), 69
Juliana, Queen (Netherlands), 64

K

Kannalikham, Tham, **207**
Kelly (policeman), 111–12
Kennedy, Caroline
father's death and, **151**
playground, 122, 186, 197
pony, 122, **155**, 186, **187**
Second Floor toy room, 167
Solarium kindergarten, 125, 233, **233**
Kennedy, Jacqueline

children, 122, **124**, 125
clothes and style, 99
floral preferences, 169
furnishings, 166
historical work on White House, 166, 168
holiday traditions, 75
hospitality, 66, **66**
Jacqueline Kennedy Garden, 181
Kennedy's death and, **151**
musical entertainment, 91, 92, **93**
President's Dining Room, 234
staff, 101
televised White House tour, 240, **241**
The White House: An Historic Guide, 243, **243**
Kennedy, John F.
assassination, 66–67, 151
children, 122, **124**, 125, **187**
Eisenhower's advice for, 32
family pets, 122
funeral, **150–51**
hospitality, 39, 66
Jacqueline Kennedy Garden, 181
on Jefferson, 39
musical entertainment, **90**, 91, 92, **93**, **197**
naval blockade of Cuba, **21**, 33
President's Dining Room, 234
Rose Garden, 176, **178**
State Arrival Ceremony, 84
televised addresses, **21**
on White House history, 246
Kennedy, John F., Jr., 122, **124**, 125, **151**, 167, 186, **187**, 197
Khan, Liaquat Ali, **64**
Khrushchev, Nikita, 122
"Kids' State Dinners," 104
Kim Keon Hee, **84**
Kim Young-sam, **205**
King, Charles Bird, painting by, **45**
Kitchen, **214**, 220, **220**, **221**, **222**, **223**
Kitchen Garden, 104, **190**, 191, **191**
Knight, Gladys, **95**

L

Laddie Boy (Harding's dog), 205
Lafayette, Marquis de, 45, 239
Lafayette Square, **174**
Lane, Harriet, **49**, 50, 53, 182
Latrobe, Benjamin Henry, 172, 173
League of Nations, 60
Lee, Robert E., 201
Legend, John, 95
"Let's Move" program, 104
Lewis, Norm, 95
Library, **vi**, **5**, 162, 164
Lincoln, Abraham
assassination, 53, 143
children, **96**, 110–11, 140, 142, 233
Civil War, 11, 201
Emancipation Proclamation, 39–40
funeral, **142**, 142–43

furnishings, 235–36
hospitality, 39–40, **40**, **52–53**, 53, **195**
music, 91
office seekers and, 12
philosophy, 245
on public opinion, 24
road to the White House, 6, 7
Roosevelt (Theodore) on, 6–7
on security, 153
Soldiers' Home cottage, 171
staff, 11, **11**, 213, **213**
Thanksgiving Turkey Pardon, 188
Lincoln, Mary Todd
children, 110
criticism of, 53
furnishings, 236
grief, 140, 142, 143
hospitality, **40**, **52–53**, 53
Lincoln, Robert, 110–11, 143
Lincoln, Thomas "Tad," **96**, 110–11, **111**, 143, 188
Lincoln, William "Willie," 110–11, 140, 142, 236
Lincoln Bedroom, 166, 235–36, **236**
Lincoln Suite, 64, 66
Longworth, Alice Roosevelt, 115, **117**, 133–34, **134**, **135**, 234, 238, **239**
Longworth, Nicholas, 134, **135**
Looker, Earle, 116
Louis Philippe, King (France), 48
Louisiana Purchase, 5

M

Ma, Yo-Yo, **94**
Macaroni (Caroline Kennedy's pony), 122, **155**, 186, **187**
Macron, Brigitte, 86
Macron, Emmanuel, **xii**, 86
Madison, Dolley
charitable works, 99
enslaved workers, 213
hospitality, **41**, 41–42, 43, 44
household management, 220
making the White House a home, 162
as matchmaker, 47, 130
piano, 91
War of 1812, 5, 42–43, 238
as White House guest, **49**, 132
Madison, James
cabinet meetings, 41
correspondence, 239
enslaved workers, **212**, 213
hospitality, 44
making the White House a home, 162
as secretary of state, 41
War of 1812, 5, 42–43, 238
Manning, Helen Taft, 118, **118**, 238, **239**
Map Room, 164
March of Dimes, **102**
Marie, Queen (Romania), 61
Marine Band, **82–83**, 91, 95, **141**, **194**, 195, **195**
Marine One, **23**
Marker, Peggy, **207**
Marshall, John, 239

Martha Graham Dance Company, 69
McAdoo, Eleanor "Nell" Wilson, **109**, 118, **119**, 136, **137**, 239, **239**
McAdoo, William Gibbs, 136
McBride, Gigi, **203**
McElroy, Mary Arthur, 55
McKee, Benjamin Harrison "Baby McKee," **112**, 112–13, **113**
McKee, Mary L. (daughter), **112**
McKee, Mary (mother), **112**
McKim, Charles, 229
McKinley, Ida, 57, 146
McKinley, William, 15, 33, 57, 144, 146, **146**, 153
Medal of Honor, 73, **73**
Mellon, Rachel Lambert, 176, 178, 181
Memorial Day (2022), **193**
menorah, 80, **81**
Mitterrand, François, 69
Modi, Narendra, **88**
Molotov, V. M., 62
Monroe, Elizabeth, 44, 130
Monroe, James
cabinet and, 24–25
daughter's wedding, 130
debts from White House years, 210
descendants, **193**
enslaved workers, 213
furnishings, 5, 44, 226–27, **239**
Monroe Doctrine, 25, 239
move to White House, 43
New Year's Day Reception, 44
protocol for foreign diplomats, 44
South Portico, 5
White House improvements, 226
Monroe, Maria, 44, 130, **130**
Monroe Doctrine, 25, 239
Monroe Room, 239
Month of the Military Child, **107**
Monticello, Virginia, 191
Montpelier, Virginia, 213
Morrison, Scott, **177**
Morrison, Susan, **89**
Mount Vernon, Virginia, 76
Munger, George, watercolor by, **43**

N

Napoleon, Prince, **195**
Napoleon I, Emperor (France), 5
National Book Festival, 104
National Governors Association Dinner, **72**
National Park Service, 181, 182
National Symphony Orchestra, 95
National Turkey Federation, 188
Native American tribal leaders, 197
NATO alliance, 35, 197
Neal, Peter, 139, **139**
Nehru, Jawaharlal, 122
New Year's Day Reception
Adams, 91
Coolidge, **40**, 61

Hoover, 41
Jefferson, 38
Johnson (Andrew), **38**
Lincoln, 39–40, **40**
Monroe, 44
range of years, 74
Roosevelt (Theodore), **12**
Van Buren, 47
Nicolay, John, 11, **11**
Niinistö, Sauli, **27**
nineteenth Amendment, one hundredth anniversary, 105
Nixon, Julie, 125, **125**, 139
Nixon, Pat
 charitable works and issues, 101
 clothes and style, 99
 daughters, 125, **125**, 139, **139**
 as goodwill ambassador, 101
 holiday traditions, **75**
 hospitality, 67, **67**, 171
 with Johnson (Claudia "Lady Bird"), **165**
 sitting room, 240
 staff, **75**
 "Summer in the Parks" program, **101**
Nixon, Richard M.
 computers, 15
 daughters, 125, **125**, 139, **139**
 Easter Egg Roll, 202
 fireplace use, 240
 hospitality, 67, **67**
 music, 91, 92
 playing piano, 92, **92**, 240
 President's Dining Room, 234
 public tours of gardens, **243**
 resignation, 7, 9, 34, 69
 State Arrival Ceremony, 84
 telephone call to moon, **26**
 Watergate crisis, 125
Nixon, Tricia, 125, 139, **139**, 167, 177, 240, **241**
Nobel Prize winners, dinner for, 39
North Atlantic Treaty Organization (NATO), 35, 197
North Carolina Spiritual Singers, 92
North Drive, **40**
North Entrance, 158, 201
North Fence, 192
North Front, **172**, **208**
North Lawn, **200**, 201, **201**
North Portico
 bowling alley, 205
 change of administration, 201
 construction, 5, 175, 226
 Kennedy family, **151**
 staff, **215**
 State Visits, **65**, 84, **87**
 Truman renovation, 231
North View, **174**
Northern Virginia Community College, 106
Norway, Crown Prince and Princess of, 62
Nugent, Patrick J., 136, 233
The Nutcracker (Tchaikovsky), 75

O

Oath of Office, 8, **8**, **9**, 112
Obama, Barack
 boarding *Marine One*, **23**
 communications, 15
 daughters, 127, 186
 family pets, **129**
 foreign policy challenges, 35
 hospitality, 73
 "In Performance at the White House" (concert series), 95
 Jacqueline Kennedy Garden events, 181
 press conferences, **30**
 portrait, 236, **237**
 recreation, 205
 Rose Garden events, 177
 Second Floor private office, 169
 South Portico, **244–45**
 State Dinners, 95
Obama, Malia, 127, 186
Obama, Michelle
 charitable works and issues, 104, **104**, 191
 china, 85
 daughters, 127
 holiday traditions, 76, **77**
 hospitality, 73, **242**, **243**
 "In Performance at the White House" (concert series), 95
 Jacqueline Kennedy Garden events, 181
 Kitchen Garden, 191, **191**
 making the White House a home, 168–69
 portrait, **169**, 236, **237**
 State Dinners, 95
 White House refurbishing, **237**
Obama, Sasha, 127, 186
O'Connor, Sandra Day, 177
Ogle, Charles, 47, 225
Oklahoma City bombing (1995), 192, 201
Old Guard Fife and Drum Corps, United States Army, **85**
Olmsted Plan, 192
Olympics, 197, **199**
Outer Oval Office, **15**
Oval Office
 Biden in, **2**, **19**, **27**, **129**
 Bush (George W.) in, **21**
 Coolidge in, **26**
 Hoover in, **19**
 Johnson (Lyndon) in, **128**
 Kennedy in, **21**
 Nixon in, **26**
 press conferences, 29, **30**
 Roosevelt (Franklin D.) in, **30**
 telephones, **19**
 Trump in, **27**
Oval Room (now Blue Room), 39, 130. *See also* Blue Room
Owen, Frederick Dale, **159**

P

Palestinian Liberation Organization, 197, **198**
Pan-American Exposition, Buffalo, New York, 144, 146
Panama Canal, 22, **22**, 34, 69, 245
Patterson, Betsy, 38
Patterson, Martha, 54, 220
Pence, Karen, 105
Pendleton Act (1883), 13
Pennsylvania Avenue, 201, **201**
Philip, Duke of Edinburgh, 64, **65**, 66
Pierce, Benjamin, 50
Pierce, Franklin, 32, 50, 226
Pierce, Jane, 32, 50
Pinckney, Roswell Newcomb, **117**
Polk, James K.
 death, 10
 enslaved workers, **212**, 213
 hospitality, 49, **49**
 on presidential duties, 10
 on shaking hands, 39
 White House improvements, 225
Polk, Matilda Childress, **49**
Polk, Sarah, 49, **49**, 99, 225
Preserve America Award, 177
The Presidential Mansion and Grounds, During the Performance of the Military Bands (engraving), **3**
Presidential Medal of Freedom, 92
Presidential Scholar program, 197
Presidential Sites Summit, **193**
President's Commission on Mental Health, **102**
President's Dining Room, **166**, 234
"President's Own" (United States Marine Band), 95
President's Park, 170–207. *See also* Rose Garden
 Children's Garden, 184, **184**, **185**
 Christmas trees, **77**
 closed to public, 115
 commemorative trees, 192, **192**, **193**
 Easter Egg Roll, **127**, 154, 202, **202**, **203**
 evolution, 172–75
 fences and walls, 172–73, **173**
 greenhouses, **182**, 182–83, **183**
 Jacqueline Kennedy Garden, **180**, 180–81, **181**, **187**
 Kitchen Garden, 104, **190**, 191, **191**
 Marine Band concerts, **194**, 195
 North Lawn events, **200**, 201, **201**
 open to public, 171, 175, 242, **243**
 playgrounds, 186, **186**, **187**, 197
 presidents at play, **204**, 205, **205**, **206**, **207**
 South Lawn events, 196, **196**, **197**, **198**, **199**
 Thanksgiving Turkey Pardons, 157, 188, **188**, **189**
 visitors, 114–15
press conferences, **28**, 29, **30**
Press Room, **128**
Price, Leontyne, 95
privacy, quest for, 158–59
Private Quarters, **158**, 167, **167**, 168–69, 225, 229, 240, **241**
Pushinka (Caroline Kennedy's dog), 122

Q

Queens' Bedroom, 64, 166

R

Rabin, Yitzhak, **198**
Ramsey, James, **217**
Randolph, James Madison, 109
Randolph, Martha, 109
Rathbone, Basil, **66**
Rauschner, John Christian, portrait by, **5**
Reagan, Maureen, 126
Reagan, Michael, 126
Reagan, Nancy
 boarding *Marine One*, **23**
 charitable works and issues, 101, **103**
 children, 126
 clothes and style, 99
 exercise equipment, 205
 floral preferences, 169
 holiday traditions, **76**
 hospitality, 69, **70**
 Private Quarters, 167, **167**
 State Dinners, 88
Reagan, Patricia, 126
Reagan, Ronald
 boarding *Marine One*, **23**
 children, 126
 china, 85
 commemorative trees, 192
 dinner guests, **37**
 exercise equipment, 205
 foreign policy challenges, 34
 hospitality, 69, **70**
 Intermediate Range Nuclear Forces (INF) Treaty, 34, **35**
 Oath of Office, **9**
 President's Dining Room, 234
 Private Quarters, 167, **167**
 Rose Garden events, 177
 State Dinners, **x**, xi, 88
 White House improvements, 235
Reagan, Ronald, Jr., 126
Reasoner, Harry, **241**
Rebecca (Coolidge raccoon), **128**
Reconstruction, 54
Red Room, **8**, 32–33, 142, 162
Reid, Angella, **219**
Robb, Charles S., 34, 136, **138**
Robb, Lynda Johnson, 125, 136, 167
Robin (Caroline Kennedy's canary), 122
Rodham, Tony, 139
Roosevelt, Alice "Princess Alice" (T. Roosevelt's daughter), 115, **117**, 133–34, **134**, **135**, 234, 238, **239**
Roosevelt, Alice (T. Roosevelt's wife), 133
Roosevelt, Archibald, 115, **116**, **117**, 154
Roosevelt, Edith
 children, 116, **116**, **117**
 on gallery of first ladies' portraits, 164
 gardens, 181
 hospitality, 58
 musical entertainment, 91
 on Panama Railroad train, **22**

254   LIFE IN THE WHITE HOUSE

sketch of Private Quarters, **158**
White House renovation, 229
Roosevelt, Eleanor
  birthday commemorated, 69
  clothes and style, 99
  hospitality, 62, **63**, 64
  making the White House a home, 163
  musical entertainment, 91–92
  participation in national affairs, 100
  Roosevelt's death and, 148
  with staff, **99**
  This I Remember, 62
  on White House family life, 97
Roosevelt, Ethel, 117
Roosevelt, Franklin D.
  airplane, 16, **17**
  birthday commemorated, 69
  death and funeral, 9, 148, **148**–49
  family life, 97, 121, **121**, 186
  hospitality, 62, **63**, 64
  Inauguration, 121, 196
  making the White House a home, 163
  musical entertainment, 91–92
  in Oval Office, **30**
  philosophy, 1, 245
  radio addresses, 1, 20
  State Dining Room mantel, 246
  swimming pool, 29
  travel abroad, 22
  World War II, 22, 25, 62, **63**, 64, 164
Roosevelt, James, **239**
Roosevelt, Kermit, 32, 116, **116**
Roosevelt, Quentin, 115, 116, **116**, **117**, 154, 186
Roosevelt, Theodore
  with cabinet, **24**
  cartoons of, 29
  children, **115**, 115–16, **116**, 133–34, **135**, 186, 233, 238, **239**
  couriers, 16, **16**
  on decision-making responsibilities, 32
  family life, 115, 116, **116**
  family pets, 115, **115**, 117
  holiday traditions, 74
  hospitality, 58, **58**
  letterhead, 3
  on Lincoln, 6–7
  moving day (1909), **162**
  Panama Canal, 22, **22**
  philosophy, 245
  road to the White House, 7
  Secret Service and, 153, **154**
  staff, 58
  "Tennis Cabinet," 205
  travel abroad, 22, **22**
  West Wing construction, 12, 29, 58, 158, 182, **229**
  White House renovation, 58, 163, **228**, 229, **229**, 231
Roosevelt, Theodore, Jr., **115**, 116
Rose Garden, 176–79
  Kennedy redesign, 176, **177**, **178**
  location, 176
  press conferences, 29
  public tours, 243

State Dinners, 177, 178
Thanksgiving Turkey Pardon, 188, **188**
Truman in, **176**
Trump renovation, 177, **178**
Trump's press conference, **31**
weddings, 139, **139**, 177
Rose Suite (later Queens' Bedroom), 64, 66
Rossin, Ross, paintings by, **6**, **7**
Rostropovich, Mstislav, 95
Rough Riders, 58
Rowe, Abbie, **225**
Rucker, Joanna, **49**
Russia, invasion of Ukraine, 35

S

"Sacred Cow" (Douglas VC-54C Skymaster), **17**
Sadat, Anwar el-, **200**, 201
Salonga, Lea, 95
Sartoris, Algernon Charles Frederick, **132**, 133
Sayre, Francis Bowes, 134, 136, **136**
Scott, Reverend Dr., **112**
Scott, Sir Walter, 132
Seaton, Sarah Gales, 44, 130
Second Floor. *See also* Private Quarters
  Clinton-era, 168
  East Sitting Hall, **136**
  exercise equipment, 205
  family library, **160**
  Garfield's death, 143–44
  Harrison (Benjamin) Christmas tree, 74
  heating, 225–26
  as Hoover reception area, 163
  Johnson-era (Lyndon B.), 167
  President's Dining Room, **166**, 234
  president's private office, 169
  Roosevelt (Eleanor) with staff, **99**
  Roosevelt (Theodore), children's behavior, 115
  State Visits, 64, 84
  Truman pianos, 164
Secret Service, **152**, **153**, 153–54, **154**, **155**, **156**, 211
Segovia, Andrés, 95
September 11, 2001 terrorist attacks, **21**, 34, 197, **199**
Seward, William H., 40
Shanks, Daniel, **216**
Sinatra, Frank, 70
Singleton, Angelica, 47
Sky Parlor. *See* Solarium
Slade, William, 213, **213**
Smirne, Rocco and Arioth, **203**
Smith, Jerry, **215**
Smith, Kate, 91
Smith, Margaret Bayard, 109
Socks (Clintons' cat), **128**
Solarium, **75**, 164, 167, **232**, 233
Soldiers' Home, 142, 171
Sophia, Queen (Spain), 69
South Drive, 186
South Entrance, 84
South Front, **230**
South Grounds
  Children's Garden, 184, **184**,

185
  Easter Egg Roll, 202
  events, 196
  Jefferson's landscaping, 173
  jogging track, 205, **205**
  Pope John Paul II's visit, 201
  putting green, 205
  stables, 186
  tennis courts, 146
  Tennis Pavilion, 205, **207**
  tree houses, **187**
  visitors, **175**
South Lawn
  baseball field, 73, 205
  closed to public, 115
  commemorative trees, **193**
  Easter Egg Roll, **127**, **154**, 202, **202**, **203**
  events, 196, **196**, **197**, **198**, **199**
  helicopter, **17**, **23**
  musical performances, 68, 91, **194**, 195
  open to public, 175, 243
  playground equipment, 122, 186, **186**
  tennis court, 205
  Thanksgiving Turkey Pardons, **189**
  tree houses, 125, 186
South Portico
  Biden family, **97**
  commemorative trees, 192
  construction, 5, 39, 226
  Lincoln hosting Prince Napoleon, **195**
  Marine Band concerts, 195
  Nixon (Julie) and Eisenhower (David), **125**
  Obama in, **244**–45
  Taft on, **196**
  wall repair, **234**
  Wilson (Ellen) and daughters, **119**
Southwest Gate, 84
Souvenir (Margaret Truman), 153–54
Soviet Union, 33, 34, **35**
Spanish-American War, 32–33, 58
Stanton, Edwin M., 111
Starling, Richard, **156**
State Arrival Ceremony, **xii**, 84, **84**, **85**
State Department, 61
State Dining Room
  Biden events, **31**, **72**
  Clinton refurbishing, 235
  gingerbread house, **77**, 78, **79**
  Governors' Dinner, **72**, **216**
  mantel, 246, **246**–47
  Nixon events, 67
  Roosevelt renovation, 229
  State Dinners, 85
  televised tour, **241**
  Truman renovation, **231**
  two-hundredth anniversary of the White House, **71**
State Dinners
  Biden, **ii**, **86**, **87**, 88, **88**, 95
  Buchanan, 50, 53
  Bush (George H. W.), **70**
  china, 85
  Coolidge, 61
  Ford, 177
  Grant, 54, **55**

"Kids' State Dinners," 104
Kitchen Garden food, 191
McKinley, 57
North Entrance, 201
Obama, 95
protocol, 84–85
Reagan, **x**, xi, 88
Rose Garden, 177, 178
staff, **218**–**19**, 220, **221**
Truman, 64
Trump, **177**
Tyler, 48
use of term, 84
State Floor
  Biden press conference, **31**
  Clinton refurbishing, 235
  crowds of callers, 158
  Family Dining Room, 234
  heating, 225
  holiday traditions, 74, 80
  museum character, 168
  open to public, 168–69
  Tiffany stained-glass screen, 227, **227**
  State Visits, 22, 61, 64, **64**, 84, 84–89, 197
Storeroom, 210, **210**, 211
Stott, Kathryn, 94
A Stranger in America (Janson), **5**
Stuart, Gilbert, portrait by, 238, **238**
"Summer in the Parks" program, 101
Sunak, Rishi, **28**
Super Bowl, 73
swimming pool, 205, **206**
Syria, uprisings, 35

T

Taft, Charlie, 19, 118, **118**
Taft, Helen (daughter), 118, **118**, 238, **239**
Taft, Helen (mother), 58–59, **59**, 118, 160, 196, 210
Taft, Robert, 118
Taft, William Howard
  car fleet, 16, **16**
  as chief justice, 7, 162
  children, 118, **118**, 239
  cow, 220
  family life, **118**
  holiday traditions, 74
  hospitality, 58–59, **59**, 196, **196**
  on loneliness of White House, 32
  making the White House a home, 162
  salary, 211
  on Secret Service, 153
  staff, 211, 227
  telephone use, **18**, 19
Taylor, Margaret, 50, 140, 158–59
Taylor, Zachary, 50, 140, 159, 213
Tchaikovsky, Pyotr, 75
Teacher of the Year Award, 177
Team USA, 197, **199**
Tennis Pavilion, 205, **207**
Thackeray, William Makepeace, 162
Thanksgiving Turkey Pardons, **157**, 188, **188**, 189

INDEX 255

Thatcher, Margaret, 69
Third Floor, 122, 168, 229
This I Remember (Eleanor Roosevelt), 62
Thompson, Malvina, **99**
Tiber Creek (Waddell), **170**
Tiffany, Louis Comfort, 227
Todd, Thomas, 130
Travolta, John, **37**
Treaty Room, **100**, 166
Truman, Bess, 64
Truman, Harry S.
   airplane, 16, **17**
   on atomic bomb, 33
   birthday commemorated, 69
   "*The* BUCK STOPS *here*!" sign, 32, **33**
   on his presidency, 245–46
   hospitality, 64, **64**
   Lincoln Bedroom, 235–36
   Oath of Office, **8**
   piano, **90**, 91, 164
   pitching horseshoes, 205
   on predecessors, 7
   road to the White House, 7
   Roosevelt's death and, 148
   in Rose Garden, **176**
   salary, 211
   televised addresses, 20, **20**
   televised White House tour, 240, **240**
   travel abroad, 22
   on White House as "a great white prison," 32
   White House renovation, 64, 80, 181, **224**, **225**, **230**, 231, **231**, **232**, 233
Truman, Margaret, 153–54, 164
Truman Balcony, **viii**, **241**
Trump, Barron, **126**, 127, 186, **187**
Trump, Donald J.
   COVID-19 pandemic, **31**, 35
   family life, **126**, 127, 186
   foreign and domestic policy challenges, 35
   holiday traditions, **27**, 78
   hospitality, 73
   Inaugural Parade, **126**
   Jacqueline Kennedy Garden events, 181
   Kitchen Garden, 191
   musical entertainment, 95
   Rose Garden events, **31**, **177**
   State Dinners, **177**
   video conference with U.S. military members, **27**
Trump, Donald J., Jr., 127
Trump, Eric, 127
Trump, Ivanka, 127
Trump, Melania
   "Be Best" initiative, **105**
   charitable works and issues, 104–05, **105**
   children, **126**, 127
   commemorative trees, **193**
   holiday traditions, 78, **78**
   hospitality, 73
   Jacqueline Kennedy Garden events, 181
   Rose Garden renovation, 177, **178**
   Tennis Pavilion, 205, **207**
   White House refurbishing, **237**
Trump, Tiffany, 127
Turkey Pardoning ceremony, **157**,
188, **188**
Tyler, Elizabeth, 130, 132
Tyler, John, 48–49, 91, 130, 132, 175, 213
Tyler, Julia Gardiner, 48–49, 132
Tyler, Letitia, 48, 130, 132, 158
Tyler, Priscilla Cooper, 48, 132, 158
Tyler, Robert, 48

U

Ukraine, invasion by Russia, 35
United States Air Force Strings, 95
United States Army Herald Trumpets, 95
United States Magazine, 175
United States Marine Band, **82–83**, 91, 95, **141**, **194**, 195, **195**
United States Navy Band Sea Chanters, 95
Upstairs at the White House (West), 219
U.S. Secret Service. *See* Secret Service
U.S.–Africa Leaders Summit Dinner, **95**

V

Van Buren, Abraham, 47
Van Buren, Martin, **47**, 47–48, 171, 213, 224–25
Vertical Void (Hepper), **181**
Vietnam War, 34, **34**, 73
Vosk, Jessica, 95

W

Waddell, Peter, painting by, **41**, 170
Walker, Robert, **49**
Wallace, Mike, **241**
Waller, William, 130
Walters, Gary, 219
War of 1812, 5, **42**, 42–43, **43**, 238
Washington, Booker T., 58
Washington, George
   birthday celebrations, 45, **46**, 46–47
   formal court etiquette, 38
   Oath of Office, **8**
   portrait, 238, **238**
   protocol for foreign diplomats, 44
   road to the White House, 7
   White House design and construction, **4**, 5
Washington, Lucy Payne, 130
Washington, Martha, 38
Washington Diplomatic Corps, 44, 71
Washington Monument, **170**, 171, **195**
Washington National Opera, 95
Watergate crisis, 125
Watson, Ed, **viii**
Webster, Daniel, 132, 213
Webster, Sidney, 32
weddings, 130–39
   Adams, John (grandson), 130
   Biden, Naomi, 139, **139**
Cleveland, Grover, 133, **133**
Grant, Nellie, **132**, 132–33
Johnson, Luci, 136
Johnson, Lynda, 136, **138**
Monroe, Maria, 130, **130**
Nixon, Tricia, 139, **139**
Rodham, Tony, 139
Roosevelt, Alice, 133–34, **134**, **135**
Tyler, Elizabeth, 130, 132
Washington, Lucy Payne, 130
Wilson, Eleanor, 136, **137**
Wilson, Jessie, 134, 136, **136**
West, J. B., **165**, **219**
West Garden Room, **129**
West Sitting Hall, **165**
West Wing
   construction, 5, 12, 158, 182, **229**
   New Year's Day Reception (1903), **12**
   newsroom, 29
   as presidential work space, 10, 12, 15
   press conferences, 29
Wheeler, Perry, 176
The White House: An Historic Guide, 243, **243**
The White House Gang (Looker), 116
White House Historical Association, xi, **xi**, **76**, **193**, **203**, 236, 243, **243**
White House Library. *See* Library
White House Police, **154**
The White House Years (Dwight D. Eisenhower), 164
Wilhelmina, Queen (Netherlands), 62
Williams, Anthony, **201**
Willow (Bidens' cat), **129**
Wilson, Edith Bolling Galt, 59–60, **98**, 99–100, 136, 195
Wilson, Eleanor "Nell," **109**, 118, **119**, 136, **137**, 239, **239**
Wilson, Ellen, 118, **119**, 134, 136, **136**, **137**, 176, 181
Wilson, Jessie, 118, **119**, 134, 136, **136**
Wilson, Margaret, 118, **119**
Wilson, Woodrow
   assisted by Edith Wilson, **98**, 99–100
   children, 118
   communications, 15
   daughter touring Eisenhower White House, 239, **239**
   daughters' weddings, 134, 136, **136**, **137**
   with grandchild, **109**
   hospitality, 59–60, 195
   League of Nations campaign, 60
   press conferences, 29
   travel abroad, 22
   Versailles peace conference, 22
   widowhood and remarriage, 136
   World War I, 25, 33
Windsor, Duke and Duchess of, **67**
Winter Olympics, 197, **199**
World Series (1990), 177
World War I, 22, 25, 33, 60
World War II, 22, 25, 33, 62, **63**, 64, 164
Wyeth, N. C., illustration by, **4**

Y

Yellow Oval Room, **77**, 84, 166–67
Yoon Suk Yeol, **84**
Yuki (Lyndon Johnson's dog), **128**

Z

Ziemann, Hugo, **221**